THE
PSYCHIC
REALM:
WHAT CAN
YOU
BELIEVE?

THE PSYCHIC REALM: WHAT CAN YOU BELIEVE?

by NAOMI A. HINTZE
and J. GAITHER PRATT, Ph.D.

RANDOM HOUSE / NEW YORK

Copyright © 1975 by Naomi A. Hintze and
J. Gaither Pratt, Ph.D.

All rights reserved under International and Pan-American
Copyright Conventions. Published in the United States by
Random House, Inc., New York, and simultaneously in Canada
by Random House of Canada Limited, Toronto.

Library of Congress Cataloging in Publication Data

Hintze, Naomi A   The psychic realm.

Bibliography: p.
Includes index.
1. Psychical research. I. Pratt, Joseph
Gaither, 1910–   joint author. II. Title.
BF1031.H56   133.8   75–10285
ISBN 0–394–49538–1

Manufactured in the United States of America
9 8 7 6 5 4 3 2 1
First Edition

Grateful acknowledgment is made to the following for
permission to reprint previously published material:

Abingdon Press: For material from *Psychology, Religion and
Healing* by Leslie D. Weatherhead. Copyright 1951 by Pierce
& Washabaugh.

The Chattanooga Times: For a letter from Mr. Sells, published
in the September 4, 1974, edition of *The Chattanooga Times*.

Delacorte Press/Seymour Lawrence: For a brief excerpt from
*Life Without Death?: On Parapsychology, Mysticism, and the
Question of Survival* by Nils O. Jacobson. Copyright © 1974
by Nils O. Jacobson.

E. P. Dutton & Co., Inc.: For excerpts from *Beyond the Reach
of Sense* by Rosalind Heywood. Copyright © 1959, 1971 by
Rosalind Heywood; and from *ESP: A Personal Memoir* by
Rosalind Heywood. Copyright © 1964 by Rosalind Heywood.

Harper & Row Publishers, Inc.: For brief excerpts from *The
Gift of Healing* by Ambrose A. Worrall and Olga N. Worrall
(1965).

Macmillan Publishing Co., Inc., and Hodder & Stoughton Ltd.: For material from *Ring of Truth* by J. B. Phillips. Copyright © 1967 by J. B. Phillips.

William Morrow & Company, Inc.: For material from *The World of Ted Serios* by Jule Eisenbud. Copyright © 1966, 1967 by Jule Eisenbud.

The New American Library, Inc.: For an excerpt from *The Poltergeist* by William Roll. Copyright © 1972 by William Roll.

Spiritual Frontiers Fellowship: For material from an article by Melissa Siebert which appeared in the December 1974 issue of *Newsletter*; and from an article by Robert H. Ashby which appeared in *Journal*, Spring 1972.

We dedicate this book to:
The parapsychologists who have shared with us the results of their investigations; the many laymen who have given us permission to use their personal experiences, together with their names; authors and editors who have allowed us to quote from their books and other publications; friends and colleagues who made constructive criticisms of the earlier versions of our manuscript; and the many librarians who never stopped looking until they found the answers to our multitudinous questions.

CONTENTS

FOREWORD
by Ian Stevenson

A reader, picking this book up to examine it more closely, may well ask himself why he should choose it instead of some other general guide to parapsychology. The number of popular books on parapsychology now available is so large that no one could read them all, and a choice of one or a few must be made. The titles and the grandiose claims can utterly baffle someone who has decided that parapsychology is here to stay but is not sure how to discriminate between the reliable travel guide for this territory and the swindler's cruise brochure.

When thinking of the present book in comparison with its few genuine competitors, I can properly recommend this one. I have observed the genesis and maturation of *The Psychic Realm: What Can You Believe?* from the time the idea first occurred for an unusual if not unique plan of collaboration. You can usually see rather well what two people who are working together are doing if you look over their shoulders, especially if they do not keep their hands covered. I have been doing this with Mrs. Hintze and Dr. Pratt as they developed this book, and they have been completely open about their movements. Since the gap between plans and accomplishment is much less for this book than for most others, I can speak confidently of what they have actually done.

They have selected certain cases and experiments that belong in the field of parapsychology, the branch of science that investigates phenomena which appear to occur without the mediation of our presently known organs of sensation and movement. It has been clear to a small number of scientists for about a century that many such phenomena occur, cannot be suppressed, ought not to be ignored, and therefore should be thoroughly investigated. Now it is becoming increasingly obvious to a large number of their colleagues and to the public that the first small group of scientists was right and their effort ought to be supported and enlarged. The experiences to be studied and the experiments to be conducted are, however, far too numerous for the tiny band of full-time professional scientists who are working in this field. An obvious result of this situation is that only a small portion of the available material can be presented in any single book written for the general public. Some selection is necessary. The authors of *The Psychic Realm* have displayed a bold, I could almost say a startling, originality in their management of this problem. They have adopted two criteria for the selection of cases and experiments included in their work.

First, they have chosen cases and experiments that (with a few exceptions) are recent and never before presented in books on parapsychology written for the general reader. In many such books the authors have borrowed from one another so that the same old cases are served up again and again. I can assure the reader that the present book is a welcome exception to that deplorable practice. Nearly all the material of this book comes from cases and experiments of quite recent times. Unless you have read the scholarly journals in parapsychology it is unlikely that you have ever heard of most of the research presented in this book. It is that new. There are indeed a few cases here that are not fresh, but the authors' approach to them always is. If a reader happens to have heard of Patience Worth, for example, or even to have read something by her, he has the chance to test his old thoughts about this mystifying personality with the new insights of Mrs. Hintze and Dr. Pratt.

Second, the authors have included mostly cases and experiments that have been given rigorous investigation and have been reported in a more formal and more detailed manner in the scientific literature. This criterion of selection lifts this book still higher above its rivals. I am not one who believes that truth is stranger than fiction, but I do think it is more interesting. Why anyone should be titillated by sensational reports of events that never happened when he could read about equally extraordinary ones that did remains for me a great mystery. And yet many writers of popular books in parapsychology have chosen to offer their readers reports of cases which, however sensational, were never thoroughly investigated, or of experiments that neglected the most elementary rules of procedure in science. If they publish a mixture of strong and worthless material, as some of them do, this simply shows that they cannot evaluate evidence and have no right to offer themselves as guides for laymen. In contrast, the authors of *The Psychic Realm* have mostly presented cases and experiments of high quality and for the few exceptions they have indicated where the weaknesses are.

Selection of the material for this book was only the beginning of the authors' task, as they fully realized. I can say something also about how they continued after they had made their choices. I do not need to tell the reader that Mrs. Hintze is a gifted writer. Anyone who knows anything about writing can see this. Still, not everyone knows equally well what hard work underlies the exhibition of a gift for writing. Let no one suppose that because Mrs. Hintze's sections read easily they were written easily. I happen to know how thoroughly she herself went over the terrain of the cases and experiments that she discusses. She is anything but a passive journalist inertly waiting for the news to fall into her ears. I myself experienced her thoroughness when she found some details less than thoroughly explained in the case of Bishen Chand as I had reported it. Her interview with me about these details reminded me of my own interviews with the original informants for the case, interviews that I had immodestly considered rather searching ones. And I know that Mrs. Hintze was equally zealous in conducting her own personal review of other cases or experiments included in the book when the further inquiries she wished to make were still feasible.

Mrs. Hintze's share of the work has been the presentation of a report of a case or experiment studied independently by a critical layman and narrated in language free of the burdens of technical jargon. What then can we say of Dr. Pratt's contribution? He is far from being a mere commentator on Mrs. Hintze's reports. In addition to informing the reader about what parapsychologists have done in each area, Dr. Pratt takes him behind the published results in parapsychology and shows him something of the processes of scientific investigation. No attempt is made to promulgate rules for planning and conducting research. The skills of the successful scientist cannot be taught, but learning them can be aided to some degree by watching a good model in action. In Dr. Pratt's sections of this book the reader has a chance to see how one parapsychologist—a particularly eminent one —views a wide range of research problems that together represent a large part of the field.

Mrs. Hintze and Dr. Pratt have each written other books as individual authors and they might have written two separate and excellent books on parapsychology. These, I suppose, could have been bound together in one volume and ethically advertised as two books for the price of one. It seems to me, however, that by their felicitous collaboration in the present work they have so increased the value of each other's contribution that the reader is now really buying not just two books for the price of one, but three. May he enjoy the bargain as much as I have.

THE PSYCHIC REALM: WHAT CAN YOU BELIEVE?

INTRODUCTION

"What are Naomi Hintze and Gaither Pratt doing as co-authors of a book on ESP?"

As it became known that we were collaborating, we were interested to note the curiosity our teamwork stirred among friends and associates. While we received mostly encouragement, there were questions, asked with a degree of skepticism: "Why is Naomi Hintze spending her time writing this kind of book when she is a successful author of popular novels?" "How can Gaither Pratt, a parapsychologist who has published mainly scientific papers, take time from his research and scientific writing?"

Adequate answers to these questions call for a separate statement from each of us, just as it became clear early in this joint endeavor that writing together about psychic phenomena would require that we stand apart throughout.

Hintze Statement: I am a layman insofar as parapsychology is concerned, but I have long had a strong interest in psychic phenomena. Since my fiction often reflects this interest, I follow fairly closely the literature dealing with the subject: that written by serious scientists and scholars working in the area, and also a number of the purely popular books produced by professional writers.

Some of the publications of the former are, quite frankly, beyond me. (My ignorance of statistical evaluation, for instance, is equaled if not surpassed by my fervent desire not to have it explained to me.) Some of the popular books are very good, but even the good ones often give me a *déjà vu* feeling of going around and around in the same old house. Why is it necessary to warm up these few stock-in-trade reports and serve them over and over? And why do they so often omit so much that people really wonder about?

It seemed to me that Gaither Pratt and I could write a

book together that would be comprehensive, introduce new material, and also translate the current parapsychological ideas into terms that could be easily understood by the average intelligent reader.

I have felt very fortunate that my acquaintance with Dr. Pratt and others in the field has enabled me to get lucid answers to my many questions: What about psychic surgery? Are the Russians really that far ahead of us in their understanding and use of psychic powers? Is it safe to fool around with automatic writing and ouija boards? What about poltergeists, reincarnation, and out-of-the-body experiences?

I was convinced that there must be many others like me who, trying to pick their way through the debris of the occult explosion, would like to avail themselves of current scientific thinking and efforts to throw new light on these psychic mysteries.

Pratt Statement: I have given full time to experimental research in parapsychology for thirty-five years, twenty-five of them in the Parapsychology Laboratory at Duke University and since 1964 in the Division of Parapsychology at the University of Virginia. During this time I have made no effort to keep up with the flood of popular books dealing with the field. I read, of course, the ones written by my scientific colleagues, but I have not been able to spare the time for the far more numerous books by purely journalistic writers.

An occasional sampling of such books more often than not left me with a bad taste and an empty feeling—but what could I, as a scientist, do? Research workers had, after all, placed their findings in the public domain by publishing them in the scientific literature. They could not be held responsible for the use others might make of the material. Like most of my colleagues, I left the rest of humanity to figure out what we were up to as best they could.

During recent years I have felt a growing sense of doubt and dissatisfaction about the "hands off" attitude of the research workers toward the popularization of parapsychology. Obviously, the public interest is going to be served. If there are those who could serve it responsibly but choose not to do so, they are at least partly responsible for the low quality of information about the field. Not surprisingly, a growing number of parapsychologists are now beginning to recognize that the professional investigators have an obligation to assist in presenting the meat and meaning of the research to satisfy the needs of intelligent public interest.

We are interested in presenting parapsychology as the study of a broad spectrum of unusual experiences, a field that is diversified in detail and at the same time a unified whole.

Psychic experiences occur in everyday life. They are not *super*natural, but natural. And these unexplained natural occurrences give rise to the questions with which parapsychology is concerned. Thus parapsychology is the branch of science that deals with ESP (extrasensory perception—the act of becoming aware of a situation or event, usually outside the organism, without the use of any of the sense organs), and PK (psychokinesis = mind-action or a direct influence of "mind over matter").

For an experience to qualify as a genuine psychic phenomenon, it must be shown beyond reasonable doubt to have involved either ESP or PK, or both. If these experiences are what they appear to be, they are important for the very reason that orthodox science says that they should not occur at all. Parapsychologists have pursued these mysteries in everyday life and also have learned to produce them under controlled conditions in the laboratory. We want to show the close connection between the unexpected personal encounters with psychic phenomena and the laboratory investigations made to increase our understanding of them.

For most readers the case reports of real-life events are more interesting than the methodical investigations the parapsychologists carry out in their laboratories and field studies. But there is a close connection between laboratory and life, and this fact is what makes the area exciting to both the scientist and the nonscientist. We hope to share our excitement about psychic phenomena in a manner which does not assume that our readers have been educated along mathematical and technical lines. And we hope to encourage some of our younger readers to undertake serious study of parapsychology that will lead a few of them to research careers in this field.

Specifically, Naomi Hintze will introduce each new chapter topic by giving accounts of actual experiences. Then Gaither Pratt will comment upon her selection of material, and will add information showing what the professional investigators have done to advance scientific knowledge on the questions that are raised.

It is our hope to open the door to this field of science for anyone who wishes to enter, and to provide a map of its principal regions. The territory that might be explored is vast, and it is not possible for one book to cover more than a small sampling of the whole psi domain. ("Psi," incidentally, is the name of a letter from the Greek alphabet that parapsychologists use as a convenient way of referring to psychic phenomena.)

Perhaps a few further words are needed about the case reports presented in our pages. We do not offer them as conclusive scientific proof of any psi manifestations. On the other hand, we have strong confidence in them as real experiences which have been reported honestly by the persons who had them or who were closely connected with the events.

There are those who hold that observations cannot be scientifically valid unless they are made under controlled conditions in the laboratory. We believe that psi events in everyday life offer a rich source for scientific study. They indicate ways in which psi seems to operate; they suggest interesting questions for research and possible ways of seeking answers in laboratory and field studies. When investigated directly and thoroughly they become valuable as scientific evidence of the reality of psi effects and as a source of new knowledge about the nature of psi.

One final word about how widespread psi experiences really are among the general population: Several surveys conducted at different times over the past century indicate that at least ten percent of the adult population (some surveys come closer to fifty percent) have had psychic experiences that were convincing to them. Translating even ten percent into actual numbers, we can estimate that in a city of 100,000 adults, there should be somewhere around 10,000 of them who think of themselves as living proof of the reality of psi—mostly of the ESP type. Yet the amazing fact is that each of these psi-prone individuals knows about the psychic experiences of only a very small number of others.

In our culture one doesn't easily speak about such things. If we stop to think about it, this is an amazing conspiracy of silence about a pervasive aspect of experience, and we predict that later generations will see it as a taboo regulating twentieth-century society in a manner as quaint as we now see that the Victorian denial of sex was for that period.

We hope to speed the change of some of these attitudes. We do not hope to convince the rigidly skeptical. If your mind refuses to consider that which has not been proved beyond the shadow of all scientific doubt, then "ten angels swearing" (to borrow from Abraham Lincoln) would not convince you of the reality of psi experience.

But if you have an open, adventurous mind—and this we feel to be the truly scientific mind—our book may raise some interesting questions about a world that is all around us, and only just beginning to be explored.

BY EXTRASENSORY MEANS: CAN MR. A COMMUNICATE WITH MR. B?

"In 1894 the first Lord Balfour wrote that no event which could easily find its niche in the structure of physical sciences, even one so startling as the destruction of the earth by some unknown celestial body, ought to excite half so much intellectual curiosity as the fact that Mr. A can communicate with Mr. B by extrasensory means."—Rosalind Heywood, Beyond the Reach of Sense (1971)

"I had a dream . . ."

This was how it started for Mrs. Penny Berendt of Warren, Michigan. This is how it starts for many persons who receive telepathic communications. Usually, though not always, the persons involved are connected by blood or emotional ties; in this instance, Mrs. Berendt barely knew the older man she dreamed about, but she felt strongly drawn to him because he reminded her of her dead father.

Sometimes, as in this case, the dream content is symbolic, but the dreamer wakens with a definite feeling that something, usually something unpleasant, has happened. Whether the impression is received in connection with a dream or in a waking state "out of the blue," the effect on the receiver, the percipient, is the same: uneasiness, almost always so compelling that some sort of action must be taken.

Penny Berendt had an experience that is an almost classic example of telepathic impression. In describing it, she wrote to Dr. Pratt:

"In 1963 my best friend's brother-in-law [Chester Williams], whom I only met twice, but I liked very much, was found dead late in the afternoon. I had a dream about him, and when I awoke between seven and seven-thirty I knew he was dead.

"I called my friend and asked her how her brother-in-law was. She said he was fine, so I told her about my dream and feeling when I awoke . . . My friend said he was to pick up his wife from the hospital because she had had a minor operation. When he did not pick up his wife, she called several times. They broke into the house very late that day and found him dead in bed."

Sometime later, Dr. Ian Stevenson, of the University of Virginia, contacted Mrs. Berendt, and she sent him further details about her dream in which Chester Williams and also an owl had figured:

"My dream: It seemed that I was in the country walking with Chester. There were many trees with dead leaves, some on the trees and many, many dry leaves on the ground. The owl was, I would say, about two feet tall and alive, but did not move. It did not seem like an unusual dream. I can still see the owl as sure as I would see it if I saw it now, but the whole dream was that way. [Neither] Chester nor I touched the owl. It was just there . . . on the ground sitting up or how you would see a regular owl. I have never seen a real one outside of that dream. I can't remember any color except the natural color of the trees and leaves that are dead like in real life. The owl was brownish. It was all on our right side. He [Chester] motioned for me to turn to the left and Chester kept walking toward the trees and owl. I don't remember anything as I turned to go left.

"When I awoke . . . that is when I received the impression without any thought to the dream. I mean the impression of knowing Chester was dead and not dying."

Mrs. Berendt described her emotional state in another letter: "The feeling I got was an awareness and a frightened feeling in the pit of my stomach. I felt a little sick. It was also a feeling that you would get if you were driving and someone would run in front of your car . . ."

She had told her husband immediately upon waking about her irrational feeling that Chester Williams, whom she had thought to be in good health, was now dead or dying. On her way to work she stopped by her aunt's for a cup of coffee. Still distressed, she related the dream about Chester and the owl. Then later at work she called her friend, as recounted earlier, only to be told that Chester was "fine," although, of course, he had been dead since about the time when Mrs. Berendt had received her strong and disturbing impression. He was presumed to have died between 7:00 and 8:00 A.M. The death certificate listed coronary occlusion as the cause of death.

Dr. Stevenson wrote to Penny Berendt's husband, to the sister-in-law of the deceased Chester Williams, to the aunt with whom Penny had had a cup of coffee, to Mrs. Chester Williams, and even to the Michigan Department of Public Health for a photostatic copy of Mr. Williams' death certificate. It all fitted together, corroborating Penny's original statements with only the minor discrepancies of memory that somehow seem to add up to believability. After all, seven years had elapsed; it is remarkable that so many remembered the details of Penny's dream as she told it to them before she knew of Mr. Williams' death.

In a monograph on the subject, Dr. Stevenson comments on the symbolism of the dream: ". . . dead autumn leaves and [Penny's and Mr. Williams'] turning in different directions—which could be interpreted as indicative of Mr. Williams' death." But he says, "The important point is . . . that the strong emotion of the impression was apparently not an accompaniment of the imagery of the dream . . . The physical symptoms she described ('frightened feeling in the pit of my stomach . . . felt a little sick') might also be among those experienced by a person dying of a heart attack, as Mr. Williams did."

Not all extrasensory communications are of the crisis variety. Following an article about Gaither Pratt in *McCall's*, scores of letters came to him illustrating the wide range of circumstances under which such psychic experiences take place:

Yosene Balfour-Ker, mother of the film star Tuesday Weld, wrote of the strong extrasensory link that exists between her and her daughter, although often they are a continent apart. Upon occasion they have had the same dreams simultaneously, and they sometimes experience the same pain.

Dwight Garland, of Burbank, California, says that he gets impressions just by talking to people. At a drive-in one night, a friend who knew about his ability suggested that he tell him what he could about their carhop. Mr. Garland said immediately, "She's from Germany, has a daughter, was married to an American sergeant and is now getting a divorce." When the carhop came back he asked her when her divorce would be final, and "she jumped straight up." But she confirmed that all the information he had somehow picked up about her was true.

Mrs. Sophia Paul, a Philadelphia schoolteacher, reported that she frequently has a strong sense of ESP with one pupil which lasts through the school term. She said: "I don't know who is picking whose brains. I know I am very perceptive to certain people, and this closeness is intensified by my affection toward that person." As an example of this, she cites the following: "When I attended West Chester State College, I was fascinated by my history professor, who later became President Charles Swope of that same college . . . About seven years ago I had a dream in which Dr. Swope was rising to speak in the auditorium when he suddenly slumped to the floor and called out to me, 'Sophia, help me. I'm sick.' As I went over to him he said, 'I'm dead.' Or perhaps, 'I'm dying.'

"The next morning the six o'clock news broadcast announced that Dr. Charles Swope was about to stand up to speak in the auditorium when he slumped down and said, 'I'm sick.' He died of a heart attack within minutes."

Margaret De Bolt, a navy wife now living in Savannah, Georgia, wrote of a Palm Sunday when she was sweeping her walk in Monterey, California. She suddenly found herself thinking very strongly of a friend whom she has asked us to call Lola. Roommates in college, their closeness was such that they sometimes used to joke about sending each other "thought signals."

Although letters and visits had been infrequent since graduation, Margaret said that on that particular morning "Suddenly my desire to speak with her was overwhelming. I actually threw my broom against the wall, hurried to the telephone and dialed her number in Silver Spring, Maryland. It was good, after a lapse of three years, to hear her voice at the other end of the line, saying, 'What a nice surprise!'

"I launched into a rather long exposition of what I had been doing. When I paused for breath I realized that Lola was sobbing and saying 'Good-bye' almost incoherently. I spoke her name several times, but there were only a few more sobs and then silence.

"Worried, I hung up the phone. Later I tried to call her again, but I got a busy signal. Deeply concerned, I felt the only thing for me to do was to wait for some explanation, since I suspected I might have called at an inconvenient moment."

A letter arrived a week later with this explanation: Personal problems had caused Lola to take a bottle of sleeping pills, a quantity of aspirin, and a water glass of gin. Her husband, about to leave the house, had heard the phone ring, and when he came back to the bedroom to find out who was calling, he found his wife on the floor with the phone off the hook. The letter from Lola said: "They did a good job of pumping my stomach out at Bethesda Naval Hospital. Thank you, my dearest friend, for that phone call. I will always believe that somehow I called out to you for help across the miles."

It has been suggested that psi powers seem to be set free by close relationships. Mike Smith used to live in Bloomington, Illinois, where he and a buddy, Rick Scott, apparently were able to "tune in" to each other's thoughts.

Mike's mother corroborates his statement that time after time he would pick up the phone before it rang and Rick would be on the other end. Once, knowing that the two boys were to meet at a certain hour, she told Mike he had better hurry if he didn't want to be late. "That's okay," Mike said. "Rick will be ten minutes late." Just then the phone rang and it was Rick, who said, "Mrs. Smith, tell Mike I'm going to be ten minutes late."

Mike likes to draw, and once Rick called up and said, "I know you're working on a picture, but what is it?" Mike said,

"Why don't you tell me?" Rick then described a water scene in which he saw a boat. "But something's crazy. The boat isn't in the water—it's up on top of a rock." Mike said, "Right. I'm calling it 'Low Tide.'"

Mike moved several hundred miles away, but the boys kept in touch. One night after dates, each sat down and wrote to the other, expounding on girls and love and life in general. The letters crossed in the mail. The first four lines were almost identical, only a word or two differed, and the rest of each letter was almost a duplicate of the other.

Mike says that they used to score remarkably high with ESP cards and ordinary playing cards when working together, but neither could score much better than chance with others.

Mrs. Henry Weiher of New Rochelle, New York, would like an explanation for what happened one morning when she was in a deep sleep. She seemed to hear the words "For God's sake, get up!" She ignored them at first, but they were repeated over and over. She got up and went downstairs, to find that the coal range in the kitchen was red-hot. Her husband had opened the drafts and gone off to work, forgetting to close them. There was also a gas stove in the kitchen and it had all the cocks wide open. Her twins, just toddlers, had apparently turned them on and were standing there in their pajamas. She is convinced that the words that roused her from sleep probably saved their lives.

Born in Germany, Angela von Baillou grew up with the knowledge that her mother, who seemed to be psychically gifted, had many experiences where a sudden impression was so strong she had to take immediate action. Once she woke in the middle of the night to tell Angela that she must get up quickly and take her in the car to find her brother. "I know he has had an accident on his motorcycle. I can see just where he is."

Angela remembers the details very well, although this happened many years ago. "It was about two o'clock in the morning when we drove along that mountain road. I stopped where my mother told me to stop. We got out of the car and my mother plunged ahead of me down the mountainside, where we found my brother. He was unconscious under his overturned motorcycle."

The discovery that one of her students seemed to be able to read her mind and know in advance what the test questions were going to be was a little surprising at first to Doris Kaneklides, a psychology teacher at Catawba College, Salisbury, North Carolina. But Doris was interested in parapsychology, and she realized after running a few ESP-card tests with the student, Adele Ellis, that the two of them, working together with Doris as sender and Adele as receiver, could come up with some remarkable scores. They went on from the cards to some experiments involving distances that were sometimes as great as five hundred miles.

In the first experiment of this sort, however, the distance was only about two miles. The setup was simple: at a pre-arranged time, 8:00 P.M. in this instance, Doris, at home, was to concentrate on an object, and Adele, in her dormitory room, was to write down any impressions she was able to pick up.

At the time agreed upon, Doris sat in her room. The object she had chosen for concentration was a charm bracelet, but she had barely started looking at it when she heard her mother cry out. She rushed to the kitchen, where she found her mother very upset. She had allowed a pretty little Corning Ware teapot, white with blue flowers, to boil dry. When she had snatched it from the flame, it had burned a hole in the nearly new counter top.

That was the end of the distance experiment for that night. They would have to try another time. In the morning Doris started explaining to Adele what had happened and why she hadn't been able to follow through with her part of the experiment. She remembers that Adele was giving her a funny look. "You'll never believe this," she said. And she handed Doris a piece of paper on which she had written: "White teapot with blue flowers."

A palm reader in New York looked at the palm of a woman she had never seen before, and said, "Oh, poor thing, you were sent away from home when you were five years old."

This was true; because of family financial difficulty, she had been sent to live with her grandmother. The same palm reader told a young man that he had been a blue baby when he was born, and treated by his family as an imbecile. This was also true.

These cases could go on and on. They have been strongly convincing to those who have experienced them, and though they do not "prove" ESP, as Dr. Stevenson said once in a speech to the Parapsychological Association, "If only a few spontaneous cases demonstrate paranormal processes—and I believe the number is far greater—then any picture of human personality which does not take account of them must be ridiculously impoverished."

J.G.P. COMMENTS:

The question, "Can Mr. A communicate with Mr. B by extrasensory means?" deals with telepathy, the use of ESP by one person to make direct contact with the mind—the thoughts, strivings, and emotions—of another person.

If the accounts seem amazing, that is one of the most surprising things about them. The extent to which psychic experiences will strike us as strange tells a lot about how hard we try in our culture to ignore such happenings. Perhaps the attitude toward psychic experiences is changing, so that the "conspiracy of silence" is gradually crumbling and the taboo against psi is yielding before the advance of scientific research.

Telepathy was the kind of psychic experience that seemed most reasonable to the British scholars who began the first organized research into such matters nearly a century ago. Their preference for telepathy as the likely explanation—instead of clairvoyance, the extrasensory perception of physical objects or events—arose quite naturally out of the accounts of ESP experiences from everyday life, since they appeared almost always to be focused upon people rather than upon purely physical situations. A spontaneous ESP occurrence usually involved direct knowledge about a personal crisis or some grave danger that a distant family member, relative, or friend was facing. The experience seemed to be a way that the percipient learned about a threat to a loved one's well-being. It was only natural, therefore, to assume that the person who was going through the crisis was taking the initiative and sending a message to let the person receiving it know of the trouble. Thus telepathy, taken at face value, was regarded as an ESP experience involving at least two persons, a sender (or agent) and a receiver (or percipient).

Examined more closely, these reports raise a number of questions. Are they reliable in that they establish that ESP really was involved? If at least some of them stand up to careful scrutiny, do they prove telepathy or can they be explained just as well in terms of clairvoyance? If telepathy occurred, was the central figure in the crisis really sending out a psychic SOS call for help, or was the percipient taking the initiative by focusing his ESP attention upon the mental state of the distant person?

The reports Naomi Hintze has described are personal accounts, and they are prone to errors of various kinds. Key parts of the events could have been forgotten or other parts added or exaggerated on the basis of faulty memory. The accounts may have been changed, unconsciously and in spite of the intention to be accurate, to make a trivial incident good or a good incident better. These doubts are appropriate enough when we are thinking of flaws that must exist in the whole mass of such material. But what we need to know is whether even some of the accounts stand up under the closest possible scrutiny. If only a small percentage of them prove to be correct, then these alone can be enough to support the conclusion that genuine ESP events do enter into daily life. We therefore look for cases in which the percipient wrote down the experience or told one or more persons about it before the facts about the distant events were confirmed. It requires patient work to check out such a report, but in hundreds of instances where the circumstances made it possible to get clear-cut evidence, the result of such careful investigation has been a strong indication of ESP at work in real-life situations.

Furthermore, in most instances a distant person seems to have been serving as an agent who sent out a message. As a rule, the cases emphasize the feature of crisis or danger, suggesting that the experience of the person caught up in the crisis was somehow a contributing factor. If this were not the case, it is strange that there are so few instances of ESP of catastrophic events without human involvement. Most of the cases, therefore, look as if they depended to some degree on telepathic communication, though once the psychic experience begins, it is not clear that the information obtained by ESP is restricted to what the sender was experiencing. In most instances the cases seem to involve an intermingling of telepathy and clairvoyance with the telepathic aspect usually but not always predominant. Let us examine a few of Mrs. Hintze's cases from this point of view.

Mrs. Berendt's dream about Mr. Williams at about the time of his death does not fit the usual pattern. If there was an agent, Mr. Williams would have been the one serving in this role. To hold this view, we must speculate that he did not die peacefully in his sleep but that he had a period of suffering and awareness of his dangerous condition. But if he sent out a telepathic call for help, why did it reach Mrs. Berendt, who was not particularly close to him, rather than his wife or even Mrs. Berendt's best friend, the sister-in-law? Or if Mrs. Berendt initiated the ESP contact, was she making telepathic contact with the person who was dying or clairvoyant contact with the fact of his death after it had occurred? Such questions, instead of casting doubt upon the value of the case, only reveal some of the complexities of a psychic experience.

Margaret De Bolt's life-saving telephone call fits Lola's interpretation that it came in response to her subconscious telepathic appeal. But it lends itself equally well to the view that Mrs. De Bolt was the active one and somehow shared her friend's state of mind as she attempted suicide. Either explanation would be telepathy.

If there was an active agent in Mrs. Weiher's case, it must have been the husband, who remembered at an unconscious level that he had not closed the draft. If we knew that the warning was recognized as his voice, this explanation would be more attractive. The twins were apparently too small to sense any danger, so we cannot suppose that the mother sensed the alarm from that source. The weight of the evidence in this case seems to me to tilt toward clairvoyance.

In the teapot incident, the sender failed to communicate what she was trying to send, while the receiver got an impression of something that happened unexpectedly and that the agent thought of as only something that interrupted the experiment. This observation illustrates how inadequate is our understanding of the part the agent is playing. A good step forward in this direction was made by Ian Stevenson in his analysis of 195 experiences when the percipient knew that something was wrong with a particular person or at a particular place, but got no details. In more than half of these cases, the percipient took some action appropriate to the ESP impression received, such as changing travel plans in the course of a journey in order to go to the person who was in a crisis. *The findings show that when the agent was thinking about or calling for the percipient during the crisis, the percipient was more likely to take some specific action.*

Though the evidence for telepathy from real life is strong, no one would question the desirability of getting independent proof in the laboratory. Ideally, this should be done in a way that excludes other possible interpretations and thus leaves telepathy as the only explanation if the results are too good to attribute to luck. Two such experiments have been done. In each of them a team of investigators chose the targets that were to be sent telepathically by speaking to each other and recording the results of the test only in terms of shared memories that no other person could interpret. Thus both experiments were conducted without any written records that would be available as targets. One of these investigations was done with unselected volunteer subjects, and the results were successful at the level that would be expected by chance only once in a hundred such tests. The other experiment was done with a selected subject who had demonstrated an outstanding ESP ability. Her "pure telepathy" result was as good as her results under other conditions when she might have used clairvoyance, and the success achieved would have been expected on a chance basis only once in a million repetitions of the test.

Since these two studies, both carried out in the forties, gave clear-cut laboratory evidence that telepathy really occurs, some experimenters have chosen to do their laboratory research with methods that resemble closely the conditions in everyday life that favor the occurrence of psychic experiences. All of these lines of research have employed a sender who was undergoing some vivid and interesting experience, sometimes even a contrived crisis situation, in the expectation that the receiver would be more successful in getting it by ESP.

The majority of spontaneous psychic experiences occur in dreams. Picking up on this clue, in 1960 Dr. Montague Ullman, a psychiatrist at Maimonides Medical Center in Brooklyn, launched a research program on telepathy in dreams. Dr. Ullman and his colleagues used a number of subjects, but the major findings were based upon a few selected individuals who were adept at recalling their dreams and also had outstanding telepathic ability. By good fortune, the subject who achieved the most striking result was Dr. Robert L. Van de Castle, a psychologist who has made the study of sleep and dreaming his special field.

The Maimonides work proves beyond any reasonable doubt that the dreams of a subject sleeping under laboratory conditions may be influenced to some degree by what an agent in a distant room is thinking about and trying to project into the dream process. The dream experiments were obviously more extensive, but even when they are reduced in this way to the lowest common denominator, the revolutionary impact of the findings remains strong and clear.

Thelma Moss, doing ESP research for her Ph.D. thesis under the direction of Dr. J. A. Gengerelli at UCLA, placed the sender in a doubly soundproofed room and had him, in random order, experience six contrasting, intensely emotional situations. One situation, for example, was to watch slides— accompanied by funeral music—showing President Kennedy's assassination. After experiencing each situation, the sender recorded his reactions to it. Meanwhile, the receiver was seated relaxed in an easy chair in another room, where he was told to record on tape every thought and change in emotion that he experienced. Results were obtained from thirty sender-receiver pairs, each of whom went through the six situations in a random order. For each pair, the records of sender and receiver were marked so as to conceal the order in which they were made, and they were given to outside judges to see how successfully they could match the two records. The judges were successful at a level that would be expected by chance only one time in a thousand, while trials made with nonemotional material gave only chance results. Repetitions of the experiment along these general lines also gave good results for strongly emotional material and chance results for nonemotional material.

In October 1974 a paper in the British science journal *Nature* reported on ESP research carried out at Stanford Research Institute (SRI). The experimenters, Russell Targ and Harold Puthoff, worked primarily with Uri Geller and another subject. Geller has become well known for his claims of unusual psychic abilities, especially the power to cause metal to bend without the apparent use of any normal means such as force or heat. The SRI investigators say they witnessed some of the metal-bending but did not study it under controlled experimental conditions, and therefore had not reached any conclusion on it.

Rather, they focused their attention upon testing Geller's ESP abilities. He was clearly successful under their well-planned and carefully followed experimental procedures.

In one experiment Geller attempted to duplicate on each trial a target drawing that one of the experimenters had made of an object. Either Geller or one of the experimenters was locked inside a room that had a double wall of metal. This isolation room was shielded against any communication by normal means—such as light, sound or radio. Only after he was separated from the experimenters did they choose at random what the target would be and make a drawing of it. Geller then concentrated upon getting an impression of the target and drawing it. If he felt he was successful, he submitted his drawing to be counted as an official trial in the experiment. If he was not confident, he was allowed to pass and the trial did not count.

Two independent judges were asked to match the ten targets to the ten sets of drawings made by Geller. Each judge did this without making any error, a result that would be expected by chance less than one time in a million matchings of the ten pairs.

In other trials no one present knew what the target was. Geller's drawing under those conditions did not match the targets any better than would be expected by chance. Thus it appears that a sender was essential in some way to the success of the drawings experiments.

Another kind of experiment involved having Geller try to call what face was uppermost on a die that one of the experimenters had shaken vigorously inside a metal box. The subject guessed the die eight times, and when the box was opened he proved to be correct on every trial. The results are, again, highly significant, with odds against chance of approximately a million to one. Clearly, Geller was successful even though no one knew the right answer and thus could have been acting as a telepathic sender.

The other outstanding subject in the SRI research was Pat Price, a retired policeman and former city councilman. He participated in an experiment in which telepathy seems likely, though it is not the only possible explanation for good results. On each of nine trials an outstanding landmark in the San Francisco Bay area, randomly chosen from among more than a hundred such possible targets, was used. A team of two to four experimenters was allowed thirty minutes to reach the target by car, and then for thirty more minutes they stayed there while thinking about the features of the location. Meanwhile, back at SRI another experimenter who had no knowledge of which location was the target had Price record on tape any impressions he received.

Later five judges, working independently, decided which one of the subject's impressions recorded on the nine trials best fitted each of the nine target locations. The subject's descriptions were not precise, and the agreement among the judges in the matchings was not unanimous. Nevertheless, in six of the nine trials more judges agreed upon the correct choice than upon an incorrect matching of target and impressions. The odds against getting correct agreement on so many trials are greater than a thousand to one. Therefore, chance coincidence is not a reasonable interpretation of the result, and we can agree with the experimenters that the subject somehow received real, though incomplete and imperfect, information about the distant scenes.

The SRI scientists said in their report that they took as their main responsibility to test under adequate conditions whether information can reach the subject by some channel other than those hitherto known and accepted in science. From their work and other evidence, we can accept telepathy as a good working hypothesis, one that has strong support from many lines of evidence, without feeling uncomfortable because we are still far from having all the answers.

X+Y=Z

"It would be a greater stretch of credulity to believe the witnesses were all insincere, incompetent or deceived, than to believe the truth of their statements, however strange or mysterious they be."—C. W. Mitchell, X+Y=Z, or The Sleeping Preacher *(1876)*

Nearly a hundred years ago a curious little book titled *X+Y=Z, or The Sleeping Preacher* was printed for the Reverend C. W. Mitchell. It consists mostly of the repetitious attestations of witnesses to the marvels performed by an Alabama minister, the Reverend Constantine Blackmon Sanders. We chose to use it because it contains some evidence of the rather rare ability to perceive clairvoyantly, and also because of its value to psychic research: it is almost the only source of information concerning this strangely afflicted and apparently gifted personality who in his dissociated state always signed himself X+Y=Z.

The author of this book said that he was presenting the "most remarkable, preternatural, mental phenomena that have come to light . . . since the days of Jesus Christ and his apostles."

He provided the names and addresses of about seventy witnesses, including ten clergymen (one a university president), six physicians, and one member of the Alabama legislature. The wonders were witnessed, as he said, not by those "unlearned and vicious; but by men and women of unblemished moral character." And there follows the rather wistful plea for belief with which we begin this chapter.

The early life of Constantine B. Sanders seems not to have been particularly "strange or mysterious." He was born to farm parents in Madison County, Alabama, in 1831. Left fatherless at the age of six, his schooling was scanty. Later in life he was to receive an honorary degree of Doctor of Divinity from the Cumberland Presbyterian Church, but when he was taken under the care of the presbytery and began preparations to study for the ministry at twenty-one, he could scarcely write his name.

Since it was known also that the uneducated young ministerial candidate was afflicted with what were referred to as "nervous spasms," there is little wonder that an older minister, the Reverend Mr. Bone, doubted that he would ever amount to much in the ministry. Mr. Bone was further dismayed one night after a church meeting when he was wakened by his landlord, who, candle in hand, announced that he was bringing the young Sanders in to share his bed. He said, "I felt no little alarm at the idea of sleeping with a man that had spasms; especially in a room alone with him, and that room isolated from the family residence."

Mr. Sanders slept for a time. Mr. Bone did not, for he was, as he said, "looking out for the fit which I anticipated."

It came, lasting for about fifteen or twenty minutes and accompanied by terrible groanings and muscular contortions. When it ended—and this would hardly seem more conducive to a night's rest—the young Mr. Sanders began to sing. But Mr. Bone assures us that "It was the most heavenly music I ever heard. Then he made a short, fervent prayer. He then preached a sermon . . . which I never heard excelled by anyone . . . Instead of being scared to death, I was surprised and filled with joy unspeakable . . . I have seen him in like condition very often since."

This condition, described in more detail by other contributors to the book, included some very alarming aspects. The woman who was his landlady while he attended the school which was to prepare him for the ministry, mentioned the terrible headaches which often accompanied his convulsions: "He often exclaimed, 'It will surely kill me.' And on one occasion he said, 'My head feels like it has opened.'"

Dr. Thach, a physician who had treated Sanders for sixteen years at the time when he contributed his testimony to the book, said that during these seizures his eyes would be so gorged with blood that frequently the blood would trickle down the cheeks in drops. Often he had excruciating chest pains and great difficulty in breathing, ". . . which I have often seen suspended for such a length of time as to induce me to believe it impossible that it could ever be restored."

Strange as the man's physical symptoms were, the little book would never have been written had they not been accompanied by even stranger psychic manifestations. Dr. Thach said, "With these paroxysms of suffering there is almost always a peculiar condition, to be inexplicable . . . which those acquainted with him generally call 'sleep,' merely from the fact that, when recovered from this condition, he is totally ignorant of any and everything that has occurred while in this state (even the length of time that has elapsed, not knowing whether an hour or a week) . . . and yet, at the time, he seems conscious of everything that is going on around him; and not only so, but of what is transpiring at any point to which his attention is directed, regardless of distance."

From his bed in Alabama, Sanders "saw" the burning of a block of business buildings in Salisbury, North Carolina, on the night of February 26, 1866. The next day he told a neighbor about it, Mrs. Mary Brown, who was from that area: "You need not have any uneasiness about your folks at home. I went to see them last night. They are all as well as usual." The event of the fire was later confirmed in a letter from Salisbury more than three hundred miles away.

At that same time, although Mr. Sanders had never been in North Carolina, he spoke of a division which might be made of a tract of land on Mrs. Brown's former homestead near Salisbury. He described a certain tree as a beginning point, then told the way the dividing line would be run, mentioning its course past the orchard, stream, stock-lot and barn with, as Mrs. Brown attested, "as much accuracy as anyone could have possibly done had he been on the identical spot of ground."

He "saw" the death of a neighbor, Lieutenant Robert McClure, when it occurred in Tennessee, nearly a hundred and fifty miles away. Guests sitting with Sanders noticed that he seemed overcome by emotion. They heard him say, "Poor fellow! How he suffers! He is almost gone! He is going! Going! Gone!" And then he told those present, "Lieutenant

McClure has just died suddenly of an internal hemorrhage near Clarksburg, Tennessee."

Young McClure, recently married, had left his bride with her mother, expecting to be in Tennessee only a short time. The following morning she received a telegram informing her of his death.

Sanders "found" lost objects—gold coins, a ten-dollar bill, a gold watch chain, and other things—seeing their location at a distance by apparently clairvoyant means.

His "peculiar sleeps" were not always accompanied by pain. Often he was said to be cheerful, and such an engaging conversationalist that guests would stay far into the night to hear him talk. At times he wrote things down and had no memory of them afterwards. On one occasion, when asked for help in locating a deranged woman who had escaped her caretakers, he referred to his notes and found information which enabled the searchers to find her.

Sometimes $X+Y=Z$ wrote in Latin and Greek. Those familiar with the languages translated these writings, but Sanders himself could not read or understand them, for he had no conscious knowledge of any language other than English.

Like the remarkable Edgar Cayce, who was to come into prominence many years later, Sanders was deeply concerned lest his unusual powers should interfere with his desire to be an effective witness to his devout Christian faith. He, too, although to a lesser degree, diagnosed physical ailments, and of course, like Cayce, had never studied medicine. He seemed to have a considerable knowledge of the human body and its ailments, however. During his periods of dissociation he examined the sick without coming in contact with them, writing diagnoses and giving prescriptions.

Dr. Thach said, "I have frequently had him to give me the exact condition of patients whom he had never seen, and who were miles distant. His prescriptions frequently contain medicines which cannot be procured in this country, which he makes arrangements to import; showing his comprehensive view of *Materia Medica* in this preternatural way."

At one time Dr. Thach is reported to have asked Sanders how one of his patients was doing, and Sanders replied, "He is no worse than when you left him, but his wife has made a mistake in giving the medicine. You left two different powders to be given, one in a white, the other in a blue paper, directing her which to give first . . . But I think her mistake will do no harm."

When Dr. Thach asked him if he could identify the powders, he did so. The next morning Thach found that, as described, the wife had made the mistake, but with no harm done.

Sanders' seizures were a source of great embarrassment to him. At times he seemed almost heartbroken, feeling that many considered him to be a trickster, a "reverend mountebank." Although he sometimes fell down in convulsions when attempting to preach, he was said to be a preacher of great power and persuasion. In spite of his many afflictions, he married at the age of twenty-five. He and his wife, Duanna, had six children, and what seemed to be a very happy family life as they moved from one small-town pastorate to another.

Scores of incidents were included in the book to show Sanders' paranormal abilities, and many of the witnesses indicated that they could have related many more. The author tells us that the phenomena occurred almost daily.

Little was known about dual personality in Mr. Sanders' day, although a few studies had been made. Since the newspaper stories that appeared about him in Louisville and Cincinnati papers were widely copied, it seems strange that they did not happen to come to the attention of anyone who was qualified and interested enough to make a psychological investigation of the case.

If this was ever done, the book gives no hint of it. Mr. Sanders is quoted as having said, "My peculiar developments will not be explained from a scientific standpoint." He said that it was impossible for him to give a comprehensible explanation, but he compared his ability to that of the telegraph, then of fairly recent invention, which received messages as well from five thousand miles as from fifty. He said his spirit did not actually leave the body to go to distant localities, but simply extended his scope of vision so that he was able to see distant events as well as those which took place close at hand.

Apparently the writings of Sanders' secondary personality

were considerable, although, insofar as is known, nothing has survived. We are told that his writings were invariably signed X+Y=Z. The trance state never produced any explanation for this strange mathematical signature. When writing or speaking of himself, the secondary personality always used the term "my Casket" for the normal Sanders. This separate, though similar, personality seemed to have warm affection and concern for his "Casket," exhorting him not to "neglect the gift that is in thee."

The only attempt at an explanation of his supernormal abilities was made in connection with his affirmation that the dying actually do see visions and hear that which is inaudible to others present at deathbeds. This took place, he said, when the body was modified by approaching dissolution. When his "Casket" had been similarly affected, very near to death on so many occasions, the veil had been withdrawn in "a preternatural way."

In mid-February of 1876, X+Y=Z gave notice that he would soon be taking leave of his "Casket," and on May 5 of that year he wrote a letter of farewell. Thus the "peculiar sleeps" ended after twenty-two years. After a time of adjustment to his new condition as an undivided personality, Sanders appeared to feel enormous relief. X+Y=Z had, however, said he would return.

And there we are, left hanging by the Reverend C. W. Mitchell and almost everybody else. The writings of X+Y=Z, referred to as "books and papers," seem to have vanished without a trace. We have not even been able to determine the date of C. B. Sanders' death. We have found some indication that others have attempted to do research on this tantalizing story, but they seem to have met up with the same stone wall.

We do have a bit of evidence that X+Y=Z may have made at least one reappearance. F. W. H. Myers, discussing trance states in his *Human Personality and Its Survival of Bodily Death* tells us of an event that took place about thirteen years after the secondary personality supposedly had taken its leave.

Myers reports that Sanders, while suffering on his bed, declared with some amusement to witnesses that he had just "seen" a man stand to volunteer to pray for sinners at a religious meeting, then kneel, and instead of praying, fall asleep. This, like all the other evidence, is backed up by more than one witness, including the man who went to sleep.

Although Dr. Walter Franklin Prince wrote some fifty pages about this case for the Boston Society for Psychic Research, he, too, was limited almost entirely to Mr. Mitchell's book. He felt that the case never had received the attention it deserved. He seemed strongly convinced of its evidential value, and calls attention to the fact that the author makes the flat statement that in no instance had Sanders ever been detected in dissimulation, fraud or charlatanism. He considered this proof that the author had no fear that his statement would be challenged, since the book was to go into circulation in the towns where Sanders had spent almost all his life.

He says, "In such small places everybody knows everybody, and everybody is under the scrutiny of many curious and critical eyes. Especially a clergyman, and a clergyman's family, and his ox and his ass, are in the sharpest focus of attention. Living all his life within a few miles of where he was born . . . his would seem to be a most unfavorable situation to carry on a career of deception for twenty-two years."

J.G.P. COMMENTS:

The 1929 report by Walter Franklin Prince, to which Mrs. Hintze referred, concludes that a number of the psychic phenomena of Reverend Sanders, as reported by witnesses, could not be set aside on any reasonable grounds by an open-minded reader, and therefore the case as a whole stood up as strong evidence for the reality of ESP. But some of the incidents could have been a hoax by Sanders—if he had wished to fool his associates and if he had been fantastically lucky in carrying out his trick a large number of times without once having been caught or coming under suspicion. For example, there might have been trickery involved when Sanders would announce where some lost object was to be found, and then it would be recovered at that spot either by Sanders in the presence of witnesses or by someone else.

But during the years since Prince examined the case, revolutionary advances have been made in parapsychology. We no longer need to agonize over whether fraud was involved or whether the exploits of the $X+Y=Z$ personality prove the reality of ESP, since this conclusion has been reached many times over on the basis of other evidence. We can, therefore, approach the material in the Mitchell book with the attitude that it was likely genuine ESP throughout and see what we can learn that may be of value in current psi research.

The first lesson has to do with the social environment, which influences research on psi phenomena. Parapsychology shares this environment with other branches of science, but there is one respect in which it has an advantage over them: the puzzling natural events that give rise to the questions with which our field is concerned *take place in the realm of experience*. The ordinary person knows that these unexplained powers of human nature exist. If he has not experienced them himself, he has not been far removed from others who have. And a personally experienced psi phenomenon creates its own insistent demand for a scientific solution.

The publication of the book $X+Y=Z$ is an early illustration of the desire for better understanding of the psychic phenomena that people know about through their own direct, inner experience. Though orthodox science does not take the psi factor into account, we do not have to be told that such happenings are important, because we feel this and accept it intuitively. If science can successfully find ways to probe the enormous physical universe, how can it neglect the clear signals of psychic experience that point to unfathomed depths of human nature?

It takes more than a great psychic gift to advance our understanding of these matters. The gifted person must be willing to be investigated. According to the record, Reverend Sanders had both the interest and the patience to cooperate to the fullest. This, plus the willingness of witnesses to testify to their observations, puts us in a good position to examine what happened to him.

The sharp change that came over Sanders when he went

into his special sleep was necessary for his psychic abilities to come into play. The statements of the many witnesses give no indication of any noticeable ESP abilities in his normal state. It seems clear, therefore, that a profound change of consciousness somehow made it possible for him to use psychic powers that must have been present but unavailable for use at other times. This observation alerts us to expect and look for quite exceptional altered states that may release really powerful manifestations of psi. His example should encourage us to expect more than the relatively modest improvements in ESP that we have obtained so far through altered states of consciousness produced in the laboratory.

We can also note that though the scope and character of the psychic experiences recorded by the X+Y=Z personality were wide and varied, in all of them Reverend Sanders seemed to be striving to become the kind of minister that he would have liked to be in his normal state. The accounts of the witnesses seem to show that he was largely occupied during his special trances with happenings in his general location as well as with the concerns of his parishioners and fellow ministers of the region. His mind seemed to work like a psychic radar that was constantly scanning the surroundings for anything of interest.

Occasionally he showed a detailed knowledge of something at a great distance, such as a fire that burned out a block of buildings in Salisbury, North Carolina, but even this event was connected with an Alabama neighbor who had relatives in that city.

Time and time again, he seemed to pick up interesting details that were of concern to those around him. They were events that might have attracted the notice of the normal Sanders if he had been in a position to observe them with his eyes or other senses. The sleeping Sanders simply had a wide scope for the play of his attention, and he seemed, according to the record, to have remained alert for events near and far, but beyond sensory range, that interested him.

The reports of his feats of recovering lost objects, especially money, are so numerous that he would today be dubbed a "finder." In the rural South during that period, money would have been a precious possession, and it seems likely that a simple, self-made minister would have felt strongly at times the effects of not having it. He may well have felt the anguish that others suffered through losing money, since there is no indication that he ever tried to keep for himself anything of value he had recovered if the owner could be identified. But this finding ability also worked when the value was not large, so it was not simply a matter of doing someone a real service.

The frequency of these incidents seems to indicate that it was not possible that anyone could have led the Reverend Sanders to the object by telepathy. His finding experiences are therefore evidence for *clairvoyance*. This mode of ESP has been investigated extensively in the laboratory during the last fifty years. As we turn our attention to some recent studies of the extrasensory perception of physical objects or events, it is good to have the Sanders case as an indication that clairvoyance, like telepathy, has its roots in the experiences of everyday life.

In 1961, in Prague, Czechoslovakia, thirty-year-old Pavel Stepanek began to take part in ESP tests that Dr. Milan Ryzl was conducting. Stepanek did not claim to have the power of clairvoyance, though as a boy, in 1945 when World War II was apparently finished in Central Europe, he had pleaded with his parents to leave their home one day and go with him to visit an aunt. When the parents refused, Stepanek went alone. Later that day the Allied Forces staged a bombing raid on Prague, the only one that city suffered, and the apartment house in which the family lived was hit. The parents were not injured, though they had to be moved to an apartment in another building.

In his tests, Ryzl was using his own homemade ESP-test procedure. The subject guessed which side of a card, white on one side and colored on the other, was facing toward him inside a cardboard cover. A convenient number of targets concealed in this way were used for a set of trials, and after each run through the set, the cards were removed, randomized, and reinserted into the covers before they were used again. Naturally, the experimenter took precautions to insure that the subject could not identify any of the targets by using sensory cues.

The experimenter said in letters abroad that Stepanek had been successful in naming around sixty percent of the colors correctly over many trials, as compared with the fifty percent expected on a chance basis. That level of success maintained for the thousands of trials done was highly significant.

In June 1962, I visited Prague and participated in an experiment with Stepanek that confirmed the earlier results. I went there again in February 1963 and worked with Ryzl in two further experiments that also yielded successful results. After our findings were published, other parapsychologists became interested, and over the next few years investigators from Britain, Holland, Sweden, India, Japan, and the U.S.A. went there to take part in the research with this subject. During 1967–1969 we were also able to bring Stepanek to Charlottesville on three occasions for more intensive periods of research at the University of Virginia than could be carried out in Prague.

From the point of view of the safeguarding of the experiments against every conceivable source of error and the strongest evidence produced for clairvoyance, I will cite two experiments done five years apart. These are not, however, the only ones that were adequate by ordinary standards.

The first experiment was carried out by Jan Blom (on the science faculty of the University of Amsterdam) and me in Prague in 1963. We worked with the subject without the help of Ryzl and did the work in a new location. Our experiment included four thousand trials spread over four days, and the target cards were concealed individually inside double cardboard containers.

We hid the cards inside the envelopes while we were alone in our hotel in the morning of each test day, doing this in such a manner that neither experimenter knew which way each card was placed in its container. Each envelope was then sealed shut. During the session one of the experimenters, working in a separate room with the door closed, randomized the envelopes and concealed them inside larger cardboard covers before each run. When Stepanek called the targets, he saw only the outside covers, and no one could possibly have any sensory knowledge of which colors were facing upward on the hidden cards.

The success rate in this experiment was 53.8 percent. This was lower than the level reached in some of the previous tests. Nevertheless the result is highly significant, since the odds against finding a score this high purely by chance are a half-million-to-one.

The second experiment that yielded very strong evidence for ESP was one done at the University of Virginia in the spring of 1968. This experiment was planned not merely to test once more whether Stepanek could "beat chance" in the total number of cards he called correctly, but also to try to confirm an effect that had been observed in earlier tests: the subject had developed personal preferences for particular concealed targets. He called certain ones the same way on as many as seventy-five to eighty-five percent of the trials, while he responded to other targets only at the chance fifty-fifty level. Since he had no normal way of knowing which target was presented on each trial, this wide difference in his way of responding to them was itself evidence of ESP.

A three-experimenter test was planned to provide maximal safeguards against flaws in the research, and highly significant results were obtained, with the odds against occurrence by chance being more than a million to one.

The period of concentrated research with Stepanek lasted for a decade. It is the largest number of trials and the longest period on record of a successful demonstration of ESP by a subject in laboratory tests. More investigators conducted experiments with Stepanek and reported their own successful results than has been true for any other ESP test subject.

Another outstanding ESP subject was Lalsingh Harribance, a citizen of Trinidad, who was also in his thirties. He gained a reputation in his country for being able to give "readings" of persons, either face-to-face or from photographs, in which he made correct statements about personal things that he apparently could not have known in any normal way. His reputation brought him to the attention of a psychologist in Trinidad, who tested Harribance for ESP, with good results.

The psychologist wrote to Dr. J. B. Rhine, who invited Harribance to Durham, North Carolina, to be tested.

In the Institute for Parapsychology the investigators tested Harribance with the standard ESP cards, without any success, and they shortly informed him that he was free to return home. The subject was not willing to admit defeat, so he visited the Psychical Research Foundation in the same city. There W. G. Roll, the research director, designed a test that seemed closer to what Harribance was accustomed to doing with his psychic abilities in daily life.

The plan adopted was to use ten photographs from a college annual, five men and five women. The target pictures were arranged face down in random order in one room, after which Harribance in another room called, from left to right, his impressions of the sex of the persons. The subject was not always successful in this test—no ESP subject has been able to produce on demand every time—but he frequently achieved phenomenally high scores in experiments when good safeguards were used against sensory cues and other possible weaknesses.

He worked as a subject for approximately five years, but toward the end of that period there was a gradual decline in his ability to produce results in the controlled laboratory situation. Harribance then appears to have dropped out of the research picture.

Dr. Helmut Schmidt was a research physicist at the Boeing Research Laboratories during the late sixties. During that same period he invented a machine which could be used for testing automatically for psi ability of different kinds. I will describe here how he used the machine in an experiment dealing with clairvoyance.

The subject sat facing a small metal box smaller than a portable typewriter. It had an on-off switch, two counters, a row of four colored light bulbs, and a row of four buttons lined up with the four bulbs. After the switch was turned on, pressing one of the buttons would cause one of the bulbs to light up immediately. At the same time one of the counters would change to register the next higher number to show that a trial had been made. If the light that turned on was the one paired with the button that was pressed, the other counter would turn to the next higher number to show that a hit was made. The order in which the lamps lit was random and was determined by the machine in a manner that could not be known in any normal, sensory way. Without the use of psi, therefore, the expected score would be approximately one-fourth of the number of trials.

In this experiment the order in which the lights were turned on was determined by a hidden paper tape that was fed into the machine. A total of 15,000 trials were made.

When the scores were evaluated, they showed that the subjects had chosen and pressed the buttons in accordance with their stated intention 260 more times than the average expected by mere luck. This score is much too high to be reasonably taken to be a mere chance happening. Therefore, in view of the safeguards that were built into the machine and that were enforced automatically, we are left with ESP as the only available explanation. And since the physical state of the machine-tape combination was already set within the machine when the subject made his choice, the most obvious interpretation of the results is that the subjects occasionally chose correctly by clairvoyance.

These few examples of recent studies of clairvoyance show that this particular psychic phenomenon can be accepted as a reality. Indeed, it is difficult to see how anyone who will examine the evidence could justify not agreeing that clairvoyance occurs, or at least that the evidence makes its reality a strong possibility.

PRECOGNITION:
A FEW NEW INSTANCES

*"If it is true . . . that the psi faculty is an innate, if often
latent, ability in each man, the ostensible paranormal
events must be a daily occurrence involving hundreds of
thousands, even millions, of people. Yet relatively few
new instances are produced in the literature of psychical
research bodies, and skeptics can ask with some justification
why this is the case if such experiences are as widespread
as we claim."—Robert H. Ashby,* Quarterly Journal of
Spiritual Frontiers Fellowship. *(Spring, 1972)*

The question posed by Mr. Ashby is a good one: Why does
one encounter the same tired old cases over and over in so
many of the books on psychic phenomena? Are these ancient
anecdotes the only ones that the writers have ever heard of?

Readers of this book will not find very many of the classics
of the field. But they may note, and wonder a little, at the
use of so many cases involving persons living in the area
where the authors currently are living. The first reason for
this is easily guessed: investigation is simplified; it's always a
sound idea, in the words of the old adage, to "put down your
bucket where you are."

Our second reason is more important. Despite the fact that
Dr. Pratt has made dozens of investigative trips to many
countries of the world, we have used many local experiences
to reinforce a point that is often lost sight of: manifestations
of psychic phenomena are everywhere. An investigator could
probably pick almost any place in the United States, or in
the world, and find enough cases to fill a good-sized book.

The majority of reported psi experiences have to do with
precognition, direct awareness of future events often mani-
fested in dreams. For example, Anna Martin, a Charlottes-

ville woman, dreams of events which, although they are often trivial, come true time after time in minutest detail.

Of particular value, from a research point of view, is the fact that she has kept a dream record for many years, and whenever possible has told the dream or given a written account to another person immediately. In many instances, the dream has become actuality before she has been able to pass on her account of it.

For a number of months Mrs. Martin mailed her dream record to Dr. Pratt. Her method of reporting is so admirable that it may serve as an example for others who may wish to keep such a record. I cite only a few from her file:

DREAM: I was fixing drinks for some people and everyone was joking about their color. They were a translucent blue, and I was explaining that they were called blue martinis. I poured some of the liquid from the shaker into a brandy snifter for serving. Comments such as "What is that?" and "Are you going to drink that stuff?" were being made as I prepared to serve the drinks.

REALITY: The next day my cleaning woman was washing windows. I went into the kitchen during the afternoon and noticed a brandy snifter half full of blue liquid on the counter. I was surprised, but said nothing, assuming she had some purpose for this unusual combination. Later, when my husband and children came home, I was working in the kitchen but had not noticed that the blue concoction was still there. The comments were the same as the ones in my dream. I sniffed the liquid and found that it was Windex, but my maid had gone and I could not find out why she had poured Windex into a brandy snifter. The appearance of the liquid and the glass which held it were exactly as in the dream.

DREAM: There was a single vivid image which appeared, so far as I am able to recall, outside of any context of association. It was that of a crescent moon, and in front of the moon there was a cross which appeared to have been traced by a finger that had been dipped in blood. The moon was yellow against a medium-blue sky, dull, but not dark enough for perfect night. The cross was a bit wavering in design, as if the finger tracing it had trembled. It was projected considerably in the foreground, whereas the moon seemed to be much more distantly located. I was alarmed to the point of waking immediately, and my dreams were disturbed during the rest of the night.

REALITY: Shortly after this dream I did encounter a crescent moon against the yet-blue sky of early evening, and I thought about the image in my dream. During the week I saw a movie in which a cross of blood was marked off on a girl's naked body. The size and proportions were like the cross I had seen in my dream. The effect of the movie was characterized by the same shock and foreboding which had prompted me to wake much disturbed. I thought immediately of the crescent moon, now further back in time.

DREAM: A great puzzle to me for years was a recurrent dream which found me getting out of bed and going to the bathroom, but with neither bed nor bath situated as in any place I had ever lived. Other details of the house were very clear.

REALITY: I finally moved into the house I had dreamed of so many times even before the house was built. (It was built for someone else and I had nothing to do with the plans.) Many details are almost exactly the same. In this house I have finally "come home" to the bedroom and bathroom of my dreams, and the deeply ingrained mental route to the bathroom is identical.

DREAM: I was talking on the telephone to a friend when our call was interrupted by a feminine voice talking very fast and not too audibly. The effect was gibberish, but it was very disconcerting. We terminated our conversation because of this interference.

REALITY: The following morning the friend with whom I was talking in the dream phoned me. I remarked that I had dreamed the night before that we were talking on the telephone and had been harassed by a woman's voice to the point that we had decided to hang up. Moments later we both heard a woman's voice in rapid conversation. It seemed to be an intrusion from some other line. It was quite annoying, so we agreed to hang up.

We move across the country now, to a Western state from which we have had a letter about a man and a woman who dreamed about each other before they met. The woman writes: "Several years ago I was invited to a house party at the home of friends in Arizona. I got there very late Friday night and was told that the rest of the guests would not arrive until around noon the next day.

"That night I dreamed that I was sitting somewhere in the sun with the light so bright on a rough white wall that it hurt my eyes. A man I had never seen before keep looking at me, and I had the thought that although he wasn't saying anything personal, he was making a pass at me.

"The next day, when the other guests arrived, we all went out onto the patio for drinks before lunch. I hadn't seen the patio the night before, but suddenly I became aware that the whole scene, especially the blinding sun on the white plaster wall, was the same as in my dream, and that one of the men who had just arrived was looking at me exactly as in the dream.

"When we went in to lunch he said, 'I'm sorry I have kept staring at you. But last night I had an erotic dream about you. Yes, I know I had never laid eyes on you, but in my dream I saw exactly how you would look.'

"Of course, I can't vouch for the fact that he really did have a dream about me. We just let it go at that because his girl friend was there and I could tell she was jealous. But I do know that my dream is more vivid in my memory than some of my real-life experiences. Maybe because it's the only precognitive dream I've ever had."

Mrs. H. D. Wigodsky, who lives in Omaha, Nebraska, has had a great many precognitive experiences, both awake and asleep, and nearly all of them have had to do with death. Card reading, however, had been different. Often she saw many happy events which later came true. ". . . but then I read the cards for my sister-in-law and saw her death. I told her I couldn't see anything. Shortly after that, she developed cancer and died. And I never read the cards any more."

Mrs. C. M. Luman, of Alexandria, Virginia, has told us of a dream which her mother had. She awoke one morning in great distress after having dreamed that her husband was sailing away on a ship with all on shore waving him goodbye until he was out of sight. Only a few days later they all went to the railroad station to see him off on a trip of a few days to New York. Mrs. Luman says, "As we stood there, waving and watching the train pull out, my mother was overcome with sadness. She told us children, 'This is exactly how it was in that dream the other night—we all stood like this, waving goodbye.' None of us ever saw him alive again. He died of a sudden illness in New York just a few days later."

Friends of Nancy Mancuso in New Orleans are so aware of her precognitive dreams that they sometimes say to her, "Please don't dream about me. Something might happen."

Within a three-month period Nancy recorded thirteen dreams and daytime premonitions that eventuated in reality. She dreamed that her mother's face would be disfigured, and it was. She dreamed that there would be a breakage at her office that would cause trouble, and a giant stapler exploded, almost blinding a co-worker. She suddenly knew when she saw a strange woman putting quarters into a change machine that she would get six nickels, and she did.

In 1960 Dr. Zoltan S. Szaloki was Director of Research at the Whitin Machine Works in Whitinsville, Massachusetts. He often made trips out of town in connection with his work, and on October 4 of that year Priska, his wife, was hurrying to get his lunch ready, since she knew the company car would be coming early in the afternoon to take him to the Boston airport. His bags were packed and ready for the trip to Atlantic City, New Jersey, to attend a textile machinery exhibition.

Dr. Szaloki was a little later than his wife expected him to be. "You'll have to hurry," Priska said, glancing at the clock. "You haven't much time if you're going to be ready by the time the car comes for you."

"I'm not going," he said.

"Not going? But I thought you had to go."

"I changed my mind. I have already turned my plane ticket in at the office."

The following afternoon was a Wednesday, and he usually played golf on that day. Mrs. Szaloki remembers teasing him a little. "I think you just don't want to miss your golf game."

He said, "No, that doesn't have anything to do with it. I just decided, all of a sudden, that I didn't want to go."

It was most unlike him. He didn't seem to want to discuss it further, so she let the matter drop. Under ordinary circumstances, more than a dozen years later she might not be remembering that day at all.

But the circumstances were far from ordinary. That night she attended the Ladies Field Day dinner at the golf club. When she offered to give a friend a ride home, the friend went to the phone to call her husband to tell him he need not come to pick her up. She came back, her face white.

"There's been a terrible accident. A plane crashed this afternoon into Boston Harbor and all four of the Whitin Machine Works men on it were killed."

Dr. Szaloki looked as if he were in shock when his wife got home. He had already received the news that his ticket had been given to Ross Newton, who was originally scheduled to leave the next day. He kept saying, "He went in my place. Oh God, he has four little children."

The accident was a most unusual one. An enormous flock of starlings, estimated at between ten and twenty thousand, had been ingested by the engines of the Lockheed Electra prop jet. Twenty-five seconds after takeoff, the plane crashed into the shallow waters of the harbor, killing sixty-two of its seventy-three passengers.

Those who have had psychic experiences once are apt to turn up again as repeaters. Mrs. Henry A. Weiher, whom we previously mentioned, was planning to visit her daughter in Massachusetts. She said she always took the morning Trailways bus and always sat in the front seat. As time for the trip approached, she became increasingly uneasy, and finally phoned her daughter to say she could not come. On the morning she had planned to go, she learned later, a lumber truck crashed into the bus and the woman in the front seat was injured and died.

Angela von Baillou and her mother went to a hotel one day, and as soon as they entered the cloakroom the mother put out her hand to touch a camel's-hair coat that was hanging there. Very much upset, she said, "I must get in touch with the man who owns this coat. At three o'clock tomorrow afternoon he is going to die." When they made inquiries of the desk clerk, he told them that the man was in his room working and could not be disturbed.

Angela says, "My mother then wrote the man a note and told him that he must not leave his room on the following afternoon. Yes, I am sure that she told him why. But a couple of days later we read in the paper that the man had died in an accident. When we contacted the desk clerk, we found that my mother's message had been delivered and that the man had promised to heed it. But he had received a frantic call from a close friend asking him to come at once. He left the hotel immediately and at about three o'clock in the afternoon, just as my mother had foreseen, was killed in an automobile accident."

J.G.P. COMMENTS:

Perhaps the concern about what is going to happen is the most universal one in human experience. Consider how frequently we use words that have a forward reach in time. *Foresee, expect, anticipate, wish, promise, plan, begin, prophesy, forecast, prognosticate* are only a few of the verbs that lace our everyday speech and express a state of mind directed to the future.

There are many areas of human activity in which information about future events is of vital importance, and highly skilled professions exist solely for the purpose of meeting this demand. We have meteorologists to forecast the weather, actuaries to predict life expectancy, opinion poll takers, and even astrologers. There has always been a strong demand for those who claim to be able to delve into the future.

Such forecasters use available knowledge and some system for interpreting it to make an educated guess about what is going to happen later. They depend on inference or reasoning, and, naturally, the results can be no better than the assumptions used and the accuracy or skill of the forecaster in applying them. This kind of work does not raise any questions of direct interest to parapsychologists. But the kinds of experiences that have been presented in the preceding pages, and the thousands of others like them, force us to recognize that these future events were not perceived in a way that depended upon reasoning or powers of inference. What could Dr. Szaloki have known that would keep him from boarding the plane before it crashed in Boston Harbor? How could Mrs. Martin have had the dream about the blue martinis in the brandy snifter that showed such surprising points of similarity to the events that occurred the next day in her kitchen? Taking these accounts at face value, there was no way that they could have been figured out in advance. This does not mean, however, that we can conclude that such reports prove that precognition is established.

We began our investigation by taking the closest possible look at cases such as those given in this chapter. Reports of experiences that stood up on first examination were then studied as closely as possible by follow-up correspondence, by seeking confirming testimony from independent witnesses, and by face-to-face interviews with the persons involved. These efforts often produced valuable additional information which gave strong reassurances that the facts of the cases under scrutiny were correct on all essential points. This was good as far as it went, but the experiences themselves were still spontaneous and widely scattered. Why not do what had been done with clairvoyance and telepathy, and devise a test for precognition to be used in the laboratory?

The first planned tests of precognition were carried out at Duke University in 1933. The beginning experiments were only exploratory, and the plan used was a very simple one. The subject was told to write his impression of what the future order of the cards would be when the pack was shuffled *after* he had finished writing his calls. These preliminary experiments gave significant positive results, but they could not be regarded as conclusive evidence of precognition, because the person shuffling the cards might have been using clairvoyance to match them to the recorded order of calls.

As the investigations were continued, careful controls were introduced to insure that there was no causal link of any kind possible between the subject's calls and the later target order.

The Schmidt machine described in the tests for clairvoyance was adapted to test for precognition. The apparatus was designed to generate a series of random targets, which are not selected before the subject presses one of the buttons, but rather, at random, approximately one-tenth second later. Thus the subject working with the machine is trying to predict a future event that will take place a split second after he has made his response.

Dr. Schmidt carried out two experiments in Seattle with his machine in 1967, with subjects who had been selected as good prospects on the basis of preliminary tests. The first experiment consisted of 63,066 trials, all made while trying to get as many hits as possible. The overall number of hits was 691 more than the most likely number expected by chance. The odds against doing as well as this merely by luck are more than a hundred million to one.

The second experiment included twenty thousand trials, and for approximately half of these the subject specified before starting a session that the aim was to get as few hits as possible. The hits made when the subjects were trying for a high score were 401 more than when they were seeking to avoid making hits. This result is somewhat better than that from the former experiment, the odds against chance being more than ten billion to one.

The subject B.D., supremely confident of his psi abilities, was tested, during his 1972 visit to the Institute for Parapsychology, for precognition with the Schmidt machine. In one series, under informal home conditions observed by two experimenters, he scored phenomenally high in nine hundred trials, reaching a level with odds against occurrence by chance of more than a million billion-to-one. In a formal laboratory test observed by Helmut Schmidt and J. B. Rhine, he scored 180 hits in 508 trials, 53 more than the expected chance number and a highly significant result. In a further informal test with one investigator present, trials were made in a dark room and with the bulbs of the machine disconnected so they would not turn on. The subject had to choose the buttons to be pressed by feel. It was possible to form an impression of the outcome of each trial from the fact that a wrong choice was followed by a single click made by the trial counter, while a correct choice brought a double click—the trial and the hit counters both advanced. This test included 329 trials with 163 hits, the highest scoring rate of all.

The above tests with B.D. were made without having the tape recorder connected to the machine. When a new experiment was started with the tape recorder attached, the scoring level dropped to near the chance level. B.D. first blamed the low results on the machine, but eventually it became clear to him that he was doing poorly for purely psychological reasons. This discovery increased his determination to succeed with the tape recorder, and over a period of eight days he raised his scoring level from twenty-seven percent to above thirty percent, approximately as high as he had scored in earlier tests without the taping attachment. This work with the taping of the records totaled more than five thousand trials with a score with odds against occurrence by chance of more than a thousand million to one.

One further example of research on precognition is an experiment conducted to test whether a subject could dream in the laboratory about something in his own future. This work was part of the program of dream studies at Maimonides, and it was done after the investigators had become convinced that they had demonstrated telepathy in dreams in the laboratory.

Dreams that later seem to come true are one of the most frequent kinds of psychic experience reported from everyday life. The common feature running through most of these cases is that the person dreams about something that he finds himself later experiencing in his own life. The experimenters decided to see if a selected subject who had experienced several such precognitive dreams was able to dream something one night about what they would have him experience the next night. The subject knew the plan and purpose of the test, but nobody knew what the "target experience" would be until after the night's dreams had been recorded.

During the day after the subject's dreams had been recorded, one of the experimenters made a random selection of a slide-plus-sound "theme" from a set of ten contrasting themes that were available for the research. The method used in making the selection was a complicated, rigidly planned procedure to select a digit in a manner that could not be influenced by the dream records. The digit indicated which theme was to be used for the subject's special experience for that night, the one that he had tried to dream about the night before. The subject looked at the series of slides on the selected theme while listening to the appropriate sounds through earphones. For example, one set of slides showed birds, and the sound was recordings of bird songs and calls.

This procedure was repeated until eight trials had been completed, as planned in advance. Three independent judges who had no other connection with the research were then asked to read over each night's dream record and grade it for how closely it resembled each one of the eight themes used in the experiment. The combined results of the judges showed that they had assigned the highest average grade to the dreams for five nights when comparing them with the correct target themes. This means that five hits were scored by the subject's dreams, and this result is significant, with the odds against occurrence by chance being more than eight hundred to one.

Methods like these have been adequate to guard against mistaking simple inferences about the future for true precognition, but we need to consider also whether the principle of the self-fulfilling prophecy can account for the precognition test results. Someone has a feeling that something is going to happen, and as a result, takes actions that make it happen. Frequently, people who experience self-fulfilling prophecies are unaware that they have made their predictions come true, but this principle is familiar to students of behavior and there is no reason for confusing it with precognition under ordinary circumstances.

In parapsychological tests, the subject often wants good results, as the experimenters also want the test to succeed, but under conditions that will give solid evidence for precognition. It is easy enough to insure that false evidence is not produced through recording errors or by other normal means. The question of the validity of the test becomes more difficult when we consider whether some form of psi other than precognition might have been used to make the targets match the calls. If so, a good score could not be interpreted as conclusive evidence for precognition.

Investigators of precognition have been fully aware of this problem, and they have taken extreme pains, as we saw in the dream study, to make the target selection objective and truly random. The experimenters say in their report of that work, however, that it is not possible to be completely sure that psychokinesis—mind over matter—has not crept into the target-selection process to bring about a good score. A number of experiments have used even more complicated methods of target selection for the purpose of screening out unwanted psi processes, and significant results have nevertheless been obtained. But anyone not willing to accept precognition can still say that the results could have been produced by other psi processes.

I should say here that the Schmidt machine was not claimed by the investigators who used it to be a method yielding clear evidence for precognition. They all recognized that the results could also be explained by psychokinesis acting upon the triggering actions of the machine to make the lamps light to correspond with the subject's responses. This opinion does not question the results from the machine as evidence of psi, and anyone may still consider that precognition is the more reasonable explanation of the results under the conditions of the test.

My personal opinion is that the laboratory results we now have from a large number of experiments, combined with the more striking and well-studied spontaneous cases, provide strong but not fully compelling evidence of precognition. We need further research into this question, and the evidence gathered thus far justifies the additional effort needed to reach a definite answer.

At present we do not have the slightest inkling of how precognition could be explained if it really does occur. If we had a theory that made sense of direct knowledge of future events, this should speed the progress of the research—or at least make the problem one to challenge the research efforts of more scientists.

TESTING:
DO YOU HAVE ESP?

"Most of the experimental evidence for ESP consists in guessing the order of thousands of unseen packs of cards in fraud-proof circumstances, and getting it right, not exactly, but to an extent which, according to statisticians, is of an order of probability comparable to that of a monkey tapping out a poem by chance on a typewriter."—
Rosalind Heywood, ESP: A Personal Memoir (1964)

Some of the members of the university community in Durham, North Carolina, during the thirties still remember the games that were played at the home of a young psychology instructor and his wife after the children had been put to bed. The games were innovative and fun. To have admitted they were intended to be much more than that might have caused a few raised eyebrows at conservative Duke University, for they had to do with the somewhat suspect subjects of telepathy and clairvoyance.

Ruth and Gaither Pratt were among those who sometimes attended the parties. The strong desire to win might have puzzled an uninitiated onlooker, since the games were very simple and went on and on with few variations: "Behind this screen is a face-down pack of shuffled cards. All of you write on the record sheet your guesses of the order of the cards in the pack. The one with the highest score wins the prize."

The concept was not entirely new to Gaither; when he had been in logic class a few years before, this same young instructor had handed out sealed envelopes and said, "Today we are going to try something different. This is a test that I think you will find interesting."

It was the kind of test that was to attract interest around

the world. The young instructor, of course, was Joseph Banks Rhine, who coined the term extrasensory perception and also was responsible for the abbreviation ESP. Because of his unique approach to the mysteries of psychic phenomena, he is considered to be the founder of modern parapsychology. His wife, Dr. Louisa E. Rhine, was a full partner in that novel research undertaking, and she has gained her own world-wide reputation through reports of ESP studies on children, studies of psychic experiences from everyday life, and four books on the subject.

Since those early days, thousands of volunteers have participated in millions of tests, the majority of them with the ESP cards (circle, square, star, cross, and wavy lines) that were devised by another young member of the psychology faculty, Karl Zener, who saw that the use of simple symbols would avoid preferences for certain playing cards and would facilitate test scoring.

The evidence furnished by all the laboratory testing that flowed from those beginnings was perhaps largely responsible for what happened at the annual convention of the Parapsychological Association in 1971. The assembled members from all over the world voted in overwhelming agreement that further tests merely to prove the existence of ESP would only be boring.

Tests involving specific aspects of the phenomena do go on, not to add further proof of the reality of psi, but to gain a better understanding of how it works. These days the tests are usually of a more sophisticated variety, and most participants find them more interesting than card guessing. An example is furnished by a study of clairvoyance and brain-wave patterns which was devised in 1972 by Dr. Rex G. Stanford and Dr. John Palmer.

The experimenters assume that everybody has some ESP. I knew I had *some*, but I never had had the chance to participate in a scientifically controlled test. When I heard that subjects were needed for this study, I volunteered, more out of curiosity about how the testing was done than in getting an evaluation of my ESP ability.

As the six electrodes were being taped to my earlobes and my scalp, front and back, the test was explained to me. I would lie down in one of the "sleep" rooms, listen to music that was intended to facilitate fantasy and possible emergence of material from the unconscious, and then I was to try to receive impressions of a securely wrapped picture that would be on a table across the room.

Meanwhile, the two investigators would monitor my brain waves and listen over the intercom to any impressions I might be able to report. Was that clear? Yes.

I was taken to the sleep room, where I lay down and the dangling wires of the electrodes were hooked up to a panel at the head of the bed. The light was turned off and I was left alone in the dark room, very much aware of the fact that there was a picture on the table over there and that I was supposed somehow to be able to "see" through the sealed wrappings. Suddenly I had a very strong feeling that I could do it. I am good at visualizing.

As instructed, I turned on the tape player, and now the room was filled with the most annoying, the most distracting sounds I had ever heard in my life. This was supposed to open the gates to my subconscious mind? I could have jumped out of my skin. How could I stand it for the eight minutes I had been told it would last? To me, the meandering discords were like the fluty sounds that entice snakes from baskets in India. Fortunately, I knew that I wasn't supposed to be trying to get anything until after this "mind-clearing" noise had stopped.

It stopped. The silence was a relief. *Now* . . .

Nothing. My mind was so cleared that it was an absolute blank. I knew that those two young men out there were waiting for me to describe what I was seeing, but there was nothing to describe. I had expected to see the sort of hypnagogic images that I get just before going to sleep, amazingly realistic scenes, vividly detailed and full of color, but all I was getting from behind my closed lids was a sort of nervous, dark emptiness, devoid of anything that could be considered a picture. The jagged, angled, geometric shape that flashed momentarily before I had a good look was nothing worth mentioning, for I knew, since I was trying so hard, that at any moment my mind would furnish me with a real picture, *that* picture over there on the table.

And from time to time I heard a voice. "Are you getting anything? Can you describe your impressions?"

I kept saying, "Nothing . . . nothing . . . sorry." I was getting anxious now.

Once one of them said, "Did you drop off to sleep just then?"

"No." Of course not. A silly question. I was much too interested in all this to go to sleep.

After about twenty minutes of seeing nothing worth reporting, I heard Rex Stanford's voice: "Well, you might as well come out here if you're not seeing anything. But we've been seeing some very interesting brain waves."

John Palmer came in and unhooked me. At the same time he removed the picture that had been lying on the other side of the room. He carried it, I learned later, still in its wrapper to Gaither Pratt for its inclusion in a sequence with the other four pictures. The picture and the sequence were still unknown to John Palmer and Rex Stanford.

While this was being taken care of, I had a chance to look at what seemed like a wasteful profusion of polygraph paper (a hundred feet, they said) with—to me—the meaningless record made by the polygraph pens. Rex explained that alpha waves, which indicate a state of relaxed attention, had been produced in slightly greater than average quantity, but that many of them were of extraordinarily low frequency, around eight cycles per second or, as the scientists say, "hertz."

"Is that supposed to be good?"

"Well, it's interesting," Stanford told me. "Those who practice certain types of meditation" (I don't) "often come up with waves like that. For our purposes it's regarded as a stage-setting performance. When the subject shows relatively low-frequency alpha rhythm prior to the ESP task, our tests show that he is more likely to succeed."

"Then I must be the exception."

"Don't worry about it. You tried, whether you got anything or not. What was of particular interest to us was that twice you went into waves of a frequency slower than the alpha range, called theta. Theta indicates a borderline state of consciousness."

He was showing me where the polygraph pens had recorded the theta waves. "Some scientists suggest that it may be during this state of mind that intuitive flashes often occur. I'm a little cautious about that, because this type of research is in its early stages and no definite conclusions have been reached. But we do feel that we have good evidence that there is apt to be better ESP performance to the degree that the frequency of the alpha rhythm shifts upward from the mind-clearing period to the ESP task itself."

I may have been looking at him rather blankly.

"In other words, the ESP subject will not do well unless his mind is activated when he actually does the ESP task."

"I am sure I would have done better if I hadn't hated that music so much."

"You really didn't see anything at all?"

"I didn't see a *picture*. I did see something, but I didn't mention it because it came and went so fast that I couldn't believe it was significant. It had a jagged, sort of geometric shape to it—like a palm tree, almost." I remembered something else now. "I also got a very swift impression of blue-green."

We went out to the other room, where five large color prints, including the one Gaither Pratt had unwrapped, were displayed side by side. Neither of the investigators knew yet which was the target picture that had been in the room with me.

But I knew. For there was my palm tree. I saw it at once. It was only part of a larger picture, perhaps the least interesting part, but it was blue-green in color, it leaned at the same angle I had visualized, and it had the same geometric, jagged tufting of leaves at the top.

I was supposed to give a score to each picture, from one to twenty. Without a moment's hesitation I gave that picture a score of twenty. There seemed no point in assigning any score at all to the other pictures, but since one of them included a foreground of blue-and-green water, I gave it a score of five. Although I was totally sure, I wanted to hedge my bet a little.

John Palmer then opened the envelope that contained the number identifying the target picture. He looked at the number on the picture. It matched; the palm tree had been in my room. They were as pleased as I was to have scored a hit.

There may not be many opportunities to participate in a scientifically controlled test of this sort, but it is very easy for an interested group to do just-for-fun experiments. For a simplified version of the test I had taken, I made several sets of pictures from a fairly large collection of National Gallery prints. Illustrations from calendars or magazines would do very well, as long as there is a picture on only one side. It would be helpful to mount the pictures on cardboard. Post-cards could also be used.

The important thing is to have a variety of color, subject matter, emotional content, etc., in each set. For instance, I have one set that consists of a picture of a dead gladiator, one of the Virgin and Child, a still life of vegetables and fruit, a seascape, and a castle. Another set, from the postcards I have collected over the years, contains skeletons from a Dixon, Illinois, burial mound, a Mary Cassatt mother and child, a cremation on Bali, Degas dancers, and a jungle painting by Rousseau.

Slip each picture into its own opaque envelope. If you are making up several sets—and you will need them—the envelopes should be marked in some way to indicate that they belong to set A, set B, or however you choose to designate them.

The procedure is simple. It should be explained to the participants at the outset that this is a test for telepathy. When the person who volunteers to act as percipient, or receiver, has gone to another part of the house, a random selection of one of the five envelopes will be made by the group. This one envelope will then be opened and the picture propped up so that all can see it easily while they concentrate, trying to send impressions to the percipient. Some will concentrate on color, perhaps, others on line or emotional content, and some may even want to make quick sketches to emphasize the particular impressions they are trying to communicate.

After a suitable length of time, perhaps five minutes, any sketches will be disposed of, and now the rest of the envelops will be opened. When all five of the pictures have been laid out on any surface suitable for easy viewing, the percipient will be called back into the room.

Just before he enters the room and looks at the pictures, it is often interesting to ask what impressions, if any, were picked up. Oddly, although these verbalized impressions sometimes will seem to concur exactly with the target picture, another picture will be the one to which he will assign first place. In case the first choice is wrong, the subject should be asked to make a second one. If that is correct, he has at least scored a partial hit.

I have used this test in schools. Children are very much interested in ESP, surprisingly knowledgeable about it these days, and are thought to have more natural psi talent than adults. So far, my "star" has been Donald Eubank, a Greenfield, Indiana, boy. He was ten years old when, in an informal family setting, he chose the target picture four times out of four.

All my "testing" is informal. My methods would cause scientific investigators to cringe. I am not trying to prove anything. That has been done, so far as I am concerned, in the laboratories. The reality of ESP is now pretty generally acknowledged by all who have studied the evidence—except, of course, for the most skeptical.

But even a skeptic is apt to be convinced when he sees his own palm tree.

J.G.P. COMMENTS:

Since the picture that Mrs. Hintze attempted to describe when she was a subject was not known to anyone present during the experiment, this may be regarded as a test for clairvoyance. There are, however, other ways in which the subjects in that test could have used ESP to pick up information about the targets.

I assisted in this research by secretly selecting the target at random from a group of one hundred pictures and wrapping it in aluminum foil and black paper. Then the concealed target was made available to John Palmer to carry to the sleep and dream laboratory where the experiment was done, care being taken that I gave him no clue about the target at that point. It is conceivable that the subject later obtained information about it from me by telepathy. Still another possibility is that the subject used precognition to look into the future to the point in time when the target picture would be identified as the correct one.

From what we have been told, it seems clear that each subject was instructed regarding *what* to do in the test, but not *how* to do it. Research workers in this branch of science simply do not yet know enough about how psi operates to be able to tell subjects by explicit instructions how to turn psi on when the investigators wish to have it occur.

If that time ever comes, and to the degree that we have also learned how to control the accuracy of ESP information, we will have reached the stage at which practical applications of psi will be possible. We are a long way from this goal now, but all pioneering research of modern science has developed through such stages. Benjamin Franklin, for example, confessed that he could not say what practical applications, if any, might eventually follow from his experiments with electricity.

If you have become seriously interested in parapsychology, you need not confine yourself to reading about what others have done. You can begin testing yourself or others for either ESP or PK and you can also apply the procedures in a way that will give at least tentative answers to questions about the nature of psi.

The suggestions offered here may be taken as an enjoyable game with a worthwhile purpose, but they can also be a first step toward a career in parapsychology. I will give some instructions about how experiments may be made using a basic testing procedure, and you may think of other things that you would like to do.

A Test for ESP: In 1930 Dr. Rhine began at Duke University the experiments in extrasensory perception based upon packs of handmade cards, their faces stamped with the ESP symbols Mrs. Hintze described. Later, printed cards were manufactured and made available to anyone who was interested in such testing. These cards were widely used in research during the thirties, forties, and fifties.

The publicity given to the research done with these cards encouraged the belief that there was some special magic associated with them, and that it was necessary to have this special pack in order to carry out an ESP test. They are certainly useful, and they are still used in some serious research, but they are not essential. One advantage they have is that there are many kinds of tests and statistical procedures for the evaluation of ESP card results.

A test for ESP, however, can be made with ordinary playing cards, and the information given below on how to score the results will be enough to judge whether the test has been successful.

The materials needed are a deck of playing cards, paper and pencil, and something that can be used as a screen, such as a cardboard box or a stack of books. Remove all of the face cards, aces, and any jokers, leaving a deck of thirty-six cards (the numbers 2 through 10 of each suit).

The subject sits on one side of the screen ready to record his calls while the experimenter shuffles the deck of thirty-six cards and cuts it on the other side of the screen. The screen should be large enough to keep the subject and the experimenter from seeing each other. A wall between two rooms provides an ideal screen. There should not be any mirror or other reflecting surface that will allow the subject to get any view of what the experimenter is doing. The subject should keep his record on paper that he has prepared for the purpose, with columns having the spaces marked off for his calls and with room at the bottom for writing the score.

The first test is for clairvoyance. When the deck has been shuffled and cut face down, the experimenter lets the subject know that he is ready to begin. As soon as the subject indicates that he is also ready, the experimenter lays the top card of the deck face down with a "snap" or "slap" on the table without looking at the face, and the subject writes his impression of the color of the card, using R for red and b for black, capital R and lower-case b to avoid the risk of confusion. The experimenter then lays the second card down on top of the first, and the subject guesses which color it is. This continues until the subject has called all thirty-six cards. Such a group of thirty-six trials, or one time through the deck, makes one run of the test.

The subject should be free to work at his own pace. If the experimenter cannot tell when the call has been written and that it is time to place down the card for the next trial, the subject may give a signal, as by saying "Next." If the subject takes a long time on each trial, he should be encouraged to put down the first impression he received instead of debating with himself about which color to call. It is not necessary for the subject to call an equal number of reds and blacks in each run. He should record his impression for each card without thinking about those he has already called. It is important not to tell the subject about any hits or misses during a run, but he may know his score after he has called all the cards in the deck.

At the end of the run the cards are compared with the subject's calls as the hits are checked and the total score is written at the bottom of the record. Be sure you are comparing the cards with the calls in the correct order. Since the cards were laid face down one at a time into a new stack as they were called, the new order of thirty-six cards must be compared with the calls by starting from the bottom of the subject's record.

To prepare for another run, the experimenter shuffles the pack thoroughly and cuts it again. Then the test proceeds through the next run in the same way as before.

Strictly speaking, the number of trials to be made in a test should be set in advance, though this decision can be made after some exploratory runs and when encouraging "off-the-record" results indicate that it is worthwhile to start afresh on serious trials. Setting the number in advance will avoid the risk that the final results were influenced by "optional stopping" or deciding on the basis of the run scores after the test has begun whether to go on or to stop.

The evaluation of the test means that we find out whether the total number of hits is larger than the expected fifty-fifty level (a score of 18 in one run) to a degree that mere chance or lucky hitting is not a reasonable explanation. Any score above 18 is encouraging. A score of 24 is good, since this number of hits would be reached by chance alone only one time in twenty runs on the average. A score as high as 27 is excellent, since this would be expected by chance only once in more than a hundred runs.

If a subject can keep up an average even slightly higher than the chance level of 18 hits over several runs, this soon reaches a level of statistical significance that is beyond reasonable chance explanation. For example, four runs with an average of 22.5 hits per run is as good as a single run with a score of 27 hits. And sixteen runs with an average of 20.25 hits reach the same level of statistical significance, with odds of more than a hundred to one against happening merely by chance.

These guidelines for the evaluation of results should be enough to tell the beginner whether his prospecting efforts have struck what looks like psi gold. At that point he must prepare himself for making the best use of his discovery by reading other books or by corresponding with a sympathetic professional parapsychologist.

It is not enough to know *what* to do. Even more important is the feeling with which the subject approaches the test. He must be interested but relaxed. He must want to know how well he can score and must be eager to "beat chance." A gamelike atmosphere is desirable, but the matter should be taken seriously and not treated as a joke. It is likely to interfere with the subject if others are watching. If several are waiting their turn, they should wait in another room, or be busy with something else while one subject is taking his test. Sessions should be kept short. If the plan, for example, is to finish sixteen runs with each subject, it would be better to do only four runs at a time on four different days than to finish everything in one session.

The main thing is that there should be a sense of adventure, a feeling of the importance of what may happen. If the outcome shows that ESP has almost certainly occurred, this *is* exciting. From the scientific point of view, it would be more marvelous by far than seeing a full eclipse of the sun.

The test that has been described can be opened to the possibility of telepathy by having the experimenter lay each card down *face up*. He then concentrates upon the color and tries to send it to the subject during each trial. This would be called a GESP (general extrasensory perception) test, since the subject could succeed by using telepathy to read the mind of the experimenter, by using clairvoyance to detect the cards directly, or by a combination of the two.

A Test for Psychokinesis: The purpose of this mind-over-matter test is to find out whether a subject can influence dice to stop rolling on the number he is wishing for. The test is similar to a large number that have been carried out in para-psychological laboratories since 1934, when tests for psychokinesis were first started at Duke University.

The materials needed are ordinary dice (any number that divides evenly into thirty-six may be used, but the same ones should be used throughout a test), paper and pen, a throwing cup, and a smooth carpet or blanketed surface on which to roll the dice. The cup can be a small oatmeal box without a top, or a salt box from which the top has been cut off. A cardboard container is less noisy than metal or glass, and also less likely to scratch or chip the dice.

Let us assume that you are working with six dice on each throw. Six throws of the dice by the subject (after he has shaken them in the cup) are needed to complete a run of thirty-six trials. During the six throws the subject should concentrate upon making as many as possible of the dice stop rolling with the even-numbered faces up. After each toss, carefully count the number of even and odd faces, record each number, and check to be sure that the total is six. After the six throws have been made and recorded, the score of hits and misses for the run should be obtained. Put a circle around the number of hits (the even faces in this run).

On the second run, ask the subject to make as many as possible of the odd faces turn up. Otherwise the procedure is the same as before.

It is important that a total test should have an equal number of trials for even and odd faces. This guards against the possibility that the dice may be biased to favor some faces more than others. It is not necessary, however, to change the target at the start of each new run as indicated above. It should be permissible to do several runs for even faces, and then do an equal number for odd.

The schedule of using the odd and even faces as targets should be planned from the outset and followed strictly. If the subject is left free to decide as he goes along what target he wishes to try for, we would not know whether a significant score was due to PK acting on the dice, or to precognition of how they were going to fall.

The general suggestions given for the ESP test, such as length of sessions and favorable testing conditions, apply equally to the PK test.

Perhaps you may wish only to discover whether ESP or PK can be demonstrated in your own research. Decide at the outset how many subjects you intend to test, and how many runs each one will do. Perhaps you have decided to test nine persons and to have each subject complete sixteen runs for ESP and the same number for PK. Using the analysis of odds given for the clairvoyance test (page 60) you could make a reasonable estimate of how good the results are, especially when you examine the results for each subject separately. This might lead you to decide to work only with a few selected individuals in further experiments. This method of using the first test to select outstanding subjects to be used in a long series of psi experiments is one that has been applied extensively and with important successes in parapsychology. Half the fun of doing research is in deciding what you want to try to find out and planning how to go about it. The questions that follow are of the sort that might stimulate experiments:

How does ESP success compare when no one knows the target (clairvoyance) and when someone knows it and acts as sender (telepathy)?

Does a subject work better when he is hungry, or well-fed?

Does he work better when he is rested and wide awake, or tired and sleepy?

Is it better to work with a background of music, or in complete silence?

What influence does the speed of calling have on the level of success?

In PK, how does the level of success compare when only

one die is thrown at a time (thirty-six tosses to complete a run) and when six dice are thrown at a time (six tosses to complete a run)?

Does it make any difference whether subjects are skeptical about psi and their ability to succeed in the test, or are convinced or open-minded about the reality of psi and hopeful about their own results?

Does a promising subject selected on the basis of his results in earlier tests do better if he is held to short test periods of just one run, or if he is allowed to work a much longer time in each session?

How does an outstanding subject do if he is asked to work in the presence of a witness? Does it make any difference who the witness is? Suppose, for example, that the witness is a person whom the subject knows to be a skeptical scientist?

In the analysis of results on page 60 the purpose was to evaluate whether the scores you are achieving are more than would reasonably be expected to happen on a merely chance basis. When you are testing whether one condition is more favorable for psi than another, you are concerned to find out whether the difference in results for the two conditions is too great to be merely a matter of chance.

We saw earlier that four runs with an average of 22.5 hits per run (or 4.5 more than the expected chance average) are significant. When you are examining two sets of results, two runs of one test and two runs of another are significantly different if the average difference is 9 hits per pair of runs. (For example, if the scores for two runs under one condition are 22 and 22 and those for another condition are 14 and 12, the sums of the scores under the two conditions are 44 and 26. The difference of 18 is divided by 2, the number of pairs of runs being compared for the two conditions, and we have an average difference in hits per pair of runs of 9 which is significant. Similarly, if we do four times this many runs, eight under one condition and eight under another, the difference between the total scores under each of the two conditions divided by 8 needs to be at least as high as 4.5 to be significant, with odds against chance of more than a hundred to one.)

There are many other kinds of ESP and PK experiments,

and many statistical methods are available for evaluating results. Some of these are described in the books listed for this chapter, and you may wish to explore them in your own testing.

ESP IN ANIMALS

". . . the faculty [psi] ought to be better developed in primitive peoples than in more sophisticated ones, and it ought perhaps to be more active in some animals than in primitive man."—A. S. *Parkes in* Extrasensory Perception: A Ciba Foundation Symposium *(1956)*

In the late 1950's Mr. and Mrs. George Wood of Greenwich, Rhode Island, wrote several letters to Dr. Pratt concerning Chris, age ten. A random selection of statements from those letters might have the reader believing that the Woods were typical fond parents who were pushing their son too hard.

Chris often entertained guests in the home with card tricks and mathematical stunts that were really quite remarkable for a ten-year-old. He had been on television several times and made many stage appearances. At least once he had been billed as guest speaker at a public affair.

Although there is much in the letters to prove that the Woods safeguarded his health and were very much concerned lest he overtax his strength, it would not be surprising if one concluded that they might have been well advised just to relax and let Chris be a normal boy.

But Chris could never be a normal boy. Chris was a dog.

In all the annals of dogdom, Chris's story has never been equaled. He was tested hundreds of times for his ESP ability. In one series of tests his score was such as would be expected to happen by chance only once in more than a hundred *billion* times.

Chris was a year old when he was given to the Woods. He was a dark honey-tan mongrel, part beagle. He was hyperactive, raced senselessly about the house. A friend remembers that the Woods often said, "That dog acted crazy. If he had been a child, we would have taken him to a psychiatrist."

A neighbor family with several children had first owned Chris. Although they took good care of him, he may have been somewhat lost in the shuffle of active family life. So the Woods, who had always owned a dog, decided that Chris might settle down if they gave him lots of love and attention.

Theirs was a quiet household with no children. Marion Wood, an artist, gave a few lessons in tray-painting to friends and neighbors. George Wood, chief chemist and director of research at a textile plant, was away all day. Chris did calm down eventually and became part of the family. He showed no signs of brilliance, and it never occurred to the Woods to try to teach him any tricks.

One day when Chris was five years old a guest brought a dog that had been taught to "say" its name by pawing out the appropriate numbers for letters, and also to do a bit of simple arithmetic. When the little exhibition was over, somebody turned to Chris, who had sat there watching, and said, "Well, Chris, suppose you tell us—how much is two and two?"

Chris looked up at his mistress and pawned her arm four times.

That night when Mr. Wood came home from work his wife told him what had happened. Disbelieving, Mr. Wood asked Chris the same question. To his astonishment, Chris again pawed out the answer.

Within a few days Chris was able to tap out the numbers quickly from one to ten and do simple sums. Within a few months Mr. Wood was bringing du Pont engineers to the house to prove that his dog could do complicated mathematical problems.

By now Chris had learned the alphabet, pawing once for A, twice for B, and so on. He was giving correct replies to questions when neither of his owners knew the answers. Mr. Wood has told me that there were at least twenty other people with whom Chris would work. Reporters came to the house to "interview" him and write stories about him. Scrapbooks at the Wood home are filled with these stories.

On several occasions the dog made hour-long television

appearances, including the Gary Moore show. He was in great demand at clubs and benefits, but any fees he was paid were always turned over to charities such as the SPCA.

Rosemary Goulding, a friend of the Woods, told me about an encounter with Chris on a night when she arrived early at their home for a lesson in tray-painting. As a witness, Miss Goulding has credentials that are a joy to a researcher's heart: a psychology major, she was graduated from Brown University, and for several years has been employed by the state of Rhode Island as a probation and parole officer assigned to the Family Court. On this occasion, no one else had arrived and Mr. and Mrs. Wood were busy elsewhere when Chris walked into the room.

At that time Miss Goulding did not know Chris very well. What do you say to a dog who is supposed to be smarter than most people? Although she had no particular interest in the race track, she asked Chris the post position of the winning horses for the daily double the next day at Narragansett. He pawed a number on her arm, and then another. She asked, "Chris, is that right?" and he pawed out "S-u-r-e."

She bet two dollars on those horses. She says she can't remember now what the numbers were, but she does remember that they won the daily double and paid eighty-four dollars.

At her suggestion, a psychologist, Dr. Henry F. Nugent, was brought from Rhode Island College of Education to test Chris. Eventually, Dr. Remi J. Cadoret and Dr. Pratt came from the Parapsychology Lab at Duke to run hundreds of tests at the Woods' home.

They used chiefly the ESP, or Zener, cards, a deck of twenty-five cards with five each of the five symbols: circle, cross, wavy lines, square, and star. Mr. Wood, a scientist himself, had every respect for scientific methods and cooperated to the fullest extent in carrying out tests that were time-consuming and tedious for himself as well as the dog.

Chris's selection of the "right" cards gave him a score that was astronomical. Still, it is somehow the little stories of his everyday behavior that stick in the memory. Miss Goulding told me of a time when she tried to call on the Woods but received no answer. She could see Chris watching her through the picture window as she rang the bell at the front door.

"I went to the side door, and then to the back door through the garage. Actually, I spent a ridiculous amount of time knocking on those doors, but I thought perhaps television might be on, so that Marion Wood couldn't hear me. When I gave up I went back to the front window, where Chris looked out at me. I said—hoping the neighbors couldn't hear me—'Chris, tell George and Marion that Rosemary was here.'

"The next morning Marion called me at my office, something I had never known her to do before. 'Did you come to our house yesterday?'

"Yes. Who told you?'"

" 'Chris. When we got home last night he seemed excited, and I told my husband that I thought Chris was trying to tell us something. George went to the refrigerator and got out a little treat for him, and then he asked Chris if somebody was here today. Chris answered yes. Was it a man or a woman? Chris said it was a woman. And when George asked who it was he spelled out Rosemary. But there was something else we couldn't understand—Chris seemed to be trying to tell us something about *doors*.' "

Dr. Martin Kaplan of South Kingston, Rhode Island, was Chris's veterinarian and saw him every month for several years. In a telephone conversation he told me, "I've never known an animal who was anything like him. Sometimes Mr. Wood would bring the ESP cards and I saw some results that were really amazing. Oddly, although Chris liked me and never seemed to mind all the shots I had to give him, he would 'talk' only to my son John, who was then in his teens. We had a race horse then, Mike Hudson, who was considered the best in New England. Once when John asked him if Mike would win a certain race the next day in which he was the favorite, Chris said he would not come in first or second, but third. He was right. On another occasion he correctly picked Mike to win."

The Woods never let Chris's celebrity status interfere with his joy in being a dog. He usually had the run of the neighborhood, frisking with his best friend, a German shepherd, but ignoring a French poodle because, according to Chris, that dog was d-u-m-b. His special delight was chasing cars, and his owners never could break him of it. They would return after a few hours' absence and say, "Chris, did you chase cars today?" Almost always the answer was yes.

In 1959 Chris had a heart attack. After that he was tested with the ESP cards only when he was in the mood, but according to Mr. Wood, he scored more hits then than ever before.

Nobody ever claimed that Chris was a hundred percent right all the time. He was one day off in predicting his own death.

Dog partisans sometimes put cats down as being mysterious, aloof, showing little sense of belonging to their owners. But consider the story of Sugar. He was owned by a family named Woods, not to be confused with the Wood family that owned Chris. Sugar was a handsome cat, cream-colored, with a Persian ancestor somewhere back up his family tree. The slight deformity of his left hip joint, easily felt as a protruding spur when he was stroked, never seemed to bother him. He was full of fight, a match for any dog.

But he had one hang-up that his family, the Stacy Woods of Anderson, California, were well aware of: this bold, fearless tomcat was afraid to ride in a car. When Mr. Woods retired from his job as school principal and made plans to take his family to Gage, Oklahoma, to live on a farm, everyone knew it would be a problem to carry that cat fifteen hundred miles in the family car.

It was no surprise, therefore, when Sugar leaped out of the car after Mr. and Mrs. Woods and their ten-year-old daughter were all packed and ready to go. No amount of coaxing would lure him back and they were unable to catch him. Reluctantly, they left him with friends, hoping he would be contented, since one of his litter mates lived with that family.

Fourteen months went by. In August 1952 Mr. and Mrs. Woods were milking in their barn in Oklahoma when a cream-colored cat jumped through an open window and landed, purring, on Mrs. Woods' shoulder. Startled, she brushed him off . . . but that cat did look exactly like their long-lost Sugar!

They fed him, and although the cat settled in as if he felt perfectly at home, they joked away the thought that it could possibly be Sugar until a few days later when Mrs. Woods, stroking the sturdy body, felt the same spur of bone protruding on his left hip joint.

Meanwhile, back in California, Sugar's foster family was making plans to go to Oklahoma to visit the Woods', worrying about how they should break the news that Sugar had disappeared after spending less than three weeks with them. Upon their arrival they were astounded to see the big cream-colored cat. They were completely at a loss for an explanation as to how he could have made the long trek, but they, too, identified the cat as Sugar, for they remembered the bone deformity very well.

J. B. Rhine of Duke University became interested in this apparent case of "psi-trailing." Statements from reliable witnesses seemed to be supportive. Behavioral data seemed to be significant. But it was the identifying deformity of the hipbone that made the case worth investigating.

Dr. Rhine went to Oklahoma, where he saw Sugar and heard about the cat's ability to fend off dogs and even coyotes. Mr. Woods told him that Sugar sometimes brought home half-grown jackrabbits as trophies of a night's hunting.

In a report that appeared in the *Journal of Parapsychology* for March 1962, Rhine said, "Such a cat would be able, if any quadruped could, to make its way over the extremely rugged terrain in the fifteen hundred miles between California and Oklahoma, provided he could find the way."

But how did he find the way?

The way-finding ability of pigeons has long been known, though not understood. Some scientists have maintained that homing is chiefly a matter of instinct, whereas others feel it is due mostly to training. Pigeon AU C&W 167 seemed to demonstrate an ability that went beyond either of these.

It was summer, 1940, when a banded pigeon fluttered into the back yard of Sheriff F. C. Perkins in Summersville, West

Virginia. Hugh Brady Perkins, his twelve-year-old son, fed the bird, and to the surprise of everyone, the pigeon stayed on and became quite tame.

That next winter the rapport between boy and bird had a sudden interruption. Hugh Brady became ill and was driven across the mountains to the hospital in Philippi, a hundred and twenty miles away. One night while recuperating from an operation, the boy heard a tapping at the window. He saw a pigeon outside on the window sill, where snow had been falling for quite some time. All night that pigeon stayed there, and in the morning the boy begged the nurse to open the window and let the pigeon come in.

Hugh Brady Perkins told me recently, "That nurse must have thought I was crazy or delirious or something the way I insisted that it was my own pigeon who had somehow followed me to the hospital and found my room. But she opened the window and let it come in. Sure enough, there was the identifying band on the pigeon's leg that proved he was mine."

The boy's parents were mystified when they came for a visit a few days later and found the pigeon, which their son had been allowed to keep in a box in his room. They had seen the bird in the back yard since the boy had left, so it could not have followed the car that carried him to the hospital. But how could it have flown over the mountains those hundred and twenty miles to find the boy's hospital window that night in the snowstorm?

The story received quite a lot of attention. Newspapers picked it up and the boy made a trip to New York to be on the radio program *Strange as It Seems*. The man who had banded the bird got in touch to say he was interested to know that one of his birds, though a maverick, had made it so big; yes, he was glad to let the boy keep him; no pigeon fancier wants to fool around with a bird that wants to "do his own thing." Although all this happened more than thirty years ago, people still write to find out more about this tantalizingly unique story.

Hugh Brady Perkins has dropped his first name now, but he still lives in Summersville. He says there's not much more to add except for the fact that the pigeon he calls 167 did not have a long and happy life as a back-yard member of the Perkins family.

"We had a box out there for him, but one day he just disappeared. I'm sure he didn't go back to the loft of his owner, because the man would have let me know. I think he must have been killed—shot, maybe. I'm sure that 167 did not just fly away."

Probably the only horse in the world ever to use a typewriter was Lady Wonder. It was not an ordinary typewriter, of course. The keys were large, made of soft rubber, and she touched them with her nose. So great was the interest in this horse that a Richmond, Virginia, paper once gave more front-page space to her exploits than it gave to the return of favorite son and famous explorer Richard Evelyn Byrd.

This is an excerpt from an interview that appeared in the *Richmond News Leader* in 1932 with Katherine Warren, a reporter, asking the questions:

MISS WARREN: "Lady, can you tell me whether there will be any bad calamities in the United States during the coming year?"

LADY: "Yes."

MISS WARREN: "What will they be?"

LADY: "Storms."

MISS WARREN: "Will they be in the East, Middle West, or West?"

LADY: "South."

MISS WARREN: "Will they do any damage in Virginia?"

LADY: "Sure."

MISS WARREN: "Can you tell me if the Eighteenth Amendment will be repealed during 1932? I mean, will people be able by law to get whiskey or anything they like to drink?"

LADY: "No."

MISS WARREN: "Can you tell me who will be nominated by the Democrats for President?"

LADY: "Roo—" She stopped, looked around, and then: "I can't spell it."

On that same occasion Lady spelled out the reporter's middle name, which her trainer probably did not know, and read out two numbers written on a slip of paper presumably known only by the reporter and a companion.

Dr. Thomas L. Garrett, a New York psychologist, saw the horse in 1946 when he was working on a book which was to be an exposé of various so-called supernatural manifestations. When Lady explained a puzzling long-distance call to him, he pronounced her a genuine phenomenon and said he was convinced no trickery was involved. The long-distance operator had told Dr. Garrett only that a man by the name of Murphy was trying to reach him.

The horse typed out the information that Murphy's first name was Pat—a good guess that might not have carried much conviction had not Lady gone on to say that Pat Murphy wanted to see Dr. Garrett about Murphy's wife, an actress named Diane Ross. An immediate check with a theatrical agent in New York determined that there was a Diane Ross, actress, married to a Pat Murphy.

Lady's mother was killed when the little black filly with four white feet and three white stockings was two months old. Her owner, Mrs. C. D. Fonda, raised her on a bottle. Her ESP ability was first suggested when Mr. and Mrs. Fonda discovered that the colt in the pasture would anticipate their calls before they had spoken. They started training her with alphabet blocks and then Mr. Fonda devised the special typewriter. Her fame soon spread all over the country.

For years Lady predicted the results of horse races so successfully that clients used to wire in for regular information. When this became illegal, the Fondas set up their own one-horse show in the barn, charging a dollar for each question.

Mrs. T. G. Lupton recalls that in 1957, shortly before Lady's death at the age of thirty-one, she took her two young daughters, Sarah and Victoria, to see Lady Wonder, providing them with dollars so they could ask questions.

When asked the first question by Victoria: "What is my name?" Lady came up with "Virginia," but she named Sarah correctly, pausing a bit before adding the final "h." Each little girl then wanted to know what she would be when she grew up. The mother remembers that she herself was thinking that it would be rather nice if Sarah became a writer and Victoria a dancer. Possibly half reading the mother's mind, Lady said that Sarah would be a dancer and Victoria a writer. Sarah was delighted at the prospect of so glamorous a future; Victoria burst into tears. It seems that neither child had cause for elation or distress, for Lady Wonder's predictions have not come true for either.

Like the human seers, Lady was sometimes only half right and sometimes completely wrong. But she is best remembered for her successes, such as her prediction of the entry of the United States and Russia into World War II, and the reelection of President Truman. When her help was enlisted in 1951 in solving the mysterious disappearance of Danny Matson, a four-year-old Quincy, Massachusetts, boy, Lady said the child's body was in the area of the Pitts Field. It was found in the *Field and Wilde's Pit*, a quarry that had not previously been searched.

J.G.P. COMMENTS:

The animal stories you have just read really happened insofar as we can determine by checking from the statements of several persons who were involved in each case.

So what? The world is full of true animal stories. Why should we feel that the ones Mrs. Hintze has presented here deserve special attention?

The answer, of course, is that in these stories the common theme is ESP. The pets did things that we do not, in our enlightened and critical age, ordinarily consider to be possible. We do not read about such facts in scientific books or encyclopedia articles dealing with dogs, horses, cats, or pigeons, simply because it is not commonly accepted either by laymen or scientists that animals possess or use ESP.

However, stories such as these have led a few open-minded scientists to question whether commonly accepted ideas are correct. Currently, several investigators are checking up on claims for parapsychological abilities in animals (anpsi).

Let us look at what has been done to study each instance

in the previous pages. Dr. Rhine and his wife, Dr. Louisa E. Rhine, with the help of several colleagues, were able to make investigations in the late twenties while Lady was still only at the beginning of her long career as a "mind-reading" horse. Their study was not limited to checking on the accuracy of the claims that had brought the colt to their attention. Rather, the investigators made repeated visits to Richmond to conduct their own tests. They published two reports on this work in the scientific literature.

In the first report, tests are described in which Mrs. Fonda was removed from direct contact with Lady. This was done by slow steps to avoid upsetting the horse. The purpose was to see if Lady could give the right answers to simple questions when she could not be guided by slight sensory cues from her handler.

The tests reached the point at which Mrs. Fonda was completely out of the picture. Lady still gave more correct answers than would be expected by mere lucky coincidence or chance. The Rhines said that the best available explanation was that Lady was getting the answers from the mind of the investigator by telepathy. But they did not say that the results gave conclusive proof of ESP. Rather, they emphasized the importance of further research.

In the second paper on Lady by the Rhines they reported that the horse was no longer getting information by telepathy. She was still performing her feats, but these appeared to depend on slight sensory cues from the owner. Now, contrary to what had previously been noted, the correct answers to questions stopped when the separation between the animal and the owner was made complete.

Shortly thereafter, Dr. Rhine began at Duke University the ESP testing with his students that led to the founding of the Parapsychology Laboratory there and launched him on his research career. The trips from Durham, North Carolina, to Richmond to work with Lady thus came to a natural end, though Mrs. Fonda and her famous equine friend continued to do business as usual for more than two decades off the Richmond-Petersburg Turnpike. The stories suggesting ESP on demand at that roadside stand continued to accumulate, but unfortunately, no other scientists ever made another serious investigation of the horse's abilities and submitted their results to their scientific colleagues.

The story of the pet pigeon that flew to its owner's hospital room was checked out by Dr. Rhine in the fifties, approximately ten years after the events occurred. No reason to doubt the basic facts as reported in the popular press could be found then, nor could Mrs. Hintze and I, in 1972, do more than correct one or two unimportant errors that had crept into published accounts.

By the time the case came to the attention of scientists, the bird was no longer available, so there was no opportunity to experiment; but even as it stands, this is one of the most impressive psi-trailing cases on record. Taken alone, it certainly cannot be said to prove that anpsi occurs, but it makes that a more challenging possibility.

Scientists have been trying to explain the homing ability of pigeons for more than a century, with intensive work on the problem during the last three decades. Most of this effort has been directed toward finding a *sensory* explanation. But the possibility remains that pigeons really do home by ESP, and that science will not be able to explain their behavior until this possibility is fully and fairly taken into account.

For several years I worked under a contract with the Office of Naval Research trying to find out if homing pigeons ever use ESP to find their way. We used a mobile loft and took the birds out of the loft before moving it to another location. Then the birds were released one at a time to see if they could find their home. These tests, tried many times and under many different conditions, failed because the pigeons preferred the familiar landmarks to the loft itself. They simply made themselves at home where the loft had been previously.

There is a test for ESP in pigeons, which could be done only with great effort and expense, that might give us the answer. This would involve keeping pigeons in a loft on board a ship and never allowing them to see land. Freed in that manner from the distracting effects of landmarks, would they be able to find the loft after the ship was moved? My hope is that someone reading these words will someday find the opportunity to carry out such an experiment to see whether it would finally coax from the birds the secret of their way-finding ability.

I confess to a more nagging doubt regarding the story of Sugar. Was the cat that found Mrs. Woods in Oklahoma *really* the one that the family had left behind in California? The sex and the color were right. The animal immediately jumped on Mrs. Woods' back, something that a strange cat would not likely have done. But all these things together were not enough to make the family believe at once that it was Sugar. Only the finding of the spur of bone on the animal's hip sometime later made them decide that it really was their own cat.

The evidence as a whole, particularly that bone deformity, was strong, but in science we need to make certain of the facts. Dr. Rhine visited the Woods' and saw the cat. He made an agreement with them that when Sugar died they would send the body to him at Duke University. This plan was not carried out because the animal eventually disappeared. Since he always seemed completely at home with them, they believed the animal must have had a fatal accident on one of its hunting trips.

The greatest value of the story of Sugar is the lesson it teaches about the true worth these animal stories have for science. They raise the question of whether ESP is used by pets and other animals to a degree far beyond anything we can point to in the human species. No single case can give us the answer. Can many cases combined do so?

Certainly numbers can help. Dr. Rhine and his daughter, Sara Feather, discussed the value of such evidence in an article in which they said they had gathered fifty-four carefully selected cases of the anpsi trailing type. No individual case met all the standards for the ideal one, but taken all together they presented strong evidence for anpsi.

The dog Chris came closest to giving the kind of test results needed to prove the claims made for one of these special animals. There was only one major difficulty: Chris did not do so well in the presence of visiting scientists as he did when his owner made the test with the help of friends who were on good terms with the dog. This is perhaps to be expected, and there was no reason whatever to question the sincerity and competence of the owner, Mr. Wood, and of others who worked with him to carry out the tests planned by the scientists.

In my own work with Chris and his human friends, we used packs of ESP cards that I had shuffled and recorded in advance. Each pack was in a closed box, numbered for identification. The instructions given to Mr. Wood and Rosemary Goulding directed that one of them should take one of the boxes into a distant room, there open it, remove the pack and give the cards a cut, but without any shuffling. This would change the starting point but would not destroy the order I had recorded.

The person holding the cards (the sender) would then look at them one after the other while the second experimenter recorded the calls that Chris, several rooms away, registered by pawing on his handler's forearm.

When the records were returned to me at Duke University, I could easily see, by checking my own records, where the cut had been made and make certain that no change had been made in the basic order of the cards. I could also, of course, recheck the number of hits and see that the score credited to Chris was correct.

This was the way in which the remarkable ESP results mentioned by Mrs. Hintze were obtained. As the test was carried out, it would have been necessary for both of the experimenters to have been in on the trick to falsify results. Knowing personally the two concerned, as I came to do during the course of the investigation, I cannot doubt their honesty. Therefore, I am convinced that the testing registered strong evidence for ESP.

Whose ESP was it, canine or *homo sapiens*? One special circumstance makes it seem more likely that Chris was really the star subject that many people considered him to be. In some runs Mr. Wood stayed with Chris while Miss Goulding went down the hall to another room to act as sender, while in other runs their roles were reversed. The results were equally good both ways.

This means that both of the experimenters would have had to get really exceptional ESP results to account for the findings solely in terms of the psi abilities of humans. The unlikelihood that this would be the case favors the interpretation that Chris was the one responsible for the remarkable ESP success obtained.

The study of the anpsi question is at a stage of healthy growth, and prospects seem good for a continuing harvest of new scientific facts. If this research effort should in due time clearly establish that the lower animals also use ESP, the impact of this discovery upon our view of the world of living things around us would be simply tremendous.

VI

ALTERED STATES OF CONSCIOUSNESS

*". . . our normal waking consciousness . . . is but one
special type of consciousness, whilst all about it . . . lie
potential forms of consciousness entirely different . . . No
account of the universe in its totality can be final which
leaves these other forms of consciousness quite disregarded."*
—William James, The Varieties of Religious Experience—
The Gifford Lectures, Edinburgh (1901–02)

A daydreaming child I once knew, the despair of his
mother, came home from school one day, very late, explaining that he had missed a word in spelling and his teacher
kept him in to write the word one hundred times on the
blackboard. When he was asked what the word was, he said,
"I don't remember." He had no doubt written the word the
required number of times, but the repetition was so boring
that it had induced an altered state of consciousness. (Concerned parents of such children might take comfort in a study
conducted by the Johnson-O'Connor Human Engineering
Laboratory. They concluded that daydreamers should stay
away from such jobs as typing, accounting, computer pro-
gramming, etc., and go into some of the more creative occu-
pations, such as teaching, advertising, sciences, and the arts,
where vivid imaginations would be an asset rather than a
handicap.)

Within the last few years parapsychologists have been
directing much of their attention to altered states of consciousness for the very good reason that psi is believed to
operate quite strongly in some of them. As indicated in a
previous chapter, dreaming is one of the states during which,
barriers down, psi often manifests itself. Everybody dreams,
even babies and even those who think they never do. Labo-

ratory tests have proved that about every ninety minutes during sleep we slip into the dream state. When subjects are hooked up to EEG equipment, observers can tell by the polygraph record of brain waves and rapid eye movements (REM) when a dream begins and when it ends. When the sleeper is wakened during this REM period, even the supposed nondreamer will be able to describe something of what he has been experiencing. Individuals vary widely in their ability to recall dreams; the creative person is believed to have more vivid dream recall, and also to have more of the so-called lucid dreams in which the subject knows he is dreaming and can even control the outcome.

Changes in blood chemistry can induce an altered state of consciousness. "Rapture of the deep" is a form of narcosis feared by deep-sea divers and caused by abnormal concentrations of nitrogen in the blood. Rational thinking is suspended, and although, as the term implies, the distortion of reality is exquisitely pleasant, the temptation not to come up is almost irresistible and sometimes disastrous. The depth at which this hallucinatory state is encountered varies for different divers. Some will begin to be aware of it at 135 feet, but others can go much deeper and stay down much longer before the symptoms appear.

Rosalind Heywood has been called "England's First Lady of ESP." Some years ago she participated in an experiment conducted by a London doctor who, through the normal mind of Mrs. Heywood, was trying to discover whether the drug-altered state of consciousness was similar to that of schizophrenia.

In *ESP: A Personal Memoir*, Mrs. Heywood said that she wished she knew what words to use to describe her experiences while under the influence of mescaline (". . . like trying to reproduce the Matthew Passion on a tin lid with a spoon"), but to this admirer she succeeded much better than any of the other accounts of drug hallucination: "I felt that in another second I should be disintegrated by sheer excess of glory."

When asked to describe further impressions, she said, "I came on a cold grey, stony El Greco-like desert, its monotony broken only by jagged rocks. There was not a leaf to be seen anywhere, not a blade of grass. Huddled far apart among the rocks were grey veiled figures, motionless, unable to communicate, 'at the bottom,' beyond despair. They were, I knew, the Lost. I have never before or since felt the total compassion I felt then. I remember pausing by one of them and thinking desperately, 'Is there nothing I can do to rouse and comfort him?'

"And the answer was—nothing. I could make no contact. I was not good enough. None less, it appeared, than the perfectly Good could help the Lost, and to do so they had to sink in sacrifice, even below them, to become the object of their pity and compassion. It was only by giving those at the bottom a chance to help others who needed it that they could be saved. And by some strange paradox, only the perfectly Good could get below them to need their love."

William James, psychologist, philosopher, graduate of Harvard Medical School, had much to say almost seventy-five years ago about the various altered states. He was impressed by the extraordinary degree to which the mystical consciousness was stimulated by nitrous oxide, laughing gas. He wrote, "Depth beyond depth of truth seems revealed to the inhaler. This truth fades out, however, or escapes at the moment of coming to; and if any words remain over in which it seemed to clothe itself, they prove to be the veriest nonsense. Nevertheless, the sense of a profound meaning having been there persists; and I know more than one person who is persuaded that in nitrous oxide trance we have a genuine metaphysical revelation."

Concerning another mind-altering drug, alcohol, he says, "The sway of alcohol over mankind is unquestionably due to its power to stimulate the mystical faculties of human nature . . . sobriety diminishes, discriminates, and says no; drunkenness expands, unites, and says yes. It is in fact the great exciter of the *Yes* function in man . . . To the poor and the unlettered it stands in the place of symphony concerts and of literature; and it is part of the deeper mystery and tragedy of life that whiffs and gleams of something that we immediately recognize as excellent should be vouchsafed to so many of us only in the fleeting earlier phases of what in its totality is so degrading a poisoning."

But James seemed convinced that religious experience pro-vided a "high" that was unequaled by anything else. He spoke of the "deliciousness" of religious fervor, and said, "Intellect and senses both swoon away in these highest states of ecstasy." As illustration, he quoted St. Theresa of Avila: "The soul after such a favor is animated with a degree of courage so great that if at that moment its body should be torn to pieces for the cause of God, it would feel nothing but the liveliest comfort."

Parapsychologists, unfortunately, never made adequate investigations of Edgar Cayce. He was a deeply religious man who has had his detractors as well as his almost fanatical admirers. His son, Hugh Lynn Cayce, director of the Associa-tion for Research and Enlightenment at Virginia Beach, is an admirer but not a fanatic. He once described his father as "a confused Presbyterian Sunday School teacher with an unfathomable gift." And he says that out of the thousands of trances, ". . . there were about seventeen times when Edgar Cayce retained memory from the altered state of conscious-ness from which he gave psychic information."

The altered state about which we hear a great deal these days is the one that parapsychologists call the out-of-the-body experience. To someone like me who has never had the experience, it all seems strange, a little enviable, and all but unbelievable. I cannot doubt the sincerity of some of those to whom I have talked, however. They at least believe they have had these experiences, subjective and hallucinatory though they may be. In many primitive societies, the phe-nomenon is accepted as fact, and among the Australian aborigines the "clever-men" are believed to be able to project themselves out of their bodies at will.

Accounts of out-of-the-body experiences date back almost as far as recorded history. It is generally conceded by Bible scholars that St. Paul was writing about himself in Corin-thians II, 12th chapter, verses 2-4: "I know a man in Christ who fourteen years ago was caught up to the third heaven—whether in the body or out of the body I do not know, God knows. And I know that this man was caught up into Paradise . . . and heard things that cannot be told which men may not utter."

Almost twenty years ago I sat with other members of the congregation of the First Presbyterian Church in Salisbury, North Carolina, and heard the new minister, the Reverend Herbert Underwood, explain that he always devoted his first sermon to an account of his own out-of-the-body experience. He had tried, as a very young man, to resist the call to the ministry. Having sunk to the depths of despair, he could not believe that God could possibly have a use for him. Suicide was on his mind when he fell to his knees beside his bed.

"Suddenly, I felt as if a thousand-pound weight had been lifted off my shoulders, and I was free, really free, for the first time in my life. I felt so free that I was buoyant, and the only way I have ever been able to describe the feeling is to compare myself with a huge cork that had suddenly been cut loose from its mooring at the bottom of the sea and shot upward to the surface with such force that it did not stop at the surface, but broke through into the air. I suddenly found myself in outer space.

"I remember three things: Above me was a brilliant, shining light, so bright that I could not look at it, even though I tried repeatedly. Somehow I knew that it was the glory of God. Below me was the earth, suspended there in space, beautiful and serene. And all around me was the sound of a million angel voices singing to the glory of God, completely surrounding me, the most beautiful heavenly music imaginable. And I was suspended there, with the light above me, the earth below me, and the music all around me. I have no idea whether it lasted a few seconds or a few minutes, because just as suddenly I found myself back on my knees beside my bed. I have never felt such indescribable joy, such exultation, such happiness, such freedom, such peace. I *knew* that God had accepted me."

Here is the story of another out-of-the-body experience that changed the life of someone personally known to me. Dr. George Ritchie is a psychiatrist now in private practice, but at the time of his once-in-a-lifetime experience he was a private in training at Camp Barkeley, Texas. He had interrupted medical school to enlist in the army, but in December 1943 he received the good news that he was to be sent back to his home in Richmond, Virginia, to reenter medical school as a part of the army's doctor-training program.

He was scheduled to leave on December 20, but a nasty chest cold landed him in the army hospital. On the night of the nineteenth he was no better, but he made up his mind that nothing was going to keep him from being on that bus which was leaving at three-twenty the following afternoon.

He had a blinding headache and was coughing steadily; when he looked into the sputum cup he was alarmed to see that it contained blood. He knew he had a high fever, but he got up and dressed and went to the ward boy to ask for aspirin. He took six of them and went back to bed. When a nurse came in and took his temperature, he remembers that she ran out of the room. Later he learned that she had recorded a temperature of 106.5. A doctor came. George was taken immediately by ambulance to the x-ray building, where somebody asked him if he thought he could stand up for chest plates to be made. And that is the last he remembers, until he opened his eyes in a little room he had never seen before.

A dim light was burning. George says he did not know how much time had passed, but he was galvanized into action by remembering that he was leaving for Richmond. Nothing must interfere with that. He jumped out of bed, and as he was about to leave the room he happened to notice that a still figure lay on the bed he had just left. The person was undoubtedly dead. As a boy, he had seen his dead grandfather, and the gray hue of the skin, the slack jaw were unmistakable. *But on the left hand was the Phi Gamma Delta fraternity ring George had worn for the last two years.*

Frightened, unable to understand any of this, he ran into the hall. An orderly stood in his way, but seemed not to hear when George spoke to him. Today he says, "I don't know if I passed through him or if he passed through me, but I kept on running, my only thought being that I had to get out of this place and be on my way to Richmond."

He seemed now to be far above the earth, but he was not sure he was going in the right direction. It occurred to him that the sensible thing was to get his bearings. He touched down in a town that he somehow knew was Vicksburg, Mississippi. Beside a telephone pole, he put out his hand to a guy wire. "But my hands went right through it and it gave me no support.

"I started remembering that figure on the bed now, and I knew I had to get back to it. I was sure that I was not really dead, but I had to get back there to Barkeley to prove it."

His desire to get back to the base hospital seemed to get him there almost at once, but there were hundreds of soldiers in that hospital in identical rooms. In panic, he went from one to the other, trying to find the one with his body. All had GI haircuts. All had khaki blankets. George was desperate before he found the little room with a figure on the bed, face covered now by a sheet, but with one hand visible. It was wearing a Phi Gam ring.

"I did my best to pull back the sheet to see the face, but my fingers would not make contact. I began to know that I was dead. I despaired of ever being able to get back into that body.

"The room began to fill with light. It showed me all of my past life and I could see it as if in cyclorama. I seemed to know that the light, growing, becoming dazzling, was Jesus, the Christ. And together with its brilliance was the feeling of love that accepted even my sins that had passed before me. No words, as such, were spoken, but I became aware that a question had been asked: 'What have you done with your life?' It may seem ludicrous, but the only thing I could think of that might measure up to standard was that I had once been an Eagle Scout!

"I knew that I was in another world, one which seemed to occupy the same space, superimposed upon the world I thought of as normal. And I became aware of a strange landscape with pillars like those of Grecian ruins. It teemed with people who were most miserable, caught up in the mean, petty concerns that had ruled them when they were on earth. Figures that I sensed were teachers moved among them. I saw a mother who followed her 'boy,' who must have been about sixty, trying to guide him, though without much success. Was this Hell, Purgatory?

"I saw other worlds that night. They appeared to be solid and real, but coexisting with the world I knew. I saw people who were concerning themselves with the pursuits that had been theirs before passing to this realm, but there was a self-less concern for Truth here. I saw a great library with all the translations of the Bible I had known. But I saw also the books of other religions that had sought for Truth. And the one shelf that held the translations of our Bible was only one among many, many others.

"Above all these other worlds, or overlappings of time, was still another world. It seemed to be very far away. The city I saw seemed to be made of light, and the beings who moved about its streets gave off that same luminous glow as the being who had shown me these things.

"Just a glimpse, that's all I ever caught, of that city before I was with suddenness back in that cubicle at Barkeley, Texas. It was much later that I learned what had happened to my body. Twice I had been pronounced dead, with nine minutes elapsing. After the second pronouncement, the ward boy had been directed to prepare the body for the morgue, but he had implored the doctor to inject adrenalin into my heart. And I had come back to life. I have since seen the entry on my chart: 'Pvt. George Ritchie, died December 20th, 1943, of double lobar pneumonia.' "

George Ritchie told me that he has talked to the doctors who signed the report. They said that it was an unheard-of miracle for him to have suffered no brain damage after being clinically dead for nine minutes. For him it was a spiritual experience that he says has changed every moment of his life since then.

By way of verification of the events of his strange night, he went back to Vicksburg, Mississippi. "I was able to direct the driver of the car to the café which I had seen on the night I 'died,' and it was, in all physical aspects of location and appearance, exactly as I remembered."

Years later Ritchie participated in a hypnotic regression experiment before a class of medical students. When he was regressed to the moment when he had stood in front of the x-ray machine at Barkeley Army Base, his heart rate zoomed, his temperature went up, and he was near collapse. The psychiatrist in charge terminated the experiment at once, advising him never to allow anyone to regress him to that moment again.

Elmer Beams died in 1960. I never knew him, so I did not hear his story first hand. But his stepson, Richard Beams, told it to me and said that he had heard, countless times, the story of his stepfather's out-of-the-body experience which took place nearly half a century ago.

Elmer was working as a fireman then on the Lehigh Valley Railroad, and on this particular summer night he was late to work and half running through the streets of Honesdale, Pennsylvania. Through an open window as he hurried he seemed to hear a voice, faint but audible: "Don't go!" It sounded like the voice of his mother, but he knew that was impossible, for she had been killed in a railway accident ten years before. Still farther along the street, through another open window, he heard the same faint voice seeming to call the words to him again; "Don't go!"

But he reported for work, putting the voice out of his mind. The engine that night was one with which the engineer was not familiar, a "camelback," with the boiler extending on both sides of the cab. As they started out of the yard, they had to stop for a bad bearing that needed repair.

Late now, they "deadheaded" (pulling no cars) toward Mt. Carmel, going unusually fast to make up for the lost time. Beams saw the "red eye" ahead, the warning to slow down. He shouted to the engineer, who pulled the handle for the air brakes. His unfamiliarity with the engine may have been what caused it to start rocking from side to side. Beams braced himself, wrapping his arms and legs around an iron bar to keep from being thrown from the swaying cab. The engine turned over, rolling across four tracks and then down over an embankment onto the mule path that ran alongside a canal.

When the wrecking crew arrived, they lifted the coal tender off Elmer Beams and gave him first aid. One of his arms was broken in four places between wrist and elbow, with two breaks above. One of his legs was broken; his skull was fractured and he had multiple internal injuries.

When he regained consciousness, on a bed in the Miner's
Hospital in Mt. Carmel, his whole body was in agony. And
then suddenly the agony stopped. He seemed to be standing
beside his bed, looking down at the battered form that lay
there. He saw a nurse come in, check pulse and respiration,
and then hold a mirror before his face. She hurried from the
room and brought a doctor.

"Don't bother," Elmer said to them, but they didn't hear
him. They brought oxygen and placed a mask over the face
of the man on the bed. And then he was no longer standing
there looking down, but back in that body again with all that
unendurable pain.

Once again the pain vanished. Again he stood by the bed
watching as the nurse made another test with the mirror.
When the doctor appeared again, it seemed to the injured
man that he stood between them and for the second time told
them not to bother. They neither saw nor heard him. Oxygen
was administered again and they revived him.

Richard Beams said, "But now here is the part that was
always the hardest for Dad to tell. I guess he thought nobody
would believe it. He himself didn't understand how it could
have happened, but twice during those first terrible hours he
'went' to his home two hundred miles away and 'saw' friends
and neighbors coming in to console his family, who had been
told he couldn't live through the night.

"Later, when Dad finally got well and went back home, he
was able to give the names of those who had come to the
house that night. He told where they had sat and what they
had said, and family members said he was right. Dad never
had another such experience, but to the end of his life he was
telling about it, hoping always to find someone who could
explain it to him."

J.G.P. COMMENTS:

There are many altered states of consciousness that all of us
recognize and take for granted in our daily lives. Literally,
any shift from one state of mind to another is an altered

state, and the number we all undergo every day of our lives is countless. Anyone can make a list of the highlights of his day, and this will likely include a large admixture of altered states. In raising the question of the relation of psychic phenomena to states of consciousness, we are primarily concerned with shifts into a special state of awareness.

Certainly the altered state Mrs. Hintze chose to emphasize, the out-of-the-body experience, is a striking one. Science understands something about these experiences, but not yet as much as we would like. We know for sure from the firsthand reports of persons who have had such experiences that they are very real for them. Furthermore, during the past two decades we have received evidence that this kind of experience is not a rare occurrence, something that happened only to persons we read about in the Bible or to mystics and other rare individuals of more recent times. Findings from these investigations show that this "gift" is indeed relatively common today. Each of us must know, in our circle of acquaintances, several people who have had at least one out-of-the-body experience.

The interpretation of claims of leaving the body would be much easier if we could take as the starting point what those who have had such experiences say about them. To examine the accounts scientifically, however, we are compelled to start out favoring the viewpoint that the feeling of traveling outside the body may be nothing more than a special kind of dreamlike experience, one that occurs with such lifelike realism that the person who has it is convinced that it is *not* a dream.

Any interpretation which says this kind of experience is really more than a special kind of dreaming must show that there are features of the experience that go beyond merely subjective, imaginative thinking. As a starting point, we may observe that one common feature runs through many of these accounts: the person is convinced that he sees things from a position in space outside the body, usually doing so as clearly as he would if he were physically at that spot and seeing with his eyes. Thus we can check up on whether the experiencer's claims about where he has been and what he saw and did there have any basis in fact.

The first investigator to submit this question to a laboratory test was Dr. C. T. Tart of the University of California at Davis. He used as his subject a young lady, Miss Z, who claimed to have fairly frequently, during her otherwise normal sleep, the experience of floating up near the ceiling and seeing her sleeping body lying below her on the bed.

Dr. Tart persuaded Miss Z to sleep for four nights in a room of his laboratory, with electrodes attached to her head for studying her brain waves during the night. The wires had the effect of "tying her in bed" so she could not raise her head from the pillow more than about two feet.

On a shelf five feet above the bed the experimenter placed a sheet of paper with a five-digit number written on it. The number was face up on the shelf, so it would only be visible to anyone who looked at it from ceiling level. This sheet was placed on the shelf with precautions that the subject could not have seen it in any normal way.

Dr. Tart's report of the experiment covers the events of all four nights, but of special interest to us is that on the fourth night Miss Z awoke from sleep and said she had just been through an experience of floating up near the ceiling and had seen the number. She said it was 25132, which was exactly right. The odds against getting the number correct purely by making a lucky guess are 99,999-to-1. We can say, therefore, that the evidence is very strong that the subject somehow knew what the number was.

The experimenter stopped just short of saying that this result proved that the subject learned the correct number through the use of special psychic powers, though the impression left by his report is that he had no personal doubt that she did so. He does not say that the result, even if we accept it as a parapsychological performance, would prove that the subject was really out of her body. She could have got the number from her position on the bed by using ordinary ESP while incorrectly believing that she was out of her body and floating up near the ceiling.

This distinction is between ESP working through the organism in the usual way and having the center of consciousness actually travel outside the body to observe what is happening from another point in space. Research programs are now under way that may help us to decide between these two possibilities. In the laboratory of the American Society for Psychical Research in New York City special devices or arrangements of objects are prepared in an enclosed box. This target arrangement is placed at a distance from the subject and beyond his normal vision. The only opening in the box is a window through which it would be possible to view what is inside. Anyone who put his eye to the window would describe the contents of the box in a particular way, since the relations among the objects as viewed through the opening would give the contents a meaning that could not be seen if the things inside were examined from any other point in space.

Subjects are selected for the study who claim to be able to leave the body at will. When a trial is to be made, the subject is instructed to let his center of consciousness travel to a position just in front of the window, look through it, and report what he sees inside the box.

The logic of this approach is based on the assumption that the use of ESP in the ordinary sense to discover what is in the box would not be restricted to what could be seen through the window, since ESP would be more likely to explore the box from all angles. If the description the subject gives is the right one for what he would see when looking only through the window, this result would provide evidence that the subject had literally projected himself out of his body to the one point in space from which he could look through the opening into the box. The experimenter, Dr. Karlis Osis, considers that his first results have given encouraging indications that some of his subjects have been able to take a direct peek into his special psychic travel detector. He thinks that these findings, if adequately confirmed, would prove the projection hypothesis. But some other parapsychologists give him an argument on this point, since they say that the subjects know that they are supposed to look through the window. They would therefore be motivated to carry out the task in the way the experimenter hoped they would, and they would be able to do so by so directing their regular ESP abilities.

Another research center where work on this problem is

seeking evidence that the consciousness leaves the body is the Psychical Research Foundation in Durham, North Carolina. There, the subject is told to make his presence known at the place to which he is instructed to travel, and an observer keeps watch at that location to see if something unusual happens. Dr. Robert Morris, the principal investigator, has reported encouraging results indicating that an unusual change in the behavior of a pet kitten took place at those times, unknown to the observer, when the subject was trying to project his consciousness to the room where the cat was being watched. The investigators have not, however, observed any effect on nonliving things.

Dr. Palmer and a co-worker at the University of Virginia have recently been working with volunteers without attempting to select persons with previous experience of leaving their bodies. Their results apparently indicate that a certain number of people can achieve this special altered state under controlled experimental conditions, when they are encouraged to do so by verbal instructions and by using special sound and visual effects. The experiments gave significant evidence of ESP in those subjects who reported that they felt they really left their bodies. Those subjects who failed to achieve the feeling of leaving their bodies gave only chance results.

Scientific experimentation may eventually lead us to conclude that the experience of leaving the body does not, after all, have any recognizable connection with psi processes. On the other hand, we may confirm that ESP is better when the subject has such an experience than when he does not.

Most interesting is the third possibility—that the evidence will establish that there is some part of the total organism, the part that calls itself "I," which occasionally leaves the body and independently carries on its essential activities of conscious awareness and psychic existence. This result would give to such investigations a dimension of importance not found in parapsychological research concerned only with psi as a faculty of the physiological organism. It would have much more far-reaching implications.

We are touching here upon the general question of survival. Traditionally this question is thought of in terms of survival beyond death, but what I am suggesting is that the concept of survival can profitably be broadened to include any instance of the existence of the psyche outside the body, whether living or dead. If survival is a fact, its scientific establishment and universal acceptance would be an advance in knowledge that would rank high in the history of human thought, perhaps higher than any of the revolutionary discoveries of the past.

As to other altered states of consciousness, until recently, dreams seemed like a promised land for psychic experiences, but largely beyond our reach. We have long known that the majority of ESP experiences from everyday life occur in dreams. But nothing seemed more personal and private than the act of dreaming until, about mid-century, a discovery threw open the private world of sleep and dreaming. The technique of recording brain activity during the period of sleep is now well known, as is the period of rapid eye movements (REM) that shows up when a person is dreaming. Add the further happy discovery that we almost always remember our dreams and can describe them if we are awakened just after they have occurred, and the stage was set for new research on sleep and dreams.

The research of Dr. Ullman and his colleagues on ESP in dreams has been considered in previous chapters dealing with telepathy and precognition. We need to remember it here also, because it is a leading example of how the apparent connection between dreaming, an altered state of consciousness that we all experience, and ESP has been tested successfully in the laboratory.

Hypnosis is another altered state of consciousness which, after years of neglect, is gradually finding its way back into the field of parapsychology. Recent studies indicate that ESP subjects perform better under the influence of hypnotic suggestion than without it. The results appear to be fairly consistent and reliable.

The main reason that Milan Ryzl, the Czech scientist we met earlier, caught the interest of parapsychologists around the world was that he reported that he had found a special way of using hypnosis by which he was able to train ordinary subjects to develop and use their ESP capacities. Many para-

psychologists went to Czechoslovakia to work with the outstanding ESP subject, Pavel Stepanek, whom Ryzl said he
had trained by his special method.

There was no doubting that Stepanek was an excellent
subject. But it was not possible to tell after he reached his
heyday as an ESP performer whether the training he received
was responsible for his remarkable ability.

Some efforts to confirm Ryzl's claims have been made by
other investigators, but without success. In 1967 Ryzl
defected to the U.S.A., and though he has remained interested in parapsychology since coming across the Atlantic, he
has not reported any further success in training subjects by
his special method.

Finally, we come to that sector of altered-states research
where the action is the fastest today and is still accelerating
rapidly: the kinds of awareness that we all experience frequently during our normal waking lives. Our daily activities
take place in a personal atmosphere of constantly shifting
moods. Parapsychologists are making a renewed effort to find
out how psi processes are influenced by the shifts in that
background state of consciousness. This research is being
done with a degree of imagination, sophistication, and technological wizardry exceeding anything previously brought to
bear upon this problem.

Research workers in parapsychology have long thought
that the most favorable state of mind for demonstrating psi
is one of reduced strain, physical and mental relaxation, a
mind emptied of active thinking or cognitive processes, and
an attitude of passive receptivity as opposed to a condition of
worry, anxiety, aggressive determination, ego involvement,
introvertive self-criticism, and deliberate effort.

The current wave of interest in meditation is a public
response that is indirectly linked with the distinction
between favorable and unfavorable states of psi. The Eastern
systems of meditation instruct their devotees in ways to
achieve a state of mind in which they are more at peace with
themselves and the universe.

Public interest has also latched onto the discovery that a
generally happy state of awareness is associated with brain
activity that shows a large proportion of alpha waves. This is

the activity of the brain that appears in the EEG record as pulses with the frequency of eight to thirteen cycles per second. The assumption is that the more the brain produces alpha, the more the subject will show ESP.

Rex Stanford and Charles Honorton, among others, have found that although there is a connection between ESP and alpha frequency, the mere presence or absence of alpha is not the whole story. The level of brain activity before the subject starts the test is important, as well as whether a shift to a higher alpha frequency takes place while he is taking the ESP test. It was also learned that subjects did better at ESP tasks when their attention was directed inward, rather than when they were alert to their surroundings.

If sensory alertness is a natural enemy of ESP, why not help the subjects to shut out the outside world and thus achieve an altered state of consciousness that is favorable for the occurrence of ESP? Parapsychologists have borrowed the techniques of sensory deprivation, developed during recent years in psychological research, to do precisely this. Subjects have been blindfolded and strapped securely in a standing position in a freely rotating swing called a witch's cradle. In this device, in the subject's private world of darkness, the body sways and turns freely at the slightest movement and with a minimum of sensory awareness.

Another sensory deprivation procedure involves fastening cups made of the halves of ping-pong balls over the eyes. The subject looks through these covers into a light to experience something like staring toward the sky during a heavy noonday fog. At the same time the subject may listen through earphones to a sound shield of meaningless noise. The indications from several experiments are that these explorations are on the right track in increasing psi results, but it is too early for definite conclusions.

A team of psychologists in Houston, Texas, have set out to describe what they call the psi-conducive state and then to produce this in the subject before he takes an ESP test. Lendell and William Braud selected relaxation as the main key to ESP success, and they prepared a tape of detailed instructions to lead the subject into this state. Their procedure set a record of successful ESP results that quickly caught the attention of other parapsychologists, some of whom are beginning to apply the Braud relaxation procedure in their own search for the best conditions for psi phenomena to occur.

While the foregoing efforts to manipulate consciousness in seeking better control over psi deserve our approval, this is true for some of the more drastic shifts in awareness only because they were undertaken by qualified investigators. For example, the beginner should not attempt to bring about a state of hypnosis in his subjects unless he has been carefully tutored in the techniques as well as the dangers.

The use of drugs—which has become so widespread, with such devastating results—is a way of seeking an altered state of consciousness for its own sake. Some work has been done to see whether ESP performance is improved under the influence of drugs, and the results have been so disappointing that research along this line has been largely abandoned. No one would be justified, therefore, to use drugs on the ground that they might enhance psi capacities.

A variety of mechanical devices are offered on the market today with the claim that they will increase psychic powers. These include machines that stimulate the vision with flickering lights, devices for teaching the control of brain activity, equipment for generating negative ions, and methods for photographing the psychic aura (Kirlian effect) and tapping the power of the cosmos (the secret of the pyramid). Many of these claims are untested, and I regard some of them as outright false. Some of them have bad side effects that may make their use harmful. One should read the ads with a critical mind. Even if you expect to prove that the equipment is safe by trying it out on yourself first, this is not a sound procedure. You may be one of those who get no bad effect, while the person you try next may be seriously upset. As for many of these gadgets, I would simply like to save you from wasting the money.

THE ABERRANT CREATURES
OF OAKLAND FARM

*"I am inclined to believe that they [ghosts] occur more
frequently than is generally allowed, and are simply kept
in the family closet, which, in our culture, is by all odds the
safest place for aberrant creatures of this sort."—Jule
Eisenbud,* The World of Ted Serios *(1967)*

Oakland Farm is a happy place. If it is haunted, the average
visitor picks up no clues. Sitting under great oaks well back
from the road, the wide white house has known almost two
hundred years of living. An unusual feature is that the pre-
Revolutionary story-and-a-half structure was cut down the
middle about a hundred years ago, and the two halves moved
apart to permit construction of a central three-story section.
The extra space has been needed, for one of the families
that lived in this house had fourteen children.

That might seem a hard act to follow, but now every winter
nearly three times that number of children troop in and out
of the house for lessons and meals. For the past several years
Oakland Farm has been a school where children with a variety of learning problems come to live and receive individual-
ized help. In addition to several teachers who live in the
widely scattered dorms and cottages, student counselors
come from nearby colleges, finding challenge in these youngsters who need special attention.

During summers the school becomes a camp, and the
number of residents doubles again. Miles of riding trails wind
over the five hundred acres of wooded hills and meadows.
Indian artifacts can still be found, as this area was once
roamed by the early tribes. Three cemeteries lend a bit of
spooky enchantment to tales told around campfires.

When Dr. Pratt and I were talking to Mrs. Margaret
Shepherd, owner and headmistress of Oakland Farm, she

said, "The first time I ever saw this house fifty years ago, I had a strange feeling about it. I just seemed to know in some peculiar way that this was my house."

A young woman then, recently graduated from Stanford University, she had come to a nearby school to take the position of assistant principal. Not until after she became engaged a few months later did she find out that her fiancé's grandmother was the owner of the house. The grandmother gave it to them as a wedding present.

The house is a complicated one, with many levels, but Mrs. Shepherd says that the first time she was brought to see the inside of it she felt that she had been in it before; she knew the exact layout and where each door would lead. Her husband had played here as a boy, but had forgotten details. She remembers that when he pointed to a closed door, saying, "I can't remember where that goes," she said, "Why, it goes down to a basement room." When they opened the door and went down the stairs, the brick-walled room was just as she had known it would be.

One room in particular intrigued her. It was on the first floor, small, with that seldom-used look of an old-fashioned parlor. Over the mantel, black braided hair made a frame around the picture of a dead child, a little girl of about six or seven. The young face with its closed eyes was lovely. The dark hair was long and flowing, as if it had been carefully brushed.

"Someone told me that the child had died of diphtheria in this house. I knew that in those days it was not unusual for families to have photographs made of children in death, since often they had no other likenesses of them. That picture fascinated me. How much they must have loved her! I had a strong sense of identity with that little girl. For a long time afterward I dreamed about her."

Mrs. Shepherd, a calm and gracious woman, gave us tea in an end room that had been part of the original house. She said, "From the first, I 'heard things' in this house. Only once was I ever afraid. I had the feeling—with that one exception —that if there were ghosts here, they were friendly and liked having me here."

We asked her what sort of noises she had heard in the house.

"Sometimes as I would walk through the rooms upstairs I would think I heard sleigh bells. And very often I heard sounds of music and conversation, but always two or three rooms away. It was like being in a hotel when a big party was being held in the ballroom. Many times I heard them on New Year's Eve when my husband and I happened to be celebrating here alone. One New Year's Eve we drank champagne here in this room at midnight. The laughter and music were very plain. I said, 'Well, they're really whooping it up tonight.' "

"Did your husband hear anything?"

"He *said* he didn't. But I think maybe he just wouldn't admit it for fear of frightening me. We were sleeping one night in the downstairs bedroom off the hall when I was awakened by a tremendous crash, as if the front door had been opened and slammed back against the wall. Heavy footsteps crossed quickly, as if they were going to the hall phone. We never locked our doors in those days, and I thought there must have been an accident and that someone had rushed in to telephone for help. I was sure my husband heard it, for he raised his head from the pillow as if to listen. But when I said, 'What was that?' he said, 'Nothing.' I got up. Nobody was in the front hall. The heavy front door was closed."

On the one occasion when she was frightened, she was alone in the house. She sat at her sewing machine in the second-floor bedroom from which attic stairs led upward. All of a sudden, footsteps, heavy and deliberate, came down the attic stairs and paused at the closed door at the bottom. Paralyzed with fright, she stared at the door, waiting for someone to open it and come out. There was no doubt in her mind that an intruder had hidden in the attic, waiting for the chance to catch her alone.

She said, "Now, of course anyone with any sense would have run down the stairs and out of the house, but I went and opened that door. Nobody was there. I searched the attic and found no signs that anyone had been there."

A guest who has slept many times in that room told her

that upon several occasions she had heard footsteps come to her bed and then stop. Nothing has ever been visible.

During the winter, some years ago, an electrician came to install a light switch on the wall inside the attic stairs. This was before Oakland Farm became a school and the big bedroom upstairs was not ordinarily used in the winter. Shortly after the installation of the switch, the housekeeper, Mrs. Clement, found white footprints on the bare waxed floor.

Mrs. Clement, to whom I talked later, said, "They looked for all the world like somebody had tracked down those stairs through that mess of plaster dust the electrician had left. The footprints went into the room, over to the rug, and then back to the attic door."

I suggested that the electrician had probably made them.

"No, no, the feet were bare and this was winter. They were great big feet, size twelve at least, with the toes all spread out as if they'd never had on a pair of shoes. So I cleaned them up. But a couple of weeks later, there were those same footprints again. This time, though, right beside them were small footprints, as if they had been made by a child wearing bedroom slippers without heels. I couldn't figure it out, but I said to myself, 'This is enough of that!' and I cleaned the plaster dust off of the attic stairs."

There were no more trackings of plaster dust, but in May there were more footprints. May is the time of year when pollen dust falls from the oak trees, sifting through every crack, so the room had been closed up until such time as the annual nuisance should be over.

Again, Mrs. Clement had been the one to find the footprints. She went downstairs and said, "Who has been in the big bedroom upstairs?"

No one, Mrs. Shepherd told her. The housekeeper was insistent that someone must have been in the room, so Mrs. Shepherd followed her upstairs. She saw the footprints, which started at the attic door, tracked through the pollen dust to the rug, and returned to the door. There were two sets of prints, one of which, Mrs. Shepherd thought, had been made by a large man, and the other by a small child. Both were barefoot. She had no idea how they could have been made.

During pollen season a couple of years later, footprints appeared again in the same sort of pattern. The big footprints were bare, as they had been before, but the small footprints looked as if they had been made by a child wearing slippers. Again, there seemed to be no possible natural explanation, for the room had been closed and unused as before.

Upon several occasions Mrs. Clement has reported that a bed in one of the smaller guest rooms upstairs has shown signs of being slept in when they were not aware of having had a guest. This has never happened since the school has been in operation. On one of those occasions she found some seeds she couldn't identify tucked under the pillow. She is familiar with the ordinary kinds of seeds, but she had never seen anything like them before. Out of curiosity, she planted them, but they never came up.

One spring evening Mrs. Clement was doing some planting on a terrace garden just outside the dining-room windows. Mrs. Shepherd was away and nobody was in the house. When all the lights in the dining room came on, she called out, "Oh, you're home early—" But when she went inside, nobody was there. She found that all the lights, the table lamps, the floor lamps, and the overhead ceiling light, had been turned on although they are not controlled by a central switch.

William Roll is the project director of the Psychical Research Foundation in Durham, North Carolina. When he called Dr. Pratt to say that he and Douglas Johnson, a well-known British medium, were looking for a haunted house, Pratt said he knew of a house they might find interesting. That was all he told them.

When the three men got to Oakland Farm, Johnson asked Mrs. Shepherd and Gaither Pratt to go out of the house, saying that he did not want to pick up any telepathic impressions from their minds. He and Roll then spent about an hour going over the house. And, as Mrs. Shepherd told us later, she learned some things she had not known before.

"Mr. Johnson told me that the small footprints upstairs in what he called the most haunted room had been made by a little girl, and the large ones had been made, not by a man, as I had thought, but by a huge Negro woman who seemed to be the child's 'mammy.' In that same room he got the impression of the little girl on the bed with what he described as a choking sickness. He said he saw a woman, the child's mother, sitting by the bedside and weeping helplessly while the little girl gasped for breath.

"When he came into this room where we are sitting now he said he saw the same black woman in here. He said she was enormous, with big bare arms—he described the size of her arms with his hands—and big bare feet. She was crying as she washed some sheets in a washtub set up on a wooden bench.

"He got the impression of a man running a still in the dining room. He said he seemed to be a bad individual, very rough, and asked me if I wanted him run off the place. In that room I'll show you what appear to be ax marks on the twelve-inch floorboards. I've wondered since then if that man might not have chopped up wood there to keep the fire burning under his still. A violent person would not care if he hacked up the floor.

"Down in the cookroom, Mr. Johnson said he could hear the sound of women sobbing uncontrollably. An older woman seemed to be the center of attention, and the other women were holding her up. He looked through the window and saw several men in black walking down over the lawn to the place where you can see that small pool. An icehouse used to stand there, partly below ground. He saw the men go down the steps into the icehouse and come up bearing a coffin.

"It seemed to bother Mr. Johnson quite a lot that he couldn't get any names. He said, 'Usually in a house like this, names come at me from everywhere, but the only name I get here is Lily. I see her as a young child in pantalettes, and also as an old white-haired lady, so it can't be the same one who died upstairs. I see the way she signed her name very clearly—this is how she made the L—' and he described it in the air.

"Grandmother Lillian, the one who gave us this house, had lived here as a little girl and she died here and she had signed her name with just such a flourishing L."

Since Oakland Farm became a school several years ago, Mrs. Shepherd has been too busy to think much about the ghosts—if any—in her house. But on an August night in 1968, one of the counselors had an experience for which there seemed to be no normal explanation. He had been attending a counselors' meeting that dragged on and on. A few minutes past ten he left and walked out toward the woods in back of the cafeteria where the meeting was being held.

The young man estimates that he was about twenty or thirty yards from the woods when he noticed a glowing orange ball, about the size of a basketball, that seemed to be caught in a tree some twenty-five feet above the ground. He went closer and then stood rooted to the spot, frightened. The ball was descending, growing smaller. When it reached the ground it disappeared.

He ran back into the counselors' meeting. "Hey—this place is haunted!" He described what he had seen.

Search revealed nothing at the spot. The counselor's watch, he noticed later, had stopped at 10:23. It did not seem to be run down, but he was never able to get it to run again.

Mr. Richard Mitchell, director of the school, said that the counselor was white and very upset when he came back to the meeting, which was still in progress. He had no idea what the glowing ball could have been, nor does he have any explanation for other lights which have been seen more recently.

I have this account from another one of the counselors: "I was walking from the winter dorms when I saw an oval light. It looked like a stretched-out football, but larger, almost two feet long, and very bright. It hung over the boxwood-enclosed graves that are supposed to belong to the little girl and her grandfather, although no names are on the graves. No, I'm not at all afraid of cemeteries—I've been past that place a hundred times at night and never gave it a thought. I walked up close to the light and stood there looking at it, just very curious, trying to figure out what it could be. It wasn't very high off the ground, about seven feet. I guess I could have reached up and touched it, but all of a sudden I was afraid of it.

"I went toward the main house and kept looking back, and it stayed there motionless until I went inside. I got somebody to go back there with me, but the light had disappeared.

"My brother was working there then and he is a real skeptic. When I told him about it he laughed and said I had to be crazy. But two nights later he was driving the Volks- wagen station wagon, and when he was in front of the little church on the edge of the property, he looked in the rear- view mirror and saw a white glow almost on the back of the car. Since the engine is in the rear of a VW he thought at first it might be on fire, but then he saw that the light seemed to be following the car, though not touching it.

"He said he had a sensation of intense cold and that it was hard for him to breathe. He kept driving and looking at that light in the rear-view mirror. The light started moving around the side then, always keeping the same distance, until it was right in front of the car. The cold was really getting to him. He was really scared now, and he turned the car around and drove back to get his roommate and a dog. But when they came back, there was nothing. They drove slowly up and down the road and never saw anything to explain the light my brother had seen."

One of the campers at Oakland Farm during the summer of 1971 will always be remembered. We'll call him Stephen. He had what a counselor described as a "Julius Caesar haircut and a Roman nose." Only twelve, he was as big as a man. His problems were much more serious than most and at the beginning of summer he was thought, though wrongly, to be retarded. Some of the counselors were challenged by this rebellious, antisocial boy and gave him special attention. Sometimes when they went for a hike they would manage to "get lost" with Stephen just so they could have time to talk, one-to-one.

There was one counselor whom the boy seemed almost to worship. It is remembered that Stephen said once, "I want to change my name to yours. Do you suppose I could?" The counselor was touched, but he had to say he didn't think that was a very good idea. "But someday maybe you'll have a little boy—then you can name him for me."

"We got so that we really loved him," says Mrs. Shepherd. "It became apparent, as summer went on, that he was a very sweet child."

When Stephen's family came to pick him up at the end of

summer they were delighted with the change in him. No longer withdrawn and full of animosity, he seemed happy and well adjusted. Never before had he been accepted by his peers, but now he had made friends with other campers as well as the staff. When they left for a family vacation at Virginia Beach, Stephen was eagerly anticipating his return to school at Oakland Farm in September.

And then the news came that Stephen would not be coming back. He had been drowned in the surf at Virginia Beach. The Coast Guard searched for three days before they recovered his body.

But one of the counselors thinks that Stephen did come back. One night he thought he heard a child outside the dorm and went to look for him. It was a dark, windy night, with strange cloud formations in the sky. In a cleared space, about seven or eight feet from him, he saw a tall figure looming. The body in dark clothes was large, and it seemed to have Stephen's face.

"No, I don't think it was an optical illusion made by shadows, or anything like that. I was pretty close to it. There was that Julius Caesar haircut, the Roman nose. I just stood there staring at it for three or four minutes, positive it was Stephen. His expression was lonely—distant—separated."

I asked him if the figure looked solid.

"Yes. I couldn't see through it. But I'm positive it wasn't a flesh-and-blood person—there was a blurring about the edges, sort of a wavering of the outlines. I can't be sure, but I got the impression that it was suspended a little off the ground. I wasn't afraid as I looked at it. Matter of fact, it wasn't until I went into the dorm and got one of the other counselors that I felt really shaken up.

"I said, 'Stephen is out there—I saw him.' My friend came running out with me. He was the one who had been closest to Stephen. But nothing was there."

Mrs. Shepherd cannot accept this. She dismisses it as imagination. "After all, nobody else saw him at that time nor have they seen him at any time since . . . And yet, I do know that Stephen was very, very happy here. If he were to come back to any place on this earth, he would come back here where he had spent his happiest summer."

J.G.P. COMMENTS:

My interest in the strange events connected with Oakland Farm was aroused when Mrs. Shepherd told me briefly about her experiences after a talk I gave in 1964 to a local group. It was strengthened when I visited the house shortly afterward and heard more about the occurrences. The feature of the case that seemed to offer the most promise for scientific investigation was the mysterious footprints on the floor of the upstairs bedroom.

Mrs. Shepherd said that if the footprints appeared again, they would be left undisturbed and I would be notified. In the ten years that have passed, nothing further of this kind has been observed.

Meanwhile, as I learned when I telephoned to ask permission to bring Mrs. Hintze out, members of the school staff have recently been seeing unexplained lights. These, as well as occasional impressions of some strange presence at the place, seem to be continuing, but they do not leave any objective trace that an investigator could study.

In the language of psychic happenings, Oakland Farm would be called a haunted place. In a haunting, the unexplained events are associated with the location and they do not, as in the poltergeist we encounter in the next chapter, seem to depend upon any particular living person. A case may produce only one type of occurrence or a variety of events recurring over a long period of time. The "life span" of a haunting is likely to be years, whereas that of a poltergeist is usually measured in days, weeks, or a few months.

Traditionally, haunted houses or places are supposed to be connected in some way with a dead person or persons who lived there and whose influence somehow lingers on. Since the aim of the investigator is (or should be) to try to explain these experiences, he must consider, among other things, whether they provide evidence of surviving personal forces. What can we say at this time about what such experiences mean?

Limiting ourselves for the present to Oakland Farm, we can certainly say that some unusual things have been experienced there. Mrs. Hintze's interviews have brought to light the more recent happenings as well as further details about the earlier events. The sincerity of Mrs. Shepherd is beyond question, so I have no reason to doubt that she is representing the facts as she remembers them.

No written record was made at the time anything happened, and this is a loss that cannot be fully covered by interviewing the witnesses later. The unreliability of memory regarding details is well known. But when, as in this case, we find that there is agreement from a number of witnesses about the main facts, we can reasonably trust that these are essentially accurate. Differences in the statements made about minor details only reassure me that each participant was describing what he or she remembered from firsthand observations.

My thoughts keep returning to those footprints. Mrs. Shepherd and Mrs. Clement agree that the impressions were unmistakable as imprints of human feet. On my first visit I had the impression that they were seen only one time by both witnesses after the prints were left in the pollen dust. More recently Mrs. Shepherd has told me that the prints were observed in the oak pollen on two occasions. Mrs. Hintze heard from Mrs. Clement about two other times when plaster-dust prints were left on the bedroom floor, supposedly having been carried by "phantom feet" from the attic. The essential points on which both witnesses agree are that the footprints did appear and that they could not have been made normally by any living person. Since most investigators of haunted houses usually agree that ghosts do not leave tangible evidence of their presence, as a parapsychologist I would, as I have said, especially welcome the opportunity to observe any recurrence of this particular effect.

I have no doubt that the sound of walking and other noises heard in the house as well as the lights seen outside were very real for the persons who experienced them. But can we say that they were real in any *objective* sense? Were there sound waves in the air which would have been picked up by a tape recorder? Would the lights have shown up on a photograph?

In the absence of evidence bearing upon these questions, we simply do not know that the effects existed in their own right. It is possible that they were normal hallucinations, events that took place only in the thought processes of the persons who experienced them, projected into the surroundings with lifelike realism, something like a vivid dream that occurred when they were wide awake.

It is a well-known fact that hallucinations do occur. They may be brought about by special mental states such as hypnosis or the use of consciousness-altering drugs. But they may also be experienced by perfectly normal persons under more ordinary circumstances. This could have been the case for most of the things that we were told about at Oakland Farm.

What can we say about the experience in which a person was sure that he saw Stephen? Clearly this episode stands apart from the others, since it is the only time that a human form was seen. It could not have been directly connected with the other experiences that went back several years, though it is conceivable that it was connected in some way with the lights seen more recently.

The experience of seeing a human figure, often in good light and with completely lifelike features and clothes when no living person was actually there, is called an apparition. The vision is so real that it is usually taken for reality at first.

Apparitions occur more often than most of us might have any reason to suspect. Studies have shown that approximately ten percent of the adult population have had at least one such experience that was convincing to them. The most thorough scientific study dealing with this question was made by G.N.M. Tyrrell, a British scholar and investigator of psi phenomena. His view of apparitions, which most other parapsychologists would share, is that they are not real physically or in any other ordinary sense, but that they are produced in some way by the person who sees them. Some apparitions are seen at the same time that the visualized person is going through a crisis, such as an accident or even death. A crisis apparition thus seems to be related to the distant events when the connection could only have been known through ESP.

Stephen's accidental drowning occurred some time before his image was seen at Oakland Farm, and the tragedy was known to the staff member who had the experience. We cannot really say in this instance, therefore, that there was anything more than known normal mental processes involved. I am not saying that this is all that the experience means, but that the evidence we now have does not allow us to come to any more far-reaching conclusion.

Does the visit of Douglas Johnson, the English medium, help us to get a better understanding of the case? I can testify to the care taken to insure that Mr. Johnson could not have heard anything about the experiences that were associated with the house. Mrs. Shepherd feels that the impressions which the medium picked up in walking through the house with Mr. Roll (who was also uninformed about these matters) helped her to correct some wrong impressions that she had formed.

But even if we assume that Mr. Johnson was accurate in his statements, we cannot say that he was directly in touch with surviving personalities of former residents. Before reaching that conclusion, we would have to exclude the possibility that he was getting impressions by ESP from persons now living or even by retrocognitive ESP from the past history of the place.

I fear that some will think that I am only a spoilsport whose specialty is ruining good stories. If so, I can only say to them that I still place a high value on the things we were told about Oakland Farm, too high to say that Mrs. Hintze's account is only a fictional short story to be read for a few moments of diversion. As a scientist, I want to know, if it is possible to find out, what it all means. What is the reality back of these experiences and of the thousands of others of a similar kind?

I share Dr. Eisenbud's opinion, as quoted at the beginning of this chapter, that ghosts are likely far more common than we ordinarily suppose. Andrew MacKenzie, a British author of books on psychic phenomena, based his *Apparitions and Ghosts* on forty-nine cases selected from a larger number sent to him by readers of his two earlier books and in response to a brief BBC appearance and three one-shot published appeals. My colleague, Ian Stevenson, has told me that rather often toward the end of an interview about some other type of psychic experience, an informant will ask him guardedly, "Do you believe in ghosts?" The question comes, Dr. Stevenson has noticed, after the informant has decided it would be safe to confide in him. If Dr. Stevenson says "Yes" or otherwise indicates that he wants to hear about any experience his informant wishes to tell him, he will then listen to an apparition or haunting type of experience very similar to those described by the nineteenth-century founders of parapsychology and, more recently, by Andrew MacKenzie. I have found myself that persons who have learned of my interest in such matters frequently volunteer information on their own experiences. The indications are that there are plenty of opportunities for scientists to investigate ghosts if they seriously wish to do so.

There has been a vast amount written about hauntings, but most of it has fallen far short of coming to grips with the problem in a scientifically satisfactory manner. It is possible to write on this subject dispassionately and appropriately. Dr. Gertrude Schmeidler, a psychology professor of the City College of the City University of New York, made a study of a case in which she used sensitives—persons who believed they could sense the presence of a ghost—to see to what extent they could pick up impressions like those reported by the members of the family who claimed they had experienced a ghostly presence. Nine sensitives were led individually through the house, each one conducted by a guide who did not know what the family had reported. The places in the house where each sensitive experienced the presence of a ghost were marked on a floor plan, and these markings were compared with the places selected by the family. Two of the sensitives were successful in choosing "haunted spots" in the house that the family had picked. Also, four of the sensitives were successful in selecting adjectives in a checklist that the family had used in describing the ghost rather than adjectives that did not describe the ghostly characteristics.

This investigation was an interesting and meritorious effort in a new direction. However, even though the results were successful in that they could not reasonably be dismissed as merely chance agreement between the family's experiences and the sensitives' feelings, the investigator did not conclude that the findings proved that a real ghost was in the house. There were three other possible explanations that stood in the way of this conclusion: Both the family and the sensitives might agree on locations in the house where a ghost was experienced not because one was really there but because there are commonly accepted ideas of where a ghost would be experienced, such as in an attic, on the stairs, or in a dark corner. The successful sensitives might have been getting their impressions from the members of the family by ESP. Even if there was something unusual in the house that the sensitives were picking up, we cannot say on the basis of this evidence that it was the ghost of a dead person.

These unanswered questions about the case do not mean that the investigation failed. Science can move forward only by slow degrees, especially in an area as difficult as the study of apparitions and hauntings. But the first requirement for progress in a new area of science is an adequate method of investigation. Dr. Schmeidler has made an important contribution in providing a new approach to this old problem.

POLTERGEIST:
THE RACKETING GHOST

*"As soon as Prayers were done, and then in sight of the
Company, the Chairs walkt about the Room of themselves,
the Children's shooes were hurled over their Heads and
every loose thing moved about the Chamber."—The
Reverend Joseph Glanville*, The Full and Plain Evidence
Concerning Witches and Apparitions *(1681)*

The telephone rang in a Miami police station on Saturday
morning, January 14, 1967. It was Mr. Alvin Laubheim, one
of the owners and the general manager of a novelty company, Tropication Arts, Incorporated. When the complaint
clerk hung up he said to Patrolman William Killin, "This guy
has got to be a nut. He says he's got a ghost at his place of
business."

Calls from "nuts" are fairly routine and a nuisance, but
Officer Killin went out to investigate. Since Saturday was not
a regular working day at the novelty company, only Laubheim, big, bald, cigar-smoking, and a shipping clerk were
present. The latter, Julio Vasquez, was a nineteen-year-old
refugee from Cuba. He was good-looking, apparently bright
and efficient in spite of his inability to express himself in exact
English.

For about a month some very odd things had been going on
at Tropication Arts. They handled souvenir items, many of
which were imported from Japan, decorated, then sold to
novelty shops. Some breakage was to be expected in a business of this kind, but during the last month literally hundreds
of items had been smashed. In particular, glass beer mugs
with wooden handles were falling from the shelves. The
baffled Alvin Laubheim explained how, a couple of days
before, he had demonstrated to his employees just how the
mugs should be placed on the shelves.

"I set the glasses up myself and I said, 'Now, if you put them in this position, they are not going to fall off the shelf.' And as I turned around and walked to the end of the counter, one of them came right down behind me.

"And then everything started to happen. Boxes came down —a box of about a hundred back-scratchers turned over and fell. We picked things up off the floor as fast as they would fall down. We tried to keep it quiet, because we knew it would hurt our business and draw a bunch of curiosity seekers. Then finally the delivery men saw things happening, and people coming in and out would see it happen, and word got out, and there were more and more people coming in. And somebody suggested that with the glasses being thrown around and the girls crying out in front from fright, we had better notify the police. So I did."

After listening to this wild and almost unbelievable story of events, Patrolman Killin started looking around the warehouse. Four open-shelved tiers running the length of the cement-floored room held the merchandise, most of which was in boxes. Finishing his tour of inspection, the patrolman came back to where Mr. Laubheim and Julio were waiting.

At that moment he happened to turn around and look through the shelves, just in time to see a glass fall to the floor and break. This was a tall highball glass, painted with palm trees and flamingoes and called a "Zombie glass." No one had been close enough to cause the glass to move. There seemed to be no normal explanation.

Killin phoned the police station for help.

This took place at about 10:30 A.M. By the time two other patrolmen and a sergeant came, around noon, the following had happened:

Two boxes standing on the floor turned over and spilled their contents.

A box of pencil sharpeners fell from one of the shelves. Julio replaced them, and five to ten minutes later they fell again.

Shortly after the three members of the police force and two other persons arrived, a box of address books fell into the aisle. Nobody was near it when it fell.

On the previous day, which happened to be Friday the thirteenth, an assistant shipping clerk, eighteen-year-old Iris Roldan, was talking to Julio when ". . . I saw a big cardboard carton start to move by itself. It fell down. I ran, screaming and crying."

On that same day, another shipping clerk, Curt Hagemeyer, said he was working at the shipping desk when he happened to glance up and see a small glass fall to the floor without breaking. "The glass came out and down . . . nobody in the aisle . . . nobody at all . . . not a soul." The glass belonged on a tier of shelves against the wall, approximately fifteen feet from where it landed. That same afternoon he happened to look up and see three small boxes move off a shelf and fall to the floor. Nobody was nearby.

On the Saturday when the police were called in, Mr. Laubheim got in touch with a friend, Howard Brooks, who was a professional magician. His first reaction was that somebody was playing tricks. He listened to the stories and spent an hour and a half at the company that afternoon without seeing anything happen.

But when he came back on the following Monday he saw two boxes fall from one of the shelves. Julio was present, as was Mr. Hagemeyer, Mr. Sackett, a policeman who was having a day off, and Mrs. Sackett. The magician saw no way that any of them could have caused the event. He is reported as saying, "I can't buy this spook theory at this point, but something did move those boxes and I couldn't figure out what it was."

Sackett said he saw the boxes in the air. They had been on the shelf together and they came out as a pair, ". . . maybe three inches removed from the other one, but they were on top of each other."

During that same week, Laubheim's sister, Joyce George, said she was looking directly at a beer mug when it "sort of scooted off" the shelf, moving straight out into the air and then dropping straight down. She also said she saw an Orange Crush bottle leave a top shelf. "It went way out in the air, then down with a bang on its neck. Then it bounced three times on its side." Someone else saw the bottle bounce and corroborated the story.

Also during that same week, one of the women who painted designs on the novelty items said she was returning from lunch when she saw a plastic tray take off from the bottom shelf of the first tier, fly to the second shelf of the next, and then fly back, landing in a large carton. Almost immediately a box on one of the shelves above turned over and spilled its contents into the same carton where the tray had landed. Although Julio and another man were in the warehouse at the time, she was certain that neither of them could have caused the movements normally.

The day before the police came, one of the employees had happened to hear Miss Susy Smith in a local radio interview. Miss Smith is a well-known writer of popular books about psychic phenomena. When she came to look things over, she at once recognized the situation as one that would interest her friend William Roll. In 1958 he and Dr. Pratt had made a study of the Seaford, Long Island, manifestations where, among other unexplained actions, bric-a-brac had flown through the air, holy water had been spilled, and a record player much prized by the children had been smashed. Poltergeist phenomena had been all but ignored by a genera-tion of scientific investigators, but their published findings in that case had marked the turning point in serious research on the subject.

One of their difficulties in observing the Seaford case had been that they did not arrive until activities were tapering off. This time it was Roll's great good luck to reach the scene at the height of the disturbance that was making such a shambles of the warehouse. As soon as he became con-vinced that for their purposes the manifestations were con-tinuing beautifully, he got in touch with Gaither Pratt, who was able to join him for three of the ten days he spent in Miami.

The local observers had demonstrated a scientific approach even before Roll arrived. At Susy Smith's suggestion, several "decoys" had been set up in spots where dislocation had been most frequent; Roll approved and continued along this line, tempting, one might say, the operating force to perform.

Eighteen times the mischievous "ghost" obliged. Once a Coke bottle which had been strategically placed crashed to the floor and shattered. A beer mug set in the same position fell off and broke. Twice, items placed in the target areas seemed to have risen at least two inches to clear objects that had been sitting in front of them.

At this point, a girl who had worked in the warehouse for a week ran crying out the door. She said she never wanted to go back, even for her pay.

Early in the investigation, it was recognized that Julio Vasquez was the focal point of the incidents. But even though nothing happened on the one day when Julio was absent with a cold, fraud on his part was ruled out. There seemed to be no way, even assuming the possibility that Julio might be working with an accomplice, for him to effect the movement of the objects.

It is interesting to listen to the tapes which Dr. Pratt made on the scene. In the manner of a sportscaster who fills in time with running commentary before the game gets under way, he began to describe the scene without waiting for any disturbance to occur. His idea was that if an unaccountable movement of one of the objects should take place, the information on the tape immediately preceding it could provide a record of what the persons in the room had been doing, and just where they were at that instant.

From the tapes: "My recorder is in a briefcase and not conspicuous, and no one pays any attention to my dictating in this low voice, almost a whisper. From where I sit I can see the whole room pretty well. Julio's shirt is white with rose-colored spots, which makes it easy for me to keep track of him when I look between the openings of the shelves.

"Talking to Julio earlier, I asked him when he came to this country. He said he first came in 1961, and that he had been working ever since 1963. His mother is still in Cuba and it seems the home atmosphere with his father and stepmother is not too congenial. I have noticed that when he and Iris joke with each other in Spanish, he is relaxed. He has a nice, vivacious smile and really is a very personable chap . . . Glen Lewis [one of the owners] is talking now with Julio about some order. Bill Roll said it was time for us to get back to our respective vantage points because he thought tension was building up . . .

"Something just now went!" (Taped sounds of Yeah! Ha, ha!) "The tray that was put up this morning on the shelf where one broke earlier crashed. I was talking to Al Laubheim here at the front. Julio was in aisle two, coming toward us. I cannot conceive of any way that tray could have been rigged so that it could be made to fall. Bill was out of the room, and it looks as if there has been more activity today when he is not present . . .

"A crocodile ashtray just fell from a shelf alongside the wall at about the end. Julio was in aisle two, and Al was standing near the end of the bench. It broke without any great noise, with a dull thud. This object fell from the shelf that is about thirty inches high to the floor a distance of six feet away. So it must have had a little projectory in coming out.

"Reporters are here. We were explaining that it was impossible to give a story to them now and have any hope of continuing our investigation when . . . crash! We found a small broken glass on the floor. We promised to give the reporters a story in the morning . . ."

When the headlines started appearing, crowds of the curious came, peering in at the windows, trying to catch a glimpse of what was going bump in the daytime. A TV station sent equipment. They hoped to be able to televise the movement of the objects, but nothing ever moved while the cameras were upon them.

The crashing of crockery and bouncing of bottles continued. One large box weighing approximately fifteen pounds moved horizontally twenty-four feet and all the contents were smashed. On one day alone, there were fifty-two incidents. A total of two hundred and twenty-four events were recorded, although this by no means included all that occurred.

Julio Vasquez left Tropication Arts on February 2. Activity ceased abruptly. One of the newspapers published a story to the effect that Julio had confessed to having accomplished the whole thing by means of strings. This later was found to be false, but no further explanation ever appeared in the papers.

Readers of this story and similar cases nearly always are left hanging. What conclusions, if any, were reached by the investigating parapsychologists? Have there been follow-up studies seeking to explain the activities of this and other racketing ghosts?

J.G.P. COMMENTS:

The literal translation of the German word *Poltergeist* is "racketing ghost" or "noisy spirit." These troublesome disturbances were so labeled at a time when they were taken to be the work of demons or evil nonhuman forces. Today investigators agree that in almost every case a particular living person is the source of the unknown energy or force that causes the physical activity.

It was my good fortune, as Mrs. Hintze points out, to have arrived on the scene in Miami while the physical activity was still going on. I paid careful attention to the situation existing at the time that something happened, and also to the circumstances preceding each event. If trickery had been involved, preparations for the hoax would have had to be made before the object was disturbed.

The company was attempting to carry on its business as usual, despite the disturbances. This meant that the two full-time shipping clerks, Julio and Mr. Hagemeyer, and other members of the establishment were moving about the large storage-and-shipping room in the performance of their duties.

It would have been impossible for Mr. Roll and me to keep track of where everyone was all the time, but fortunately, we found a feature that made our task easier: the poltergeist force did not act unselectively upon just any of the thousands of objects stored throughout the warehouse, but only upon those sitting in a few spots on the shelves. We therefore concentrated our attention upon those particular locations.

As previously noted, the practice had been started, before our arrival, of placing "decoy" objects in those likely spots to see if they would be moved. Witnesses told us that a number of times these test objects had been disturbed.

After putting our own test objects of the kind the poltergeist seemed to prefer in locations where the activity had been most concentrated, we kept a careful watch to make certain that no one tampered with our arrangements. A number of these objects fell or were hurled from the shelves. We were quite sure that no trickery was involved.

We never happened to see an object *start* to move, but in a few instances witnesses said they had done so previously. Early in the case, a local TV crew had focused a camera for more than an hour on a spot on the shelves from which objects had been thrown repeatedly. Nothing happened. Meanwhile, several things were thrown off the shelves at other spots that were not being watched.

Most poltergeist cases have been elusive in this way. Objects usually are disturbed only when no one is looking. The skeptic may seize upon this fact as supporting his opinion that stories like "Mysterious Disturbances Wreck Local Home" make headlines only because the prankster has not been caught in the act.

I recall that when I was investigating the case in the Herrmann household at Seaford, Long Island, a professor at the Duke School of Religion advised me in a friendly and fatherly manner not to take such things seriously. As a young minister he had solved a fraudulent case where a mother and daughter, dissatisfied with life on the farm, secretly manufactured household mishaps in the hope that the father would agree to move to town. Another warning came to me at the same time in the mail from a total stranger. He told of a group of small-town boys who, tired of hearing their elders talking about mediums and communications from the dead, cooked up a plan to terrorize the town. They made a "ghost" race down the main street at night by tying a sheet to a string held by two boys running along the rooftops. He said that the kids were smart enough in that instance to fool their gullible parents, and warned against my letting Jimmy Herrmann, the youngster involved in the Seaford case, do the same thing to me.

Although I fully agreed that the poltergeist investigator cannot be too careful in checking the facts, I could not accept the logic of my well-meaning advisers. True, we have

investigated cases where fraud has been responsible for some
of the occurrences. But one weak link in the chain of evidence does not mean that the whole chain must be discarded. Rather, all the links must be shown to have some
proven flaw before we can completely disregard the claims.
If, over the years, we had found only one indisputably genuine poltergeist event that went contrary to the accepted laws
of physics, we would know that we had made contact with
another level of reality that is worthy of parapsychological
investigation. Perhaps no case now on record could be said
to provide perfect evidence, but there are dozens that defy
all reasonable efforts to explain them in ordinary terms.

In the report that Mr. Roll and I published about the
Miami disturbances, which ran to forty-six printed pages, I
described in detail ten separate disturbances of objects that
took place while I was in the warehouse storage room and
observed what took place before, at the time of, and after
each happening. In no case was I able to find any way that
the displacement and breaking of the object could have been
done in any normal way.

Altogether, our report describes eighteen disturbances
involving special targets that had been placed at locations
on the shelves that were found to attract the poltergeist
force, and in half of these incidents one or both of the investigators was looking directly at Julio when the object was
mysteriously moved from its perch. Julio was in no case close
enough to have caused the movement, nor was anyone else
in a position to have done so.

We were able to conclude from our investigation that a
number of the events could not have been caused in any
normal way, and therefore involved energy and action
beyond the scope of the forces that physics has already
recognized. What kind of force is it? We do not know. But no
previous period of history has witnessed so much scientific
interest in this question. At least one thing is in our favor:
poltergeist cases are not uncommon. They have been
reported since ancient times, and there is no indication that
such happenings are declining as civilization advances into a
more sophisticated age.

In fact, the "racketing ghost" has shown itself to be quite

adequate to cope with some of our technological advances. In 1967 a case erupted in a law office in Rosenheim, Germany, a small town near Munich. Fluorescent light bulbs went out repeatedly; they were found to have rotated in their sockets so that the connections were broken. Sometimes the bulbs fell to the floor and broke. The telephones went haywire, with certain numbers being dialed repeatedly when no one was near the instruments. The number for the correct time was dialed many times, as well as a number used in direct dialing of long distance. Thus the office was billed for phantom long-distance calls that were not actually made. When the utility companies were called in to make repairs, they could find nothing wrong. The incidents seemed to be centered around a nineteen-year-old girl who worked for the law firm.

While this case was active, it came to the attention of Dr. Hans Bender, director of the Institute for Parapsychology in Freiburg, who was known to be interested in poltergeist activities. Bender asked Friedbert Karger, a physicist on the staff of the Max Planck Institute, to look into the matter. Dr. Karger reported on his findings at the annual convention of the Parapsychological Association in 1968 and said that the Rosenheim events showed that physics must recognize a different kind of energy in addition to those previously accepted, this one uniquely dependent on man.

When a colleague and I visited Dr. Karger in Munich in 1972, he was still completely convinced that the disturbance in Rosenheim had been paranormal. He told us that the electric-power company had brought in an instrument which checked the amount of current flowing through the electrical circuit. This instrument, a Siemens Unired 1-line tester, was enclosed in a case and sealed, including recording needles under glass that made a continuous record of the power flowing through the line. Dr. Karger said that when he was present and looking at this recorder, nothing unusual happened, but if he looked away for a few seconds and then looked at it again, in that short interval the graph showed that the needles had fluctuated wildly, as if the power had increased many times. No one was near the instrument during the short time he looked away.

Then Dr. Karger brought another instrument from the Max Planck Institute and hooked it up to the same power line as the instrument that was connected by the electrical company. The arrangement was such that from the point of view of physics, any power that flowed through one measuring device also had to flow through the other one. Yet the new device attached by the investigating scientists showed nothing unusual, although what looked like great surges of power continued to be recorded on the first instrument attached to the line by the electric-power company. Dr. Karger took both recorders to his laboratory for testing and found them to be in perfect order.

What kind of person is usually the focal point for poltergeist manifestations? The general picture of the poltergeist personality, based on the study of a large number of cases, is that of someone who is experiencing the problems of growing up during the difficult years from around ten and through the teens. Less frequently, a case is centered on a person in the early twenties. Only rarely does an older adult take the central role in a poltergeist outbreak.

As a rule, the person who apparently "causes" the events is suffering from unusual strain or anxiety. Outwardly he may appear quite calm, but inside he may be boiling with resentment. Instead of exploding in an obvious, ordinary manner, the poltergeist agent lets off steam by unconsciously causing the mysterious noises or movements of objects. This psychological interpretation is strongly suggested by the facts, although it cannot be said to be scientifically proved at this time.

Julio Vasquez was not directly aware of causing the disturbances in Miami, but he seemed to experience a welcome release of tension following an occurrence. In one instance he told Mr. Roll just after one of the events, "That made me feel good."

Julio was an unhappy young man. His difficulties in adjusting to life as a Cuban refugee and his problems at work finally overwhelmed him, and he eventually was dismissed from his job.

Mr. Roll brought Julio to Durham for a round of examinations. A complete medical examination and a test of brain activity made by recording electrical waves at various points on the scalp revealed nothing abnormal about his physical condition. The psychological tests, however, confirmed Julio's conflicts and difficulties caused by his separation from his mother and grandmother, who had stayed in Cuba, and his resentment at having to work in positions that were beneath the level of his abilities.

In addition, Julio was given laboratory tests for ESP as well as PK tests in which he was asked to use his "mind over matter" powers to control the fall of dice. He showed nothing beyond chance results in the ESP tests, and his total results with the dice were not far enough beyond the chance level to prove that he was successful. Yet the end of the cage in which the dice were tumbled mechanically mysteriously popped open several times even though the door was fastened by four spring latches. It had never come open while being used for other subjects on other occasions. When the cage fell open during Julio's test, the dice spilled out on the floor. Much more often than should happen by chance, the dice stopped rolling on those particular trials with the faces upward that Julio was trying to get. These facts, taken together, suggest that when the PK ability worked in the laboratory by mysteriously opening the rotating cage, it also worked to control the falling dice.

Still another event was observed in the laboratory, and this one was more like the disturbances we had recorded in Miami. Instances of a poltergeist invading the laboratory are very rare, and Mr. Roll's description of this occurrence in his book *The Poltergeist* is worth quoting:

"At 9:35 P.M. we were taking a break in one of the offices. Julio was standing in the doorway to the hall with a cup in his hand when we suddenly heard a crash. When we went out to look, we found a large decorative vase or bottle which had been on a table on the other side of the hallway in pieces on the floor. The base of the bottle and the glass stopper were intact, but the neck had broken into about fifty pieces, the area of impact being five feet or so from the bottle's position on the table. It had been about sixteen feet from Julio and had moved toward him.

"Chuck Honorton and John [Stump] were standing opposite Julio just inside the doorway and had him in partial view both before and during the incident. Obviously, he could not have reached it. Was it possible that Julio had tied a string around the bottle earlier in the evening and then pulled it from his position in the doorway? His left arm and shoulder were not visible to Chuck and John, so the string theory was attractive. Supposing he could have pulled a string, the questions remained how he could have fastened it to the bottle and what happened to the string afterward. The moment we heard the crash, our attention naturally went to Julio. We saw no string or other reaching device in his left hand nor anywhere else on his body.

"The string theory faced another difficulty. When the bottle fell, Julio and I had only been at the FRNM [Foundation for Research on the Nature of Man] about an hour. The first half of this we spent in general conversation with the FRNM group so that Julio could become acquainted with them and with the PK equipment. At 9 P.M. we began testing, and worked continuously, using four PK machines, until we took the coffee break shortly after nine-thirty.

"During the time we were at the FRNM, there was no occasion for Julio to absent himself from the rest of us. When we moved from one room and machine to another, we went as a group.

"It also seemed impossible for Julio to have prepared the event earlier that day. Julio and I had been together all day except when he was examined by Dr. McPherson at Duke Hospital. In short, it did not seem possible that he could have fastened a string to the bottle or prepared this incident in some other way either while we were at the FRNM or before."

In 1958, as Mrs. Hintze mentioned, by the time Mr. Roll and I arrived in Seaford, Long Island, the disturbances in the Herrmann home had largely ended. We were, however, able to observe at first hand the last few mysterious events, and we interviewed witnesses to the earlier happenings and thus verified the accuracy of the official record compiled by

Mr. Joseph Tozzi, the police detective assigned to devote full time to investigating the case.

The Seaford case provided a vivid illustration of the strong public interest in these happenings. Anyone wondering about the impact of poltergeist occurrences on the public only needs to examine the news media of that period, starting with February 1958. World-wide coverage was given to the story in the daily papers, the weekly and monthly magazines, and through radio and TV. This public fascination reached a climax in the documentary presented in October 1958, when the Armstrong Circle Theater TV program presented a simulated rerun of the main events, with the Herrmann family and other principal witnesses appearing in real-life roles and with Douglas Edwards interviewing me about the scientific importance of poltergeists.

Roll and I concluded about this case that there was no acceptable manner in which the disturbances could have been caused normally and that the parapsychological explanation—recurrent spontaneous PK produced unconsciously by Jimmy—was therefore the only one available. But the chief value of that investigation was the emphasis it placed upon the need and the prospects for studying further cases as they became available.

An important contribution to this field was made by Dr. A. R. G. Owen while he was a faculty member of Trinity College of Cambridge University. He started out as a skeptic, but he was a skeptic with an inquiring mind. When he learned about a case involving an eleven-year-old girl, Virginia Campbell, who lived in the small Scottish community of Sauchie, he went there and talked at length not only with the members of the family, but also with their minister, two medical doctors, and Virginia's teacher, all of whom had witnessed some of the unexplained happenings.

Among these were knocking or sawing sounds, some of which were recorded by a BBC crew and broadcast on the TV program "Scope." At different times the witnesses saw movements of objects in Virginia's room when she was in bed, but awake. These included the rotation of her pillow when she was lying on it and not moving her head, the sliding of a chest full of bed linens several inches away from the wall, and the raising and lowering of the lid of the chest when no one was near enough to touch it.

Most of the disturbances took place in the bedroom Virginia shared with her cousin, but the poltergeist also followed the victim to school. When the principal became aware of the case, he told the teacher, Miss Margaret Stewart, that Virginia would be staying home for a while, as she had apparently become involved with a poltergeist.

Miss Stewart did not know what the word meant—she thought it must be some kind of illness. After two days Virginia returned to school, and Miss Stewart told Dr. Owen that she saw several objects move in the classroom near Virginia without being able to discover any way the girl could have made them move. When the children were doing assigned work at their seats, she saw Virginia with both hands on top of her hinged desk cover, trying to hold it down while it was apparently rising up by itself against the downward force she was exerting.

Later the teacher was seated at her desk looking at Virginia's paper while the girl was standing several feet to one side. A yardstick on Miss Stewart's desk began to vibrate and fell to the floor, and one end of the desk slipped several inches forward into the room. At another time the teacher saw an empty desk behind the one where Virginia was sitting rise a few inches off the floor and then slowly settle back down again.

Accepting the reality of the poltergeist effect, Dr. Owen made a thorough study of the vast literature on earlier cases, and wrote a comprehensive book on this topic. Subsequently, he resigned his position at Cambridge to become the director of New Horizons Research Foundation in Toronto, an organization listing parapsychology as one of its areas of interest.

Clearly, scientists have taken up the challenge of the poltergeist. Clearly, also, the time is rapidly approaching, if it has not already arrived, when it will be more respectable to be interested in these mysterious cases than it will be to arbitrarily label the belief in such happenings as mere superstition.

At the end of 1974 I had an opportunity to study a new

poltergeist case, one that showed some novel features unlike those commonly found. In this instance I heard about the happenings soon after they began and while they were still taking place. Thus I was able to arrive on the scene in time to witness many of the happenings. The family was very much against having any publicity about the case, and I agreed not to divulge their names or the location of the case.

Initially, the family had called the police to investigate what they took to be a prankster who was banging on the windows or doors and then quickly ducking for cover. The police became convinced that there was no prankster after they had themselves heard the knocks when no one was in a position to have made them. At that point they telephoned me and requested an investigation of the matter.

In interviewing separately two members of the police force, I learned that they had twice, while observing the front of the house, heard loud banging on the glass of the front door and at the same time had seen a hand striking the glass from the inside. The second time this happened they could see all the members of the family together in the kitchen while the banging was taking place. This was at 10:00 P.M., when the family was leaving the house to spend the night with a relative.

Early the next morning the police returned to the house and checked the door glass and several of the windows for fingerprints or any disturbance of the dust. They found no evidence that anything had touched the surfaces.

I was able to tape many of the knocking sounds during the five days I spent in the house. We had, as the events proceeded, learned what positioning and activities of the family members were likely to make the noises occur, and when a relative visited the home I was able to have the bangings occur on the back door for her benefit by telling the two children, ages nine and ten, to walk up the steps from the basement and pass near that door and into the kitchen.

In the course of taping the loud knocks we discovered that soft tattoo-like sounds, which were so low that we had not noticed them, were also occurring at the windows. During the course of one day several examples of these low sounds were recorded, and over that period of time they progressed from being merely a rapid sequence of low knocks to a series of sounds with a quality of primitive music, varying in pitch, intensity, and rhythm. While the microphone was placed on the window ledge to pick up these sounds, the voices of all the persons in the room can be heard on the tape in conversation in the background. Thus it is possible to be sure that there was no one near the mike who could have been making the noises in any ordinary way.

Quite suddenly and unexpectedly one evening the phenomena changed to movements of objects when no one was in a position to have caused them to move normally, and at the same time the knocking sounds stopped. At one time I was seated facing directly toward an upholstered swivel chair when no one was near enough to it to touch it. The chair tilted backward on two legs and banged forcefully into the wall. At another time I recorded the sound of a magazine flying through the air. It landed three feet in front of me. I saw the last half of the flight and thus could trace the origin of the movement to a rack on the floor in one corner of the room where no one was located at the time. These are only a few examples of the events in this case that I was able to witness and study while the disturbances were happening and from which I was able to conclude with confidence that genuine poltergeist effects were taking place.

KULAGINA

"We had hoped to hear that they [the Russians] were making important strides. Instead, we find out they're having psychokinesis demonstrations to show that their most famous woman psychic can concentrate on a small plastic sphere and make it suspend in midair . . . We can't see what difference it makes if a plastic ball in the Soviet Union falls down or not . . ."—Alan Van Dine
(The Saturday Review, *June 3, 1972*)

As one of the thousands of child soldiers during the siege of Leningrad, she fought bravely and with some distinction until incapacitated by a severe abdominal wound. After World War II she married, had three children, and lives now in a fourth-floor walk-up of a modern apartment building. The apartment is adequate, not luxurious; the rooms are small and she and her engineer husband share them with their married daughter, a son-in-law, and a grandchild. The rent might well be cause for envy in the United States: that sort of apartment in Leningrad rents for eight to ten dollars a month.

Her name is Nina Kulagina; also at times she has been called Nelya as well as Ninel, which happens to be Lenin spelled backward. She has a telephone which is probably tapped; her movements are restricted—she cannot, for instance, decide to take a vacation trip to the United States, although there are many here who would be delighted to have her as a guest; any letters she receives from abroad are almost certainly scrutinized, and if delivered at all, may reach her with deletions; what would seem to us but a minor infraction of the law could put her in jail—and indeed, for a time did so.

In other words, Nina Kulagina lives, with a few exceptions, the life of a typical housewife in a Soviet totalitarian society.

The exceptions are what interest us, for they have caused people from all parts of the world to be interested in her. A dozen or more scientists from different countries have made the difficult and expensive trip to Russia just to see with their own eyes what this remarkable woman can do. She has been tested by some of the visiting scientists, intensively studied by Russian scientists, and not one of them has ever accused her of fraudulence. But news stories in *Pravda* have denounced her. Her children were subjected to taunting in school. A sensitive, shy person, not very strong physically, it is not surprising that at one time it all became too much for her and she suffered a nervous breakdown.

Nina Kulagina is cursed by—the lucky possessor of?—the talent for psychokinesis, known also as PK, or telekinesis. Many believe she can affect the behavior of objects with her mind.

If we can believe those who have observed her, she can indeed levitate a plastic ball without physical contact; move a variety of objects, among them a vase weighing about half a pound; keep a scale from moving downward when thirty grams are placed upon it; stop the beating of the disembodied heart of a frog and then start it up again. Once, challenged by a skeptic, she induced in him heart symptoms suggestive of an acute coronary thrombosis. She reversed the process when the man became ill and frightened.

Kulagina never performs for money. She has spent countless hours under scientific observation, often wired up with sophisticated monitoring devices to register heart action, brain waves, etc. Although she can and often does perform without preparation, it sometimes takes many hours before she feels that she is ready to try to demonstrate what she can do. Some of the sessions last as long as seven hours, during which her heart rate rises as high as 240 beats per minute and her blood pressure rises alarmingly. In one half-hour she has lost as much as two pounds in weight, and after a difficult session she often suffers lack of coordination, dizziness and vomiting, with much bodily pain and sleeplessness.

It was in the early 1960's that she read, as did many people throughout the world, about a Russian girl, Rosa Kuleshova, who was supposed to be able to see with her fingertips.

Kulagina realized that she could do this too. She had noticed that when she reached into her sewing bag for embroidery floss it wasn't necessary for her to look in order to pick the desired color.

When she mentioned this to her medical doctor, he brought her to the attention of Dr. Leonid L. Vasiliev, who had been awarded the coveted Lenin Prize and was then experimenting with psychic phenomena. As he was testing her for her skin-sensing ability, he happened to remember a subject in Greece during the twenties who claimed a talent for psychokinesis and whom he had seen, in an old film, making a compass needle move, apparently by concentrating on it.

He produced a compass and asked Kulagina to try to move the needle. She did it at once. No doubt he was more surprised than she was, for as a scientist with much interest in parapsychology, he knew that this was the rarest of psychic gifts. "Go home," he told her, "practice and come back."

Numerous stories have been told about Kulagina's early PK ability. One that has been rather widely circulated has to do with a time when her pent-up anger supposedly caused a pitcher to slide from a shelf and crash to the floor. But Kulagina herself told Dr. Thelma Moss, a visiting parapsychologist from UCLA, that that story was not true.

In a paper her husband wrote, he told of how she began her early experiments at home. To quote from an abridged translation: "The first experiment was carried out by the subject alone in a dark room. She put a black envelope of a kind usually used for enclosing photographic material on the table near the edge. She sat on a chair at a distance of approximately two meters from the table. As she told us later, for a rather long time nothing happened. Nevertheless, she fixed her gaze on the envelope and focused her attention wholly upon the purpose of having it move. Suddenly the envelope started to move slowly and slipped over the edge of the table and fell to the floor. When thereafter Kulagina tried to repeat the experiment, she attempted to remember and keep in mind exactly what she felt during the movement of the envelope."

Kulagina's work with Dr. Vasiliev was interrupted temporarily by Kulagina's arrest. Since everyone who writes even briefly about her seems always to feel it necessary to mention this difficulty with the authorities, I feel the obligation to say that this unfortunate occurrence in no way proved that there was ever any fraud connected with what she was able to do for Vasiliev or any other scientist. We are not even sure what it was that she did that warranted arrest. One version of the story has it that she was arrested for inability to repay a large sum of money; another, that she was engaged in black-market activities.

If the latter was true, we must remember that even a minor infraction of the strict laws governing such transactions in the Soviet Union could carry a heavy penalty. What is important is that the infraction has served as a handy weapon for opponents of parapsychology ever since. Vasiliev was one of those who apparently felt her transgression to be a minor one, for it was his influence and his money that helped to free her. Until his death in 1966, he continued to experiment with her.

Other scientists then took up the work with Kulagina. The most active investigator was Dr. Genady Sergeev, a physiologist and mathematician specializing in the analysis of brain waves. Edward Naumov, a coordinator of Soviet work in parapsychology, took an active hand. Dr. Zdenek Rejdak, a Prague parapsychologist, tested her when he visited Leningrad in 1968. Sergeev, in particular, talked freely with visiting scientists from other countries and often arranged for them to make their own tests.

And yet Sergeev published very little about his findings in Soviet scientific journals. Some scientists, Dr. Pratt among them, feel that it may be because the phenomena are so foreign to the Communist view of man.

But some of the Kulagina films have found their way illegally to the West. Members of the Paraphysics Laboratory staff in England viewed one of the films more than a hundred times, analyzing it frame by frame without finding anything in the least suspicious.

An early film shows Edward Naumov with Kulagina. We see them sitting together at a round table: Kulagina alert, with wide, beautiful eyes and an expressive face. Her white blouse is simple and becoming, the sleeves short. She submits with acquiescent good grace while Naumov, seeming to feel that he must show the viewers that there are no strings, passes his hand down between her and the table twice, from her head to her lap, slowly and deliberately.

On the bare surface of the table he then places a matchbox, some other small objects, and a compass on a wrist strap. Kulagina's hands hover over the compass horizontally, her elbows akimbo, and her long fingers extended toward each other. Her hands come to within two or three inches of the compass and we can see plainly that nothing happens: the needle does not move.

She draws her hands away now without taking them out of the viewers' sight, and as they approach the compass again, we can see that the needle moves a little. Then, as her hands make sweeping circular motions, the needle makes four complete revolutions. Sometimes the movement was clockwise and again counterclockwise. Now the compass case itself starts to move. Turning and sliding, it would have fallen from the table if Naumov had not caught it.

This sequence is followed immediately by another shot of the same compass, but now it has been placed on a small snack-style table. Again the compass moves until it is about to fall over the edge, but at this point Naumov covers the compass with his hand and suddenly flips the table over, showing us the underside as if to prove there is no apparatus underneath. Kulagina's hands lift as if in surprise at this, but her face shows no annoyance and she proceeds calmly when the table is positioned again, and she makes the compass needle turn as if the interruption had not bothered her.

In the next shot, back on the round table again, the camera moves in close for a good view of the matchbox, upended, a salt cellar, a cigarette also standing on end, and some other small objects together with a pile of matches, perhaps twenty. As Kulagina's hands hover tensely, the salt cellar moves toward the matches, pushing them ahead, their careless positioning now remaining as steady as if they had been glued together in that formation. But when they reach the edge of the table they fall off one by one, and the salt cellar is caught just as it is about to go over the edge.

Of necessity, the films have been spliced to avoid the showing of long stretches during which nothing happens. One film with a viewing time of less than half an hour took seven hours to complete. Rest periods were necessary for the subject, whom we see at times trying hard without effecting any discernible movement. At those times the stress is very evident. Her dimples deepen as if she is clenching her teeth. Several times we see her characteristic gesture of frustration when she brings her hand down flat on the table or claps it against her forehead. Dr. Pratt has one still photograph in which her usually smooth, young-looking face takes on the appearance of an exhausted, much older woman.

One of the films was made in a garden setting in which a dog played around Kulagina's feet; one short sequence in this film showed a neighbor manicuring the subject's nails, presumably to prove that no magnetic filings or dust were attached to them and that no tiny magnets had been concealed under her fingernails.

An effective way of registering motion is shown in a color film taken by Dr. Pratt. He had sprinkled red aquarium gravel on the surface of the table, and a small metal cylinder, moving by fits and starts, makes an easily discernible path through the gravel. Another color film, made by Dr. Jürgen Keil from the University of Tasmania, showed a plexiglass cube measuring four inches on each edge, in which a ping-pong ball had been fastened to one end of a flexible spring, the other end of which was attached to the top of the cube. Kulagina was able to bring the ball down to the "floor" of the cube and then move it along horizontally. When she relaxed, the spring snapped back to its original position.

When Kulagina first started experimenting about ten years ago, the objects she was trying to influence moved away from her; she can still cause this to happen, but now they usually move toward her. At first she did not hold her hands near the objects; early films show that she sat with her hands in her lap, leaning forward and making a slight swinging motion with her body.

There seems to be little difference in her ability to move magnetic or nonmagnetic materials, but she feels that anything made of gold, such as a wedding ring, can be moved most readily.

Shape is important. A cylinder placed vertically is more easily moved than one in a horizontal position. Cigarettes, carefully balanced to stand on end, move with an almost skimming motion over surfaces that are not always smooth; one film shows a cigarette so placed moving over a textured lace tablecloth. In one sequence, Kulagina shreds the cigarette she has just moved, perhaps to show a skeptic that it contained nothing magnetic, such as a pin, that might have enabled it to be drawn along by the action of a magnet under the table. Incidentally, the workers at the Paraphysics Lab tried this. They found it very hard to keep the cigarette balanced, although they were able to move it for an inch or two with the pin-and-magnet device. Kulagina's cigarette, almost certainly without any magnetic help, traveled a much greater distance before toppling.

When a transparent plexiglass covering is placed over the objects, she seems at first to have difficulty getting action started, but once started, all proceeds with comparative ease. Sometimes one thing will move in one direction and something else in another. Sergeev told Dr. Pratt and Dr. Keil that matches placed in a star-shaped pattern had been observed to move in several directions at once.

Kulagina cannot perform during storms, and dislikes making the effort during warm, humid weather. Since she seems to possess some telepathic ability, it is not surprising to learn that she is very quick to sense skeptical or critical attitudes. Very often she has to ask certain persons to leave the room until she gets into her task; once she gets things under way, their return does not seem to bother her particularly. Sometimes, sensing friendly acceptance, she has been known to give impromptu demonstrations without being asked.

Dr. Pratt has a letter describing a time when this happened. Naumov had invited two laymen, Elsie and Bill Sechrist, both much interested in parapsychology, to come from the United States to lecture on Edgar Cayce. Naumov was able to arrange for them to meet Kulagina and her husband in Leningrad, and when the Sechrists invited them to have dinner with them at their hotel, they accepted. This is the way Mrs. Sechrist's letter described the events of the evening:

"Through our interpreter, we asked many questions about her psychic abilities. She was very cordial and offered to demonstrate for us. I assured her, however, that it was not necessary, as we had already seen the moving pictures demonstrating her abilities and had talked with Naumov and Victor Adamenko, physicist, who had witnessed the phenomena. I explained that I was aware of the great effort often involved in their demonstrations and did not wish to tire her just to satisfy my curiosity in seeing her demonstrate 'live.'

"After talking for more than an hour we went to the hotel dining room . . . And it was in that wholly unorthodox 'laboratory' and on a dining table (with a cloth on it) that Nelya demonstrated for us. She insisted on showing us so that we would be able to say to American audiences, 'Yes, we did see Nelya Kulagina move objects through concentration.'"

Quite unexpectedly, it seems, she moved a piece of bread about four inches square. Mrs. Sechrist says she did not see the whole operation because she was distracted by their interpreter, "who let out a shriek and with an expression of fear backed away from the table."

Kulagina then repeated the experiment for her hostess, with a slight variation. Taking off her gold wedding ring, she placed it in the center of the table and put a piece of bread on it. "After just a few seconds, the ring and bread moved hesitantly (stop and go) until they reached the edge of the table and fell into her lap.

"Amazed that she did it so quickly, I asked, 'Nelya, how is it that you were able to do that so quickly when I have read that at times it has taken you hours?' She said very simply, 'Never have I been so well prepared psychologically. You did not even *want* me to do it.' She added that skepticism made it most difficult for her to demonstrate."

The Sechrists made a second visit to Russia the following year together with a group of people from ARE (Association for Research and Enlightenment). Kulagina again demonstrated, and a member of the group, Charles Thomas Cayce, Edgar Cayce's grandson, took her pulse as she was moving objects. He said her pulse was so rapid, he could not count it.

Mrs. Sechrist's recollection is that Kulagina moved three objects: her gold ring, a piece of bread, and the top of a fountain pen. "The strain on her face this time was greater than when Bill and I first saw her, but it was also done rather quickly. (She told me that she knew she could work with this group because of their open minds.) No one at the table doubted that we were witnessing psychokinesis at its best. Nelya is a simple, unassuming person who—as she told my husband and me—is doing this (although it may kill her) for science and for her country."

Dr. Pratt, after his six trips to Russia, seems to have been another one of those who has established good rapport with Kulagina. When Soviet authorities denied his request for an international group of scientists to be allowed to meet in Leningrad to study this remarkable subject, he and Keil decided that they would go as tourists, taking their chances on seeing Kulagina without prior arrangement.

And so it was that on a Sunday night in September 1972 they knocked, unannounced, on the door. Kulagina's husband answered, recognized them, and invited them most cordially to come in. They had brought gifts—some books from Czechoslovakia and a pound of instant coffee, which is almost unobtainable in Russia. Kulagina, with her customary warmth and hospitality, insisted on preparing food for them, and after that she gave an impromptu demonstration although they had not asked her to do so.

Dr. Pratt's diary-style account says this: "Then we put some of the test objects we hoped to use later on the table." ("Later" being Tuesday for a planned demonstration that never took place.) "Keil and I were both seated across a small dining-room table from Kulagina. She soon began making characteristic motions with her hands on both sides of a small plastic jelly dish I had brought from the plane, all the while saying that she had not done anything for a year or more and didn't know whether she could succeed.

"In . . . perhaps one or two minutes, she stopped her motions and breathed deeply three or four times as if trying to muster her energy for a major effort. After that she immediately started in again concentrating upon the jelly dish. Her actions were qualitatively quite different. She was obviously trying, which I had not felt she was doing before. The jelly dish was resting upon the open pages of a slick-paper book we had brought from Prague. Back of the dish, about four inches farther away from her, was a small block of wood I had brought with me. Suddenly the block of wood moved slightly in her direction, slightly toward her right and rotating slowly in a clockwise direction as it did so. Both Keil and I saw this, as we immediately confirmed between ourselves. Then we both saw it move again in the same way.

"We were not making any efforts to turn this social occasion into a formal session. But shortly afterward I brought out a completely sealed plexiglass cube (approximately four inches on each edge) which contained two colored dice and a small quantity of red aquarium gravel. Kulagina seemed fascinated right away with this device, and she began concentrating in an apparent effort to make the objects inside move. Again, the cube was resting on the page of the book we had brought. The dice did not move independently, but suddenly the whole cube slid one or two centimeters toward Kulagina.

"These observations prove nothing, but they were nevertheless impressive to Jürgen Keil and me. Kulagina had not moved from the table from the time we put the objects down until they moved, and one or both of us had her under observation the whole time. They were our objects, and they were resting on 'our' surface. We never observed any motion suggesting that Kulagina was preparing a trick, and she would not have known to prepare it before we unexpectedly produced the objects."

The more formal experimentation did not take place, as hoped for, on the following Tuesday, because of the intervention of Soviet authorities, who, though they are alert to the evidence Kulagina's abilities present, apparently are not willing to allow foreign scientists access to *their* subject.

Admittedly, this woman's abilities, remarkable though they seem to be, do not come close to exerting the force that was exhibited in the spontaneous manifestations at Rosenheim.

But anyone who has ever been impressed, as I have been, with the way the merest touch on the button of a self-service elevator will cause several tons of equipment to zoom skyward must be aware of the potential possessed by a person with psychokinetic powers. If such a power exists in any mind, it is, as Paul Brunner, the investigator for civic works in Rosenheim, said, ". . . an alarming thought to consider what catastrophic results could happen in the realm of technology if such forces, outside the will power of technicians, would influence relays and upset functions of all kinds."

J.G.P. COMMENTS:

Jürgen Keil and I first heard about the PK effects of Kulagina when we attended an international parapsychological meeting in Moscow in 1968. A Russian physicist who was there had earlier visited Kulagina. He said that within five minutes he had observed events that physics cannot explain. He recommended that parapsychologists should concentrate their efforts on phenomena like hers, where the effects are directly observable and it is only necessary to prove that the movements are not due to fraud to establish that they are paranormal. The issue of chance does not arise and there is no need for statistics.

Later in the meeting the film described by Mrs. Hintze, the one showing Naumov working with the subject, was presented by Dr. Sergeev. The second half of the film, not yet available in the West, showed the subject demonstrating PK while connected to equipment for registering her brain waves. The waves picked up from the back of the head became many times stronger than normal when one of the objects started to move, whereas the record of waves from other parts of the head were unchanged.

Keil and I agreed that the film about Kulagina was the most interesting part of the meeting. Of course, the movie by itself was not scientific proof, since it is easy to create illusory effects in a film. The movie industry is based largely upon this fact. But the film we saw was endorsed by Sergeev, who was accepted as a qualified scientist by his colleagues. Nevertheless, we knew that such an unexpected finding needed to be independently confirmed, and we resolved to try to make our own study of Kulagina. This is how we came to make, between us, five visits to Leningrad over the next few years. Two of the visits were used only for meetings with the scientists who had worked with Kulagina, but the other three included opportunities to observe Kulagina moving objects.

Other Western scientists have also seen her work. One is Dr. Ullman, previously mentioned in connection with the Maimonides dream research; and another is Mr. Benson Herbert, the director of the Paraphysics Laboratory in England and editor of the *Journal of Paraphysics*, where the Kulagina film analyses and some other reports were published.

The observations of Kulagina by visiting scientists were made under informal conditions and were not so extensive as we would have liked. In considering the question of evidence for PK, however, it is more appropriate to choose a few special observations that gave the strongest indications of paranormality than it is to list a large number. Also, observations made by visiting investigators are more suitable in general because they have been reported in more detail.

Even though the visitors studied Kulagina under less than ideal conditions, she did not have control over the arrangements as a magician must do in performing his tricks. On the contrary, we went with our own objects and with special devices that Kulagina did not know about in advance. Thus the subject had no opportunity to arrange a trick way of moving objects under these conditions. Furthermore, after the session the investigators brought their devices away for further study to see if there was any way that successful results could have been produced by fraud. By such means the investigators largely overcame the handicap of not being able to study Kulagina in the laboratory. And it is important to stress that only one unmistakable instance when an object moved under conditions that cannot be explained normally would be strong evidence for PK.

In my opinion one result observed by visiting investigators and also filmed provides such an instance, and we should, therefore, examine it closely. This is the series of movements of the ping-pong ball suspended by a weak spring inside a plastic cube, as mentioned by Mrs. Hintze. One side of the cube was open, and the spring had one end attached to the ball and the other end glued to the inner surface of one side of the cube. Kulagina learned about the device and saw it for the first time when it was placed on the table in front of her.

The film shows that Kulagina touched the outside of the cube in changing its location on the table. In its final position the open side was toward Kulagina, and the spring, attached to the top surface, supported the ball about a half-inch above the floor of the cube. At no time did Kulagina reach inside the cube or touch the ball or spring, as a magician would have had to do to attach a fine thread.

Even if an invisible thread had been introduced, it could not have caused the movements of the ball shown in the film. First the ball is motionless, held suspended by the spring. The next view in the film shows the spring stretched directly downward, with the ball resting on the bottom surface of the cube. Then we see it pulled slightly upward by the spring and immediately pressed down again several times. It is clear that a force is being exerted to keep the ball down against the pull of the spring.

The ball then stays down on the floor of the cube while it moves slowly in the direction of the subject. As this sliding movement occurs, the spring is stretched further and further. Kulagina's hands, visible above the table, are held on opposite sides of the cube but without touching it. As the ball reaches the front edge of the cube the subject appears to relax, and the spring snaps back, pulling the ball upward into the cube, where it shortly settles down and comes to rest once more in its original position.

Consider what would have been required to produce this sequence of motions by working a trick. An invisible string attached to the bottom of the ball could have pulled it directly downward if the thread passed through a hole in the bottom of the cube or some sort of eyelet that was low enough to allow the ball to be pulled all the way down. But this thread could not make the ball move across the floor of the cube. To accomplish this by trickery would require a second string attached to the ball to move it forward at the same time that just enough tension was maintained on the first string to hold the ball down. Even so, it is difficult to conceive of any way that these two forces could have been applied so as to make the ball stay on the floor of the cube throughout its journey to the front edge.

If a magician wanted to perform such a trick, he would prepare his equipment in advance, and anyone who examined his equipment afterward would see the preparations. In the Kulagina demonstration, neither she nor anyone who might have assisted her had any opportunity to make the arrangements that would have been needed. Even if it could be assumed that they somehow managed to do so, this would have been evident afterward from the changes made in the apparatus. Later examination of the equipment by the investigators showed no changes in it.

A ping-pong ball is nonmagnetic, so it could not have been pulled down and made to creep across the surface by a magnet held below the top of the table. It is true that the spring itself would be attracted by a magnet, but there are difficulties in the way of explaining what occurred in this way. Kulagina is seen in the film to be sitting at the table with both her hands above the table in full view. Even if a magnet was available to her, and this could have been brought into position under the table without being noticed, it is difficult to see how it could have been handled so as to produce the movements of the ball without being obvious to the observers and in the film.

And how, in any case, could a magnet account for the ways the ball moved at the beginning? The spring was stretched vertically downward, so the ball rested on the bottom. Then it was pulled up a short distance by the spring and was quickly brought back down several times in close succession. If the magnet had not been strong enough to hold the spring, it would not have been able to recapture it once it had broken free and had moved farther away from the magnet. We have tested the matter with a strong magnet and found that we could not duplicate the effects Kulagina produced.

·   ·   ·

A change in matter that does not involve simple movement of objects has been reported by the Russian investigators. This is the occurrence on unexposed photographic film of markings that would normally be caused by light striking it but which appeared in their work with Kulagina when no light could have been present. They wrapped an unexposed strip of film in light-proof paper and then placed an object on one end of the cover and asked Kulagina to try to move it by PK along the length of the film. When she succeeded, later development of the negative revealed a broad streak running lengthwise on the film, as if it had been exposed where the object traveled. When the same object was moved normally over another wrapped strip of film at the rate of the movement produced by Kulagina, the negative showed no effect. None of the visiting scientists has attempted to confirm this finding.

On one of my visits I was carrying a Polaroid camera, the first one that the Russian scientists had seen. When we met Kulagina, the Russians asked her to move an object they had placed in contact with an unexposed roll of Polaroid film. She succeeded, but when the film was later developed through the camera, no exposure marks were found. This test thus failed to confirm the results with regular film, but it was interesting to me in that it showed how strongly committed the investigators were to the discovery of the photographic PK effect.

The strong brain waves picked up from the back of the head when Kulagina was making an object move, as mentioned earlier, are unusual, but they do not prove that the object was moved by PK. The peculiar EEG record shows only that Kulagina was in a special physiological state at that moment. The same thing is true for all the other changes in her behavior that occurred when she tried to make an object move: increased heartbeat, rate of breathing and blood pressure; loss of weight; the strain of great effort causing fatigue and headache, etc. These observations of her physiological conditions are important in helping us to understand the PK effects, but they are not by themselves evidence that PK had occurred. Even if the unusual physiological changes occurred during a session, the experiment would be recorded as a failure if Kulagina was unsuccessful in moving any objects or fogging a film.

There was one kind of physiological effect that gave strong evidence of PK because of the manner in which it was detected. This was an effect picked up by a sensitive device that was not attached to the subject but was only lying nearby when Kulagina was trying to move objects. When she succeeded, some effect was also picked up on this special sensor that Sergeev had invented, and the effect was recorded in the form of waves by a marker pen on a polygraph. The fact that some unknown force from the subject was able to trigger this device at the same time as an object moved gives strong independent evidence that the movement was not produced by fraud. It is unfortunate from the scientific point of view that Sergeev has not published information on the construction of his sensing device. Until this is known or another device that works in the same way has been built, independent confirmation of this particular result is not possible.

The emphasis placed upon selected examples of Kulagina's performance does not mean that the case for PK rests upon these alone. There is a large amount of other evidence that has been convincing for those who were witnesses of the events and which should at least persuade others that a new frontier of parapsychological research has been opened up.

I hope we can all look forward to the time when Sergeev will be able to make a full report on all of his work with Kulagina. He told me in 1970 that he had completed more than a hundred successful experiments and that he had long since become fully convinced of the genuineness of Kulagina's effects. Since reaching that stage, he said, they were planning and carrying out experiments only for the purpose of learning something further about the nature of the subject's psychic phenomena.

The Russian scientists theorize that the results depend upon some kind of energy in the living organism that is released, as our knowledge now stands, only by rare individuals under special circumstances. The investigators in the USSR use terms that emphasize the relation they assume exists between the PK energy and better-known energies in biology and physics, such as bioenergy and bioplasma.

In the West, on the other hand, the thinking has run more along the lines of some psychic explanation involving energy that is more closely connected with consciousness and the subjective side of human nature.

The Russians tend to think that Kulagina's PK force is a general effect from the subject's organism that moves objects sporadically but is not directed in a precise way by the subject's intentions. Some facts from the research seem to lend support to this "field force" interpretation, such as the registering of a general effect by the Sergeev sensing device simultaneously with the moving of an object. Also, in one of the films the needle of a compass that is sitting to one side starts to swing back and forth when Kulagina is obviously concentrating wholly upon moving an object directly in front of her.

It is entirely conceivable that research will ultimately show that we are not concerned in parapsychology with only one kind of energy, but that different phenomena can be adequately understood only when we are able to distinguish different kinds of causation that are involved in different psychic phenomena. We need to keep our minds open to different possibilities while pressing on with the search for more definite answers.

A few years ago Dr. Rejdak and I were discussing in Prague the research with Kulagina. He said that all we need from her is enough information and enough conviction about her ability to enable us to find others like her. I agree, and we do seem now to be on the way to achieving this goal.

One American subject was inspired by the film of Kulagina, and through great effort over a period of two months she succeeded in moving objects. She had her own film made showing her success, and she later gave brief demonstrations of her ability to a few individual parapsychologists. But for personal reasons she has found it necessary to stop working as a PK subject.

Another promising subject is Matthew Manning, who is reported to have been involved in a poltergeist case some time ago and who subsequently developed an ability for voluntary PK when he was encouraged to try. He attended a conference on PK held by the New Horizons Research Foundation in Toronto in July 1974. A brief report states, among other things, that he moved a compass needle when passing his hand to and fro above it at a distance of nine to twelve inches. While he concentrated upon a stainless-steel knife that was held by someone else at a distance of about ten feet, it was observed to be bending, and at the end of the period it remained bent.

A movie was made which shows an uninterrupted view of Manning's hands. A key shown to be straight at the outset was held lightly in Manning's closed hand. When his hand was opened the key had become bent. Afterward the film shows it continuing to bend while Manning is holding it only by the large end.

Other encouraging cases have recently been mentioned in the parapsychological literature and work with some of them is continuing, but we really need to study many more persons who have developed an ability for directly observable PK. There is always room in my postal box for a letter from anyone who can move objects or affect the state of matter by will power alone and who is willing to work at it for the sake of science.

Since this chapter is primarily about Kulagina and has touched briefly upon other similar demonstrations inspired by her example, we should not leave the reader with the impression that this is the only type of research that has been done on PK. Indeed, a vast amount of work has been done and written about on this problem since the mid-thirties, most of it by testing subjects for their ability to influence dice to stop rolling, with a greater number of target faces showing than would reasonably be expected by chance.

THE MIRACLE HEALERS

"After doing my very best for eighteen months to find some shred of evidence that somewhere there was someone who had miraculous healing powers, I concluded that no such person existed."—William A. Nolen, M.D., Healing, A Doctor in Search of a Miracle *(1974)*

"Healing presents difficult problems for the investigator . . . Nevertheless, several well-investigated cases exist in which an instantaneous and apparently inexplicable healing seems to have occurred."—Nils O. Jacobson, M.D., Life Without Death? *(1973)*

"And Jesus said [to the daughter of Jairus], 'Get up, my little gazelle.'"—Mark 5:41 (Alexander Findlay translation)

Apparently it sells. The various branches of the media have been surfeited recently with programs and articles and books about the miraculous healing of everything from plants to people. My innate, though cautious, wish to believe moves uneasily from dismay to utter disbelief as I twist the dials and turn the pages.

There is the child evangelist, enchantingly gap-toothed, with about as long an attention span as any other seven-year-old, not sure which camera to look at as he shrugs, scratches, and says, "I dunno. I just put my hands on 'em and pray real hard and they get well."

On another program, crutches are thrown aside and a sweating preacher mops his brow and shouts, "Praise God! Amen! Hallelujah!" as do the members of the packed congregation who are not in trance or evidencing glossalalia. I hear, but don't write down, the box number where the millions of viewers are invited to send their love offerings.

A best-selling book describes the polygraphed distress of plants when shrimp in another room are dropped into boiling water. Books about the miraculous healing of human ailments range from those by nonmedical writers whose uncritical enthusiasm could have the terminally ill selling their farms and heading for the Philippine psychic surgeons, to those written by British psychiatrist Louis Rose and American surgeon William A. Nolen, neither of whom found one cure that answered their criteria for a miracle.

What is to be believed?

Tony Agpaoa is but one of the psychic surgeons in the Philippines, but his name is the best known, he has made the most money, and his films have been most widely shown. A typical film shows the patient, usually corpulent, lying down and exposing the abdomen. After Tony has kneaded the fat for a brief time, "blood" flows, and shortly he brings out what is supposed to be the offending tumor, or whatever. When the "blood" has been wiped away, the abdomen is revealed without any sign of an incision, the patient gets up smiling, praising Tony and God, and walks away.

The true believers are convinced that Tony operates with his bare hands, miraculously opening the flesh and then as miraculously closing it again. There is never any anesthesia, any knife, any pain, subsequent infection, or recuperation period. Investigation has revealed that animal blood or some sort of red dye, perhaps betel juice, is palmed, squirted during the manipulation, and the tissue, anything from chicken gut to pig parts, is revealed briefly and usually disposed of before anybody can get a good look.

Out of professional curiosity, Dr. Pratt recently went to a lecture given by a husband-and-wife team who were promoting a psychic-surgery tour to the Philippines. Anything but high pressure, they were gentle, they were honest according to their lights, and they were certainly true believers. Why wouldn't they be? The husband, several years before, had been told he had terminal cancer which had metastasized, spread through his body, and medical doctors gave him only a short time to live. Desperate, the couple had gone to the Philippines, where they were convinced the *espiritistas* (spiritual healers) had healed him of his cancer and also of his varicose veins.

The wife told the audience, "The varicose veins were just

pulled out and held up like spaghetti." She'd had her share of operations too, and said, "They also removed my migraine headaches. I had a hernia removed, and I had a bladder that had dropped put back into place, and my bursitis was cured. Altogether, we've had about twenty operations."

During the question period Dr. Pratt asked for an explanation of why it was that in the few cases where investigators had been able to avail themselves of the tissues removed, they had turned out to be animal parts.

The woman said she was glad he asked. Unbelievers asked this sort of question all the time and it was good to have a chance to explain: "In the Philippines the atmosphere is changed when the Holy Spirit comes down, and so is the tissue. It changes from human tissue into animal tissue."

Now the husband took up the defense. He said that pressure from the American Medical Association had brought about the unfavorable newspaper reports about these psychic surgeons. "It's a real affront to their [American doctors] earning powers—oh, yes, it's just that simple."

Learning that the Federal Trade Commission had obtained a restraining order that prohibited three West Coast travel agencies from offering "psychic surgery" tours to the Philippines, I contacted the Federal Trade Commission for further information. I am indebted to Gregory L. Colvin, an attorney in the FTC Regional Office in Seattle, for what I found out about the hearings which began there on September 9, 1974.

Although the three travel agencies had been promoting the tours for two or three years at most, some two thousand persons had taken the trip. The FTC attorneys were demanding that the agencies inform each of those persons that psychic surgery was only sleight of hand and they could be in danger medically if they believed they were cured. Also, the FTC was asking restitution of a thousand dollars to each person who had taken the "psychic surgery" trip.

Attorneys for the defense argued that the FTC was violating the First Amendment, freedom of religion, and produced at least one physician (retired) who said he had worked with the Philippine surgeons and believed their powers to be real. They also brought to the stand a person formerly blind who said his sight had been restored, and a woman who claimed

to be an expert in psychic phenomena and testified that the
espiritistas did have the power to open and close the body
with their bare hands.

The witnesses for the FTC were more numerous and more
vocal, and some of them testified for hours. The first witness
was Carol Wright, from Shellsburg, Iowa, who had first gone
to the Philippines in January 1972 with her father. Believing
him to have been cured of cancer by the *espiritistas*, and
convinced of the reality of the paranormal healing as practiced there, Carol and her husband Donald had returned in
July of that year to learn the techniques. During instruction
by several of the healers, they soon became aware of the
fraud involved. She said that secreted upon the person of the
operator were wads of cotton, known as "bullets," which had
been wrapped around clots of cow's blood together with such
items as strings, nails, stones, cockroaches, and parts of animal tissue, including eyes. (In an article Carol and her husband wrote for a Philippine magazine, *Woman's Home
Companion*, they described an incident that took place during
an eye operation. Making it appear that the patient's eye was
being temporarily removed for treatment, the "surgeon" held
one up. It was probably a pig's eye and had been used so
long it had turned green. When the patient's brother pro-
tested, the operator explained that the nerves had died and
that dipping the eye in holy water would heal them.)

On the second day of the hearings Donald Wright simulated the operation on a towel when it was ruled that he
could not demonstrate on a live person. He made a depression in the towel, ran a moistened pad of cotton over the
depression, broke open a "bullet" he had palmed, and spread
concealed membrane which created the appearance of open
flesh. Bits of tissue were then produced, the "incision" was
closed, the "abdomen" swabbed, and the "operation" was a
complete success.

A professional magician, whose stage name is André Kole,
testified that the Filipino faith healers gave the most fantastic
performances he had ever seen. He said, "At first, I was
shaken. I thought I was witnessing the supernatural." What
seemed to happen was that a practitioner made an incision
in a woman's back just by moving his finger above it in the

air. What really happened was that the incision had been
made by a razor blade hidden in the cotton that, moments
before, had swabbed the site. The few seconds necessary for
the superficial incision to start bleeding had lent reality to the
illusion that the motion through the air caused the skin to
open.

A Boeing electronic technician took the stand to relate
what had happened to his friend in a Manila hotel room
when Tony Agpaoa accidentally broke open a cancerous
tumor on the patient's cheek. The patient had bled profusely
and lost consciousness. The technician said he yelled, "Help
—call a doctor!" Whereupon Tony grabbed up his parapher-
nalia and ran from the room.

Dr. Ronald L. Chard of Children's Orthopedic Hospital
testified that delaying or interrupting conventional treatment
could be disastrous. "I am not neutral when families of dying
children ask me about psychic surgery practiced in the Philippines. I advise them against taking such a trip." Four of
his child cancer patients have been taken to the Philippines
and four have died.

Other physicians took the witness stand, and one of them,
Dr. Otto Trott, said that the condition of one of his patients
had been made worse by the daily massaging by faith healers, and had died when a dislodged clot had traveled to his
lungs.

FTC attorney Colvin summed up his argument on the
twelfth day of the hearing by saying, "This is not faith healing in the traditional sense . . . What there was included
trickery, magic, and sleight of hand . . . Travel agencies
should be restrained from future promotion of such tours."

On February 21, 1975, Judge Daniel H. Hanscom issued an
order which, though subject to appeal, would require that
the firms stop making such misrepresentations and promoting
trips for "psychic surgery," and that they give a written
notice to persons who have taken or contemplate taking such
tours. He said, "Psychic surgery is pure and unmitigated
fakery . . . The respondents' misrepresentations have the
capacity to cause the gravest and most serious . . . injury to
individuals and to the public generally. Not only do such
representations have the tendency and capacity to cause

seriously ill persons to travel long distances at great expense
. . . but such representations have the tendency and capacity
to worsen the condition of the sick, and even to cause the
death, through interruption of normal medical care . . ."

Kathryn Kuhlman is probably the most famous and the
most popular healer in the United States today. Gorgeously
dressed, with background assists from music and flowers, she
has a weekly TV program on which she charismatically pro-
claims her belief in miracles and never stops smiling as she
presents her guests, who often give sober and moving testimony describing cures of everything from congenital bone
deformities to cancer.

The audience gave her a standing ovation when she
appeared on the Johnny Carson *Tonight Show* in the fall of
1974, and yet Dr. William A. Nolen, who had appeared on
an earlier Carson show, had said that in his opinion she had
done more harm than good. One section of his book *Healing:
A Doctor in Search of a Miracle* had been devoted to Miss
Kuhlman, and although the book had not been published
then, the section on Kuhlman had been excerpted by
McCall's magazine in the August issue.

Some ridiculous figures have been published about her age.
One, in 1967, said she was eighty-four. Even if that figure is
twenty years off—or thirty—it still seems ridiculous. Her slim
figure is that of a girl. Her posture is beautiful; her walk as
she strides onto the stage is quick, full of vigor, and her voice,
with its breathy little chuckles, maintains an emotional high,
as if she's had two martinis. Sometimes she speaks very fast;
sometimes with slow, dramatic pauses: "Kathryn Kuhlman is
noth-ing. I have never . . . cured . . . any-body. Do not call
me a faith healer [fast]—it is the Holy Spirit that works
through me." And she says on every program, slowly, empha-
sizing the consonants, "I believe in miracles . . . because . . . I
believe . . . in God."

When she appeared on the Carson show she said she
doesn't know how the healing works, or why it sometimes
doesn't work. Some of the most unlikely persons are healed,
and some of the most deserving, with the most faith, are not.

"Oh, I don't know why, Johnny! I die a thousand deaths! I just love those people!"

Johnny said, "You really do love everybody, don't you?"

"Yes. Yes, I do. I love everybody." That throaty little chuckle. "I even love Dr. Nolen!"

That would take a bit of doing for most people. Nolen had professed doubt that any good she was doing could possibly outweigh the misery she was causing. He said he had made careful follow-ups of her "miracles" and had not found one that answered his stipulations for genuine cure: Was the case medically certified before and after the alleged cure? Had the person begun to improve as a result of medical treatment? How great is the tendency of this disease to cure itself spontaneously? Could the illness be considered psychosomatic?

Kuhlman now was appearing on the Carson show at her own request. "Let us agree with Dr. Nolen that many of the illnesses are psychosomatic, but do you realize that is one of the hardest cases in the world to cure?"

Nolen might have agreed with that, but I had thought she might have proof to refute his statement that not one of her claims to a cure of an organic disease such as cancer could stand up to scrutiny.

For months I had watched her television program. At times, that overcharged smile and burbly enthusiasm had turned me off, but I had been impressed many times by the calm joy of those who *knew* they had been healed. Surely among them there must be one case that would meet the rigid requirements for a miracle. I chose one that seemed worth following up.

Ian Stevenson had made his own study some time ago of the Kuhlman claims. He had investigated only six cases, but his conclusion also had been that not one of them could be considered a cure of organic disease. And so, even before we began to work, Gaither Pratt and I agreed that investigation of the one case that had most impressed me was probably a waste of time. It would be a miracle if we found a miracle.

The case I had selected, that of pretty teenaged Lisa Larios, did seem to fulfill every one of the medical requirements: Lisa's disease was not psychosomatic; it had been diagnosed by x-ray before and after the instantaneous healing that was claimed at a Kuhlman service in the Shrine Auditorium in Los Angeles; she had bone cancer of the sort that could not logically expect remission or regression; her parents had been told by doctors that there was no hope of any cure.

Dr. Pratt wrote the Kathryn Kuhlman Foundation, not at all sure of a reply, but he received an immediate answer giving the address of the girl who had caught my interest. He wrote to her. Very soon he received a letter from her and also from her mother, giving the doctor's name and permission to secure the medical records pertinent to the case.

Lisa wrote a four-page letter in answer to the questions Dr. Pratt had asked. She said, in part, "I began getting sick and having pain in February 1972. I couldn't walk at all without terrible pain. I was operated on May 25, 1972, and the doctors found bone cancer. My hipbone was like butter, it could have been scooped out with a spoon, and . . . was full of holes like Swiss cheese. My parents were told that my life might be prolonged by chemotherapy and radiation, but there was no hope for me to get well.

"I was told by my neighbor, Bill Truett, of Kathryn Kuhlman and he enthused us to go and see her. We went July 16, 1972, and I was cured. Before the healing, I was sitting in the wheelchair section with all the other sick people. At the time K. Kuhlman kept pointing in my direction and said there was a healing of cancer and to stand and take my healing. I felt a great warmth in my body, especially in my stomach. After I was healed, I went up on the stage to talk to her and she told me I was cured, but to have the healing verified by my doctor.

"Since that day I put away my crutches and my wheelchair. I have been perfectly healthy in every way. I ride my bike. I swim. I do all kinds of sports at school. Since that day I have no pain. I eat and sleep well. Anyone not knowing of my illness would never guess I have been sick a day in my life."

I called Lisa's mother in California. Yes, she said, Lisa was still perfectly fine and healthy. There had been no recurrence of any trouble whatever. I said I had hoped Kathryn Kuhl-man might mention Lisa's cure when she was on the *Tonight Show* with Johnny Carson.

"Well, we were right there in the audience," Mrs. Larios said. "Miss Kuhlman had brought us there and Lisa was all ready to stand up if she asked her to. But I guess the time ran out, or something."

"Then you really do believe that Lisa had a miracle healing?"

"Oh, I know she did. We had been told by doctors that she had only six months to live. But later, when I took her to the hospital for a checkup, the doctors said, 'We can't believe what we are seeing on the x-rays, but there is evidence of healing.' "

We have not seen the hospital medical record of Lisa's illness, but a medical person who was professionally involved with the case has given us a summary of the developments. The patient entered the hospital on June 8, 1972, with a bone tumor in the right hip that was diagnosed as cancer. Chemotherapy was given until the patient was discharged on June 18. Lisa was supposed to return for irradiation therapy, but the mother canceled plans for treatment. On further medical evaluation of the case two months later, no symptoms of cancer were found, and x-ray of the hip showed that healing was progressing. By August 1973, x-rays showed the bone structure to be within normal limits.

Lisa's apparently miraculous improvement seemed to begin at the Kuhlman meeting in the summer of 1972. In the spring of 1975 the girl still seems to be in perfect health.

Olga Worrall has been associate director of the New Life Clinic in Baltimore for the last quarter-century, and she is so different from Kathryn Kuhlman that it is hard to believe they're in the same business. Olga could, if she wanted to bother, name several distinguished ancestors, some of them members of Europe's titled nobility. And there the glamour stops.

She talked about healing at a parapsychology symposium at Blue Ridge Community College in June 1974. Although she wore—sensibly, because of the frigid air conditioning—a

hat and fur jacket, it would have been easy to believe that
she was a neighbor who had just taken off her apron and
dropped by after putting a pie in the oven. Here was no
"show biz" performer. Everybody calls her by her first name.
Like her late husband, Ambrose, she has been psychic from
childhood, but she does not go in for mystical hocus-pocus.
She is a believer in God's ability to use her as a channel for
healing, but she indulges in no religiosity.

The Worralls said in *The Gift of Healing,* "In our opinion
it is not correct to speak of our ministry as miraculous healing
or faith healing. It is healing. It is normal, natural, a part of
the law of God's universe . . . miraculous only in the sense
that all God's laws are miraculous."

Instantaneous healings are rare. Sometimes healing takes
place gradually, sometimes not at all. In the most desperately desired healing of their life, there was no healing. Their
own twin sons, two months old and beautiful, died of infant
diarrhea in 1929 within three days of each other. It took time
for the Worralls to recover from this numbing loss, but their
belief in their ability to act as healing channels was not diminished and they wanted to make use of it.

They began with children. One of the first youngsters Olga
was able to help was a little boy, four years old, whose eyes
were so badly crossed, his parents had been told that before
he could go to school he would have to have surgery to
correct the wild, undisciplined rolling. When his parents
brought him to Olga she put her hands on his head. She says,
"I held in my mind the vision of Christ touching the boy's
eyes and healing them."

The crossed eyes began to improve and in three months
were completely normal. When he went to school he was
able to take part in all activities. Four years later he didn't
even wear glasses.

Although Ambrose, an electronics engineer, held various
full-time executive positions with the Martin-Marietta Company in Baltimore, he and Olga gradually became famous as
a healing team. They worked mainly through churches,
although they did not make any stipulations regarding
creed. They did require that a patient must be willing to see
a doctor, but they never required that a patient have "faith,"

believing the patient's coming to them was indication enough of the necessary open-mindedness. They never accepted any fees or even "love offerings."

At first they found the going rough. Some of the strict fundamentalists considered their work to be "of the devil." Doctors were suspicious. Those attitudes have changed considerably. Many doctors began to refer patients to them, and have even brought members of their own families when conventional medical treatment has failed. Since Ambrose's death in 1972, Olga has continued to conduct healing services at the Mt. Washington Methodist Church in Baltimore. Dr. Robert G. Kirkley, minister, and Fred H. Ohrenschall, a Quaker businessman, join Olga at the altar for the laying-on of hands. Those present at the quiet service are prepared by a half-hour's teaching and a half-hour of meditation and prayer before going to the altar. For those who cannot be present, a "distance" healing service is conducted each night for five minutes, beginning at nine o'clock.

It cannot be said that the medical men have a pet healer. But if they had to choose the one to whom they object the least, my guess is that their choice would be Olga Worrall. Sometimes she appears as the only unorthodox healer at medical conferences. In October 1972 she was on the program at Stanford University when more than four hundred physicians, engineers, and biophysicists attended a four-day conference on parapsychological medicine. Cautious open-mindedness was shown toward unorthodox healing. *Time* quoted, but did not name, a doctor who said, "Clearly, it does work in some circumstances. If we could harness it, it would be beneficial to many patients."

The Very Reverend Dr. Leslie D. Weatherhead, minister of London's City Temple and honorary chaplain to Her Majesty's Forces, believes in paranormal healing, but with some reservations. In his book *Psychology, Religion, and Healing*, he reports investigation of many cults and religions which have made claims for paranormal healing, some of them quite extravagant.

The Roman Catholic Church leans over backward *not* to make extravagant claims for the healings at Lourdes in southwestern France—in fact, they admit very few healings —and yet that shrine is probably the most widely known healing shrine in the world. An estimated two million people visit it every year. In 1949, together with his son, a medical doctor, Weatherhead went on the pilgrim train from England with a hundred patients who were hoping for a cure.

Much of what he found was very impressive. Above and behind a large altar, built at the mouth of the grotto where the vision of "The Lady" was allegedly seen by fourteen-year-old Bernadette Soubirous, hang crutches and braces which have been discarded by those who believed themselves cured. Ramps for wheelchairs lead up to the top of a cliff where a beautiful church, "The Rosary," is floodlighted at night. To augment seating, an underground basilica was built, second only to St. Peter's in Rome in the number of worshippers it will hold. At dusk thousands of pilgrims bearing lighted candles form a long procession, repeating the creed and led by a priest whose voice is electronically amplified. Weatherhead describes it as a most moving sight, one that can provide a meaningful spiritual experience.

He was impressed in quite a different way by the baths formed by the waters of the stream which burst from the ground at the spot where the devout young peasant girl knelt, as she believed she was directed in 1858, to scratch the dry ground.

The water from this stream is piped into sectioned bathing chambers and flows out so slowly that each sufferer bathes in water which his predecessor has just used. Weatherhead commented, "Since there are people who have come a long way, people who are far from clean, people who are too ill to be continent, and people with discharging ulcers, skin diseases, running sores and inflamed eyes, it must take a great deal of faith to be plunged beneath water which bears only too obvious signs of its filthiness, hoping to be cured. When I visited the baths, I asked the priest in charge whether he was not afraid of having an epidemic on his hands. But to my surprise, both the doctors in charge of the English pilgrims took daily baths themselves. They were, of course, Roman Catholics. One of them has since written me that he regards the freedom from infection as in itself a miracle."

Acknowledging that some of the cures may be genuine and citing them in his book, Weatherhead still found them negligible in proportion to the millions who have made the pilgrimage: "There is probably no stream in Britain which could not boast as high a proportion of cures as the stream at Lourdes if patients came in the same numbers and in the same psychological state of expectant excitement."

He also said, "Some patients manifest a temporary improvement in the mental atmosphere of Lourdes, where suggestibility is heightened by mass devotion, the processions, and general excitement. Back in the little hometown, there can be devastating relapses. In fact, patients under the guise of an emotional religion have had inadequate psychological treatment, accompanied by just that publicity which Christ deprecated." He cited several scriptural examples where Jesus said, "Go and tell no one."

Although Dr. Weatherhead deplored the publicized healing services "thronged with people who want a sensation more than they want God" his belief in the efficacy of prayer is not to be discounted. "If it be agreed that modern research into 'psi' phenomena opens up for us an unsuspected faculty in man, surely we ought to press this faculty into God's service. We pray with more earnestness if we have a clue as to how prayer 'works' . . . When a thousand people pray, God may use their mind waves to carry his healing energies to [the sufferer's] body.

"Let us never forget there is a spiritual power that has not been withheld. It has only been unappropriated."

J.G.P. COMMENTS:

Everyone is a healer, and therein lies the difficulty.

The body is protected by the wisdom of the cells. This natural endowment insures that everything possible will be done to maintain, and to regain when necessary, the normal state of good health. Without this self-restorative process, no amount of healing effort applied from outside by orthodox medicine can do any good. The cut finger is healed by the body, not by the Band-Aid. The nagging cold does not really give up after a fortnight. The body musters its resources and defeats the viral infection.

But you are also your own healer in a wider sense. We have a mental side of our nature that is closely linked with our physical condition. The mind may trick the body into showing symptoms of illness that has no organic basis. Later, this psychological side of one's nature can reverse the process and the symptoms of a nonexistent organic illness can be removed. Usually the individual is not aware of the psychological basis of such events. When such a cure is achieved under the powerful suggestions of a faith healer, it may seem as if a miracle has been performed by forces from outside oneself.

All of this is not to say that cures of organic diseases that medical science cannot explain are not possible, but only to point out that the burden of proof is upon those who claim such cures. The question of the genuineness of any claimed instance of paranormal healing is one that can only be answered after a thorough study of the case. The investigator who is not medically trained will need to consult those who are able to evaluate the medical history of the patient. Had previous diagnosis established beyond all doubt by objective methods, such as an x-ray examination, that an organic illness existed at the time the unorthodox healer treated the patient? Was the removal of physical symptoms following the healing experience just as clearly established? Was the illness and the stage it had reached such that the disease could not have disappeared naturally, as happens occasionally and inexplicably in regular medical practice?

Such questions point to possibilities that have to be faced and dealt with before we can say that an otherwise incurable or fatal organic disease was cured by a healer's psychic powers alone. If we think of the problem only in terms of the thousands upon thousands of people who turn to unorthodox healers for relief, it will be difficult it not impossible to come to any scientific conclusion. We should not be surprised, therefore, that scientists have as yet rendered no verdict on the claims made by psychic healers, though they have examined the claims.

It would be foolish, of course, in a medical emergency to entrust oneself to a person claiming special healing gifts while ignoring the help that is available through orthodox medicine. The fact that a healer has appeared on television or been the subject of a book is certainly not acceptable scientific evidence of an ability to cure.

One study was made nearly twenty years ago by D. J. West, M.D., a British psychiatrist who has done distinguished work in the field of parapsychology. He made a careful examination of the eleven miraculous cures recorded at the Shrine of Lourdes between 1935 and 1950. In no instance did the history of a case both before and after the cure contain the specific information that would justify the conclusion that a miracle had occurred. Usually the evidence did not prove that the organic disease that was diagnosed really existed, so the improvement could have been reached psychologically rather than through a physical change. In other cases there were reasons for thinking that the cure could be explained in normal medical terms. By giving this critical evaluation of these eleven medical cases, Dr. West was not denying that health may be improved by a visit to Lourdes. His investigation was not concerned with whether a change for the better had occurred, but only with the nature of the change. Cures there were, but grounds for proclaiming them miraculous in the sense of being beyond scientific understanding were not found.

Many of those who have turned to an unorthodox healer say that they received help. We have no reason to doubt their claims that they felt better, and sometimes this means they genuinely were better. The problem of interpretation arises when we try to say that the benefits were bestowed directly by or indirectly through the healer.

Parapsychology has over the past few decades produced clear evidence that psychokinesis (PK), or "mind over matter," occurs where nonliving materials are involved. Can PK also influence living systems? If the unorthodox healers are accomplishing the marvels they claim, they must be making a practical use of mind over matter in curing the sick. But since, as we have seen, we cannot get a satisfactory scientific answer to our question from healers dealing with real patients, parapsychologists have reduced the problem to manageable size and to basic elements that can be handled by controlled experiments in the laboratory.

This research got started early in the sixties with an examination of Colonel Oskar Estebany, who had had a career as a cavalry officer in the Hungarian army. During the course of that service he gradually came to believe that he had a healing power in his hands which was effective in restoring sick horses to health more rapidly than they could be cured by ordinary medical treatment. His reputation spread, and his special healing powers were in wide demand for treating both animals and humans. By the time Colonel Estebany retired and moved to Canada he had a firm belief in his own powers to benefit the ill through the laying-on of hands.

Word of Colonel Estebany's reputation as a healer eventually reached Dr. Bernard Grad, a biochemist on the staff of the Allan Memorial Institute of McGill University. Dr. Grad recognized the importance of the claims if there was any truth in them, but he recognized also the necessity of testing the question by making observations under conditions that made it possible to be sure of the results. This meant the planning and conducting of controlled experiments. Fortunately, the healer was willing to cooperate, and a long program of careful research was carried out.

The first experiments were done in 1960 with laboratory mice that had been wounded by cutting a small patch of skin from the back of each one. The wounded mice were assigned to three groups. Over a series of days the animals of one group were treated by Colonel Estebany, who simply placed his hands on the cages containing the wounded animals. Those of another group were treated in the same way by persons who claimed no healing powers. The mice of the third group were given the same amount of handling under the same conditions in the laboratory but without any laying of hands on their cages. In two such experiments the wounds of mice treated by Colonel Estebany healed significantly faster than those in the other two groups.

Dr. Grad then shifted his research to the biological process of seed germination. He made a number of tests to see whether barley seeds given water that Colonel Estebany had treated by holding the containers between his hands grew faster than did other seeds given the same amount of water from untreated bottles. Adequate care was taken to insure that those who compared the rate of growth of the seedlings grown under the two conditions could not know which ones received Colonel Estebany's treated water. The findings confirmed the results of the earlier mouse experiments: there was a significantly faster rate of growth of the seedlings nourished by the water Colonel Estebany had treated.

Studies of this cooperative healer were then taken up in the United States in the late sixties by Sister Justa Smith, Ph.D., a Franciscan nun on the faculty of Rosary Hill College in Buffalo. She focused her research upon whether Colonel Estebany could favorably influence the enzyme activity of cells. She found that he could. More recently Dolores Krieger, Ph.D. and R.N., on the staff of the Division of Nursing Education of New York University, for the first time asked whether a specific change could be found in persons who undergo Colonel Estebany's laying-on of hands. She reported significant increases in hemoglobin in persons he treated as compared with other similar individuals who had not felt the touch of the healer's hands.

These investigations should provide convincing evidence for anyone prepared to be convinced that Colonel Oskar Estebany has *something*. While this is only a first step, it is a most important one. We now have real reason for thinking that there is a scientific question about healers that is worth pursuing. We are far from understanding the effect, but we can say with confidence that the knowledge required to do so will be worth whatever effort and time it may cost.

In Bordeaux, France, Jean Barry, M.D., asked volunteer subjects to attempt to influence the rate of growth of a fungus. Since the organism selected was one that is harmful to health, the subjects were told to slow down its growth. When the results of treated and untreated fungus cultures were compared, those that the subjects had tried to check by their will power had grown significantly more slowly. To accept chance as the explanation of the statistical results, it would be necessary to say that the experiment had by mere luck hit upon an outcome that would be expected to happen only once in more than a thousand such tests.

At the University of Iceland, Erlendur Haraldsson, Ph.D., and Thornsteinn Thornsteinsson tested whether subjects could speed up the rate of yeast growth in test tubes. They found that the yeast did grow faster in the tubes in which the subjects wished for rapid growth than in tubes that were not treated but otherwise handled in the same way. Among the seven subjects used in the study, three were healers (two "psychic" and the third a physician). All of the significant results were contributed by these three subjects.

One further laboratory study of a quite different kind may be appreciated as bringing the study of healing a small step closer to the claims for success in real life. Graham and Anita Watkins, a husband-wife team working at the Institute for Parapsychology in Durham carried out experiments in which subjects were asked to shorten the time taken by anesthetized mice to regain consciousness. The subjects were successful in this task.

Clearly, these comments on psychic healing are not nicely finished and neatly illustrated discoveries. Rather, the findings are still at an earlier stage than is the case for most of the topics we have already considered.

The material from patients in real life such as Mrs. Hintze has presented is interesting, but it is very difficult to evaluate adequately from the medical point of view. We were fortunate, for example, that the one case she chose from the Kathryn Kuhlman show has a medical history that seems to support the claims for a miraculous cure. This does not mean that we may conclude on the basis of this one case that a miraculous healing really took place. For one thing, there was the period of ten days following the diagnosis when Lisa underwent chemotherapy. The doctors did not think that this was adequate, as shown by the fact that they planned further treatment by radiation therapy. It is nevertheless conceivable that the short period of chemotherapy did the job in this instance, and that the visit to Kathryn Kuhlman was only coincidental to the recovery, not its cause. After all, the history of medical science has records of many spontaneous remissions in which patients who appeared to be fatally ill got well for no discoverable reason.

I do not mean to deny that Lisa's recovery has any value as evidence for paranormal healing, but only wish to say that it is not enough by itself for a general conclusion. On the basis of our investigation, it has some weight on the positive side of the issue.

"AGAIN I COME—
PATIENCE WORTH MY NAME"

"Let any man announce himself a psychic if he would feel the firm ground of respectability slip from beneath his feet."—Pearl Curran, "A Nut for Psychologists" (The Unpartisan Review, *March-April, 1920*)

The ouija board has been around for a long time. On its polished surface are the letters of the alphabet, together with numerals from one to ten and the words "Yes," "No," and "Goodbye." A small heart-shaped planchette, or pointer, with three legs accompanies the board, and it is on this that the operators place their fingertips lightly, hoping the little thing will take off and spell out a message from "the other side." Concurrent with the occult explosion in the late sixties, sales of Ouija by-passed the long-time favorite game of Monopoly.

"Oui-ja," a combination of the French and German words for yes, had quite a flurry of popularity before World War I also. In the *St. Louis Globe-Democrat* during those early years I find that the visiting president of the New York Psychic Society had a few words to say about this popular toy: "The board has about as much psychic value as a doorknob."

Preachers were denouncing the board as a diabolic device, but pulpit denunciations never bothered the pretty head of a certain St. Louis housewife. Pearl Curran was thirty years old when she made her first acquaintance with the ouija board, and the very fact that its use was deplored in certain circles might have intrigued her, for Pearl seemed to take pleasure in being different from other middle-class Middlewestern women of her day. She was not rich, but she was idle, since her husband's income was sufficient to provide her with a maid; she smoked cigarettes; she preferred the cinema to church, and cheerfully admitted that she had never read a chapter of the Bible all the way through despite having been sent to Sunday School by her nonchurchgoing parents "because they were ashamed not to send me." The feeble flame of her interest in learning was quenched when she was put back a grade in school, and at the age of thirteen she became a drop-out, although she did continue, somewhat sporadically, her interest in piano and vocal lessons. She never had been abroad and had no desire to go. Reading anything more demanding than the women's magazines or an occasional light novel bored her.

Actually, the ouija board was beginning to bore her too after a year of fooling around with it. Her friend Emily Grant Hutchings was the one who had bought the board and brought it into Pearl's house. Emily, a fairly successful writer, was more or less a believer in the possibility of getting something meaningful to come from the spirit world, and she often had to coax Pearl to sit at the board while the pointer laboriously spelled out, in addition to gibberish, some words that she considered evidential.

A few messages did seem to have come from Emily's deceased mother and from Pearl's father, who had recently died. Pearl's mother was usually present, acting as scribe when something seemed worth writing down, and one time, when she asked for word from her husband, she was rewarded with the following: "Oh, why let sorrow steel thy heart?" Again, "All those who lately graced your board are here, and as the moon looks down, think ye of them and their abode as a spirit lake, a spirit song, a spirit friend, and close communion hold twixt thee and them. 'Tis but a journey, dost not see?"

Rather insistently, during some of the sessions in the summer of 1913, the board was spelling "P-A-T" over and over. Pearl Curran's husband, John, taking a dim view, teasingly told them that he was sure his dead friend Pat McQuillan was trying to speak to them. And Pat, he warned them, was one who sometimes used language that might be offensive to delicate ears.

On the sultry night of July 8 of that year, Pearl and Emily

sat at the board while their husbands played cards in an adjoining room. When the pointer took off in an unusually lively manner, Pearl's mother recorded these words: "Many moons ago I lived. Again I come—Patience Worth my name."

Was it possible that a discarnate spirit was identifying herself? They remembered the letters P-A-T and excitedly began to ply her with questions: When had she lived? The pointer seemed uncertain, moving from the numbers 1649 and 94. Did this mean she had been born in 1649 and died in 1694? "Where was your home?" "Across the sea." "In what city and country?" The pointer parried: "About me you would know much. Yesterday is dead. Let thy mind rest as to the past."

They did not let their minds rest. Before long even John Curran had put his skepticism aside and started keeping the record. The neighbors began dropping in to witness this peculiar thing that was happening at the Currans' house. Nobody in those early days dreamed that Patience Worth's fame would spread around the world, that her unrhymed poems would be included in anthologies, and that her novels would be acclaimed as masterpieces.

Intimately acquainted with foreign scenes, a passionate lover of nature, a keen observer with deep spiritual insight, Patience gradually revealed herself as a personality that contrasted in almost every way with the living person through whom she had chosen to speak.

Who was Patience Worth? Voluble though this communicator was, it was not easy to get much personal information about her alleged life on earth. But during the almost quarter-century when Pearl Curran was told so much and was "shown" certain scenes, something of a biography was pieced together: A spinster of the seventeenth century, she lived in rural England, possibly Dorsetshire, where she described various landmarks such as the seashore, the cliffs, and a monastery.

Walter Franklin Prince, research officer of the Boston Society for Psychic Research and later president of the Society for Psychical Research in London, wrote an interesting, though repetitive and highly defensive, book, *The Case of*

Patience Worth, in which he seemed to lean toward the belief that she was just what she said she was, the spirit of a girl who had lived in the seventeenth century.

He wrote: "We see a small, red-headed peasant girl, toiling at the humblest tasks, often chided by her mother and sometimes by the parish minister, a young woman of voluble and witty propensities, fond of finery and not averse to the other sex, considerably curbed in all these inclinations because of the ideas of the day and the narrowness of the religion, but with a sense of humor which largely sustained her. She loved her mother, though she was 'filled o' righteousness and emptied o' mercy.' Sometimes she peeped at the reflection of her bonnet's ruff on the polished brass kettle, and kicked her shoes upon the stones because she must wear her [curly] locks 'wetted smooth.'

"Her attempts at 'holy singing sounded like unto blasphemy and the dominie once, a-harkin', stopped for to pray.' She was something of a heretic, and much of her reminiscent humor is at the expense of the church and its minister. 'Well I remember a certain church, with its wee windows and its prim walls, with its sanctity and meekness, with its aloofness and chilling godliness. Well I remember the Sabbath and its quietude of uneasiness, wherein the creaking of the wood was an infernalism, the droning and scuffling of the menfolks' shoes and the rustle of the clothes of the dames and maids, the squeaking of the benches and the drowsy humming of some busy bee who broke the Sabbath's law. Aye, well I remember the heat that foretold the wrath of God, making the good man [minister] sweat. Aye, and Heaven seemed far, far . . .

" 'The good man oft denounced sin and fearsome flauntings, but lawk! he squinted a whit. I had a silver buckle on my boot, and no man knew it save the good man. He looked soberly, with the soberness he turned upon the Word, at the buckle. Aye, and thy handmaid sent him a wee upward look. Aye, and he rubbed his chin and coughed mightily and spat. And when the next Sabbath came he raged mightily against buckles. And hark—he looked to find the buckle after the Word. It was there, and lawk! I curtsied that he should see it not.' "

At about the age of thirty Patience left for America. Pearl Curran, in one of her visions, "saw" Patience making preparations for the trip, together with some of the details of the ship's crossing. Shortly after her arrival she was killed by Indians. When someone present at the board asked the name of the chief, she replied with typical tartness, "Would the questioner, were he at the end of a blade, be asking for the name of his slayer?"

Mrs. Curran reported a vivid mental picture of Patience's last moments. She saw her, ". . . a small, wee figure in gray, come out of the copse of pines on the bluff-top, speeding, speeding to the bluff, then half-running, half-falling, down, down to the beach where the waters seethed. Within her breast an arrow stood and the small hands held it as she ran and fell, and half raised to her knees . . . The dear eyes looked across the sea, straining to find the dear homeland afar. But all grew misty and the yearning eyes grew dim, and she sunk upon the sand by the seas' waters like a wounded swallow, a mere bit of gray along the vasty shore."

Patience added some of her own words to this vision: "And thy damie went her speeded unto a new land nay man knew. And the far curve o' all the sea that shut all a-whither faded, faded. And the wakin'. Ah, that I might tell thee all, all the joyin', unto all brothers, unto all men."

If the words that came via the ouija board had not been championed by some of the most influential literary personalities of the day, it is doubtful that the proliferation of these strange communications would have spread much beyond the Currans' circle of friends and acquaintances. But in October 1914 Casper Yost, one of the editors of the *St. Louis Globe-Democrat*, came to observe one of the sessions that were taking place at the Curran home two and three nights a week. A deeply spiritual man with a fine appreciation for literature, he marveled at the wisdom and wit of Patience's aphorisms, the beauty of her poetry, often instantaneously composed when a visitor made a request.

She said of Death: "Cheap pence paid for Eternity and yet man whines."

She spoke of the mysteries of God, the simple beauties of nature in language that was fresh and vivid: "poppies that

bleed in their joy"; "a hot moon, smiling with swelled lips."
She personified Night as a hunter with silvery trumpet calling
the stars "And when the first note is sounded, behold, one
star comes forth and leaps the hurdles of the West. And the
pack follows."

War had become uppermost in the minds of her growing
audience. This was her instant poem on that subject:

"Father, is *this* thy will? God, the din!

Blood, thick-crusted, still living, I saw it fall unto the dust;
Hunger, gnawing life a wolf, whose teeth do whet upon my
vitals crouching before me—

A hideous thing, whose hands show dripping, and whose
tongue doth feed upon the new-sprung streams, licking life
from living things!

Father, is this thy will? . . ."

Women's rights also had become a topic for lively discussion. When a listener asked for her comment, she said, in
part:

"The tide hath gone . . . when a wench be found in a
kirtle . . .

Behold! Womankind shall lead . . .

Leading man to the brink of day.

And he, finding the day made perfect

Through the agony of womankind,

Struts!"

Often Casper Yost sat at the board with Pearl—as did many
others—asking questions, becoming more and more convinced that the time had come for Patience to be introduced
to the readers of his newspaper. In early February 1915 the
St. Louis Globe-Democrat announced that on the following
Sunday it would "begin publication of a series of articles on
what is perhaps the most marvelous psychical phenomenon
the world has ever known. An 'intelligence' which claims to
be the spirit of a woman who lived over two hundred years
ago is composing, here in St. Louis, poems and story-plays
whose beauty amaze all who read them. Nothing like them
has ever been published, and no matter what one may think
of the claims of supernatural origin, one must be profoundly
impressed by the intellect that produces them."

The articles continued for five Sundays, telling about the

coming of Patience Worth, quoting her proverbs, her stories, her poems, including one that had been recorded in October of the previous year, which began, "Ah, God, I have drunk unto the dregs and flung the cup at thee . . ." Yost said, "There is nothing in literature that grips the mind with greater force, almost breath-stopping in its awfulness, than the first two lines . . ."

He told his readers that he was convinced no charlatanism was involved, as he had known the persons who were receiving these messages for many years. Not until the series had run its course were the names of the principals revealed.

The interest in Patience Worth spread rapidly. Literary critics were almost unanimous in their praise with a cautious "near great" to "greater than Chaucer or Shakespeare." Ouija board communications were nothing new, and although they sometimes purportedly came from famous deceased writers, this was the first time the product had anything of literary value.

Psychologists and researchers of psychic phenomena investigated the case. Chief among the latter was Dr. Prince and he called it the most important one of its kind. After ten months' study of the data, he wrote: "Either our concept of what we call the subconscious must be radically altered, so as to include potencies of which we hitherto have had no knowledge, or else some cause operating through, but not originating in, the subconsciousness of Mrs. Curran must be acknowledged."

There were the inevitable detractors who said Mrs. Curran was merely a clever trickster who had concealed her literary ability all along and now sought to become famous by this somewhat bizarre means. Prince took it upon himself to find out if this was possible. He spent nearly a year questioning everybody who had ever known Pearl Curran, and when he wrote his book he outlined his reasons for believing that it was impossible for a woman of her limited interests, education, and resources to have written, unaided, the blank verse and stories which now poured in a literary avalanche from the board. It became necessary to hire a secretary and a stenographer.

By degrees, Pearl became independent of the ouija board.

She got so she was able to call out letters that popped into her head, although the pointer was moving in meaningless circles. After six years she found that she could call out the words without bothering to spell them. The next step was to discard the board. She began writing with a pencil, and later directly on the typewriter.

Telka, a sixty-thousand-word novel of medieval England, was written in thirty-five hours. None of the words in that book came into use after the beginning of the seventeenth century; almost without exception, they were words of one or two syllables, and ninety percent were of Anglo-Saxon derivation. Pearl said she didn't even know what some of the words meant when they came to her.

The Sorry Tale, a very long novel of the time of Christ, was praised by Biblical scholars, who said there was no inconsistency with historical record. A *New York Times* reviewer said, "She invents new miracles, she retells the old ones, she fills out with incidents the lives of Christ and his disciples, but the touching beauty and simple dignity of the figure of Christ are treated always with reverence and there is nothing in the tale to which the most orthodox could object . . . In detail, one vivid scene after another passes before the reader, pictures from the life of dissipated Rome, as Theia remembers and tells of their lewd horrors, of the shepherds upon the hills, of the men and women of the city, of Herod's palace, of the desert. And through it all goes a sense of life, of reality, of having been seen and lived until all its scenes were familiar."

When *Hope Trueblood*, a novel of Victorian England, was published, some English reviewers thought it had been written by an Englishwoman. Unaware of the strange authorship, they referred to Patience Worth as a gifted new author, one who would be well worth watching.

One of her most highly respected champions was William Marion Reedy, editor of *Reedy's Mirror*, a St. Louis journal of opinion and literature which was sold around the world. Reedy, one of the judges to select the winner of the first Pulitzer Prize in poetry, delighted in publishing and promoting new writers, and the list of his protégés is still impressive today: Carl Sandburg, Edna St. Vincent Millay, Edgar Lee Masters, and Emily Dickinson.

Reedy said, "When I read the poems of Patience Worth in the *Globe-Democrat,* I was inclined to think they were a bit of clever literary fakery." An agnostic and excommunicated Catholic, he thought the idea of a disembodied spirit coming through from the other side preposterous. ("I don't think any person dead has ever come back to tell anybody anything.") And yet this scoffer came back again and again to the Currans' home, remaining to ponder, if not to pray, as he questioned Patience at length concerning God, the hereafter, and the much-debated question of the day: predestination and free will. Patience said on that subject, "I tell thee they do take out the word o' Him and set it atween the palms of their own hands and squeeze out the word until it fitteth the palms."

Patience did not claim omniscience or preen herself on her own perfection. These lines from one of her poems express her attitude toward herself clearly, and were of the sort that must have endeared her to Reedy:

"I know you, you shamster! I heard you honeying your words,
Licking your lips and smacking o'er them, twiddling your thumbs
In ecstasy over your latest wit.
I know you, you shamster!
You are the me the world knows."

Reedy said he felt he knew her "better than those whose hands I grasp . . . she is arch and coquettish, with a mind of no small power, altogether lovable." He often sat at the board with Pearl, where Patience, in reference to his corpulence, addressed him impudently as "Fatawide."

I cannot discover whether or not Reedy ever made any evaluation of the following poem, but others have acclaimed it as being one of Patience Worth's finest:

"I have heard the moon's beams
Sweeping the waters, making a sound
Like threads of silver, wept upon.

I have heard the scratch of the
Pulsing stars, and the purring sound
Of the slow moon as she rolled across
The Night. I have heard the shadows
Slapping the waters, and the licking
Sound of the wave's edge as it sinks
Into the sand upon the shore.
I have heard the sunlight as it pierced
The gloom with a golden bar, which
Whirred in a voice of myriad colors.
I have heard the sound which lay
Between the atoms which danced in the
Golden bar. I have heard the sound
Of the leaves reclining upon their
Cushions of air, and the swish of the willow
Tassels as the wind whistled upon them.
And the sharp sound which the crawling
Mites proclaim upon the grasses' blades,
And the multitude of sounds which lie
At the root of things. Oh, I have heard
The song of resurrection which each seed
Makes as it spurts . . ."

Patience wrote over five thousand poems, and in the 1918 *Anthology of Magazine Verse and Year Book of American Poetry* her poems received higher ratings than those of Edna St. Vincent Millay, Amy Lowell and Edgar Lee Masters. Nearly four million words were written during the almost quarter of a century that Patience Worth was communicating.

Henry Holt, a discriminating publisher, much interested in psychic phenomena, published three of her books, saying that he considered it literature of a high order. He took the view that the writing may have originated in the "cosmic soul," speculating that there might be inflow from "strings of postcarnate personalities—if there are such."

Assuming that Patience Worth was a disembodied spirit, one of rare talent and intelligence, why did she choose to express herself through the limited mind of Pearl Curran, to whom she sometimes referred as "the follied one"? When questioned about this, Pearl said that Patience had done much searching of "crannies" before she was able to slip into this one at a time when she (Pearl) was very tired and her mind in a vacuum state.

Patience's love for Pearl was often expressed, but so was her scorn, though kindly enough, for this intelligence she seemed to regard as inferior to her own. Once when Pearl expressed boredom with the somewhat heavy utterances that had been coming through and asked for something dainty, Patience replied, "I shall distill a dewdrop through a buttercup for thee."

But she was patient when Pearl was not quick to grasp her meaning, and once when the spelling of a proper name, Legia, in *The Sorry Tale*, was giving trouble, Patience explained, "Thou hast an eye, thou hast an arm, thou hast a Legia!"

Pearl said it was like turning the pages of a magic picture book. Sometimes she felt herself to be a part of the scenes described, tasting strange fruit, feeling the texture of the cloth. She was never in a trance during the times she received dictation, but she would obviously slip in—and as readily out —of an altered state of consciousness. She remained aware of what went on about her, hearing the ring of the telephone, greeting arriving guests with a nod and a smile. "I could feel my nose itch and scratch it, note an air of criticism on the face of one of the company, and the worshipful expression of another, think what I was going to have for midnight lunch after they had gone, and write right along on the poem."

Eventually Pearl may have got the idea that writing was easy, for after several years of being the channel for Patience Worth, she had a try at writing some stories of her own. She sold a couple of them quite readily to *The Saturday Evening Post*. By today's standards, they seem like dreadful potboilers, full of the slang of that day, but perhaps to Pearl it was refreshing to get away from archaic language.

Here is a sample from one of the stories, *Old Scotch*: "You're going to wear something nifty. It's no go, kid, in your togs. Miss Peabody don't go in this burg as a modiste. Sister, I'm going to tog you out in some nifty cloth. I got a black velvet, one-piece, that will set you off to the nth degree . . ."

Patience seemed to take a tolerant view of this sidetracking of her amanuensis: "'Tis but a babe's mixin' . . ." And she continued to communicate her own words with little or no diminishing of their literary quality.

Nothing fails like success. The world began to take Patience Worth for granted. After the successful publication of several books and hundreds of poems, certain critical assessments of her work seemed to turn publishers against her. Reedy died, one of her staunchest supporters. Casper Yost, although he never lost faith, was unable to prevail upon Henry Holt to publish his book *The Task*, which analyzed Patience's religious philosophy. Her own, *The Pot upon the Wheel*, languished for want of a publisher.

Patience seemed undismayed, her early words expressing her philosophy well enough: "A pot of wisdom should boil to nothing ere a doubter deemeth it broth worth tasting." To the end of Pearl Curran's life the mysterious flow of literary productions continued.

Pearl died in California on December 5, 1937, and her hometown paper, the *St. Louis Globe-Democrat*, made the announcement with this headline: PATIENCE WORTH IS DEAD.

Some thirty years later Irving Litvag, whose book *The Singer in the Shadows* is the most readable, most comprehensive of all the writings on this subject, interviewed as many as possible of the survivors who had known Pearl Curran. He said, "They remembered her with awe and love."

The awe has not diminished. Patience Worth–Pearl Curran is still considered one of the most perplexing of all psychic enigmas. She was also a truly wonderful writer.

J.G.P. COMMENTS:

I remember vividly the first time I saw a ouija board. It belonged to my aunts, who began working with their new ouija board around 1920, a few years after Mrs. Curran was cajoled by her friend to try it in St. Louis. Our approach was skeptical, half in jest but ready to turn serious at the first sign of anything unexpected. Like thousands of others, my family got nothing and we soon grew tired of the game.

Probably a small percentage of ouija users of that period occasionally got information that they could explain only in terms of their own psychic powers or as communications from someone in the spirit world. Mostly these experiences were kept private within the family or a small circle of friends. They went unnoticed by scientists because there were better kinds of evidence and better methods for dealing with the questions that were raised.

The communications that came through Pearl Curran were the one striking exception. The Patience Worth ouija productions were very special in literary quality, they came whenever Mrs. Curran was ready to receive them, and they continued over a period of many years. Fairly quickly after Patience Worth appeared in 1913 the communications came to the attention of persons who appreciated their literary merits and who saw to it that the case was made widely known in books. These developments naturally challenged qualified scientists to study the case and try to find out what it all meant. Taken together, these circumstances assured that Patience Worth would have a permanent place in history.

Her main literary sponsors in St. Louis, Casper Yost and William Marion Reedy, approached the case as skeptics, and they remained skeptical regarding Patience Worth's claims that she was the surviving spirit of a seventeenth-century English woman. But they were totally unable to believe that literary compositions of the unique and extraordinary quality that were pouring from the ouija board were the conscious production of Pearl Curran.

To the scientists who looked into the matter, the basic issue was whether the writings that flowed from Mrs. Curran were clearly beyond her own conscious or unconscious capacities. The more the case was studied, the more the weight of the evidence favored the view that Patience Worth produced with apparent ease literary works that were not consistent with Mrs. Curran's education, experience, and native abilities. Moreover, they were beyond anything that could be explained in terms of all that we know about the way that even the greatest geniuses of literary creativity produced their works. This is not to say that the Patience Worth writings are superior to what human genius at its best has been able to accomplish, but only to point out that the manner in which the writing was done has, for all we know, not been equaled by any of the world's greatest writers.

For example, poems adjudged by experts to be of exceptional quality flowed from the board as fast as Mrs. Curran could spell out the words (or later, in spoken words, as fast as they could be recorded). These poems were finished; there was no need for correction or revision. Complicated works of fiction that were consistent and superior in plot, characterization, diction, and other major aspects were similarly poured out in final form over a series of biweekly sessions. At each new sitting the writing task was taken up again exactly where it had been left off previously, usually some days before, without any hesitation and without any noticeable difficulty or confusion. The writing was often carried forward alternately, even in the same session, on two or more literary works without any hesitation in shifting from one to another.

One example of this last type of literary dexterity is worth giving in detail. Walter Franklin Prince, the chief psychic investigator of the case, set the stage by explaining to Patience at some length that he knew she had done this sort of thing many times but he suspected that she had worked out and memorized in advance what she wanted to say, so that the task itself was a mere recitation of what she had practiced beforehand. Therefore Dr. Prince announced that he was giving her two tasks which he wished her to carry out by alternating at frequent intervals between them. One task was to write a poem with the title "The Folly of Atheism." The other was to produce a dialogue between a wench and a lout at a fair. Dr. Prince says that his instructions were followed by a statement from Patience indicating that she understood and accepted the task and then by a period of silence of about eight seconds. After that, the words fulfilling the assigned task were uttered without interruption as fast as they could be taken down. When the recording ended, unscrambling the omelet was simple, because the points of shifting from one theme to the other, every three or four lines, were obvious from the differences in language and style.

The Folly of Atheism

"Who doubts his God is but a lout;
Who piths his wisdom with egotry
Hath lost his mark. To doubt
Is but to cast thee as a stone
Unto the very heart of God.
Who doubts his God hath but announced
His own weak limitation;
Hath tied his hand and fettered of his foot.
To doubt thy God is but to stop
The everlasting flow of mercy,
To die of thirst and lose thee
In the chaos of thyself."

Dialogue Between a Wench and a Lout at a Fair

"Ha'e ye seen the mummers settin' up a puppet show a thin the fieldin'?
Aye, I see'd 'em fetchin' past, and buyed o' a ribbon and a new latchet, and a shoon bucklin and tasseled thongs.
Aye, and I fetched me a whistle, and heared the doings of the village—that Mark, the smithy haed a new wench, and she be heft.
Aye, a wide tale. I heard it, but heeded it nae, I bein' feastin' 'pon the new thong.
Weel, 'gad! Did ye see the dominie wi' his new breeks, and a sabba' shirt?
Weel, can ye heed it—and him at the fair? A wide tale, eh?"

Mrs. Hintze has given some examples of the best of the Patience Worth poetry. I ask her pardon for adding one more. An admirer of Patience had written in to request that we should be provided with a prayer suitable for a child. When this task was presented, the ouija board hesitated for an uncharacteristically long time, and statements were made by Patience about how hard she was working to get the prayer right. After a few trial starts, the finished product emerged:

"I, Thy child forever, play
About Thy knees at close of day;
Within Thy arms I now shall creep
And learn Thy wisdom while I sleep.
                    Amen"

Though both Naomi and I have spoken of Patience Worth without putting the name in quotation marks, we have not intended to say that we accept without question her own description of her earlier life in England and the claim that she returned to earth after several centuries through the happy discovery of the channel provided by Pearl Curran. Rather, we share the feeling of those who were closely connected with the case who agreed that the ouija-board utterances gave such a strong impression of a vivid, coherent, rich "personality" that it deserved to be treated as a real person—without implying a literal acceptance of the claims.

Was Patience a creation of Mrs. Curran's unconscious mind? This possibility cannot be excluded with absolute finality, but accepting such an interpretation would mean accepting that Pearl Curran had, hidden deep within her, abilities and information completely unlike anything her own personality seemed to encompass.

The difficulties confronting a normal interpretation of the case force us to keep our minds open to the possibility that Patience Worth was, in a literal sense, a surviving spirit of someone who died and who had found a way to communicate with the living. The bearing of the case on this possibility has been carefully considered by Dr. Robert Thouless, a Cambridge University psychologist, now retired. "As evidence for survival, the Patience Worth writings are unique in kind. Novels and poems are powerful and original. It may well be that a subconscious personality of Mrs. Curran could have written literary works far beyond the power of her own . . . personality. The odd part of the Patience Worth productions is, however, their linguistic quality: their use of English words belonging to the date claimed for Patience Worth's

life, their usual (though not invariable) avoidance of words
introduced into the language later than that time, and, most
importantly, the use of archaic dialect words that have only
been tracked down by scholars *after* they had appeared in
the Patience Worth scripts. It is a case that we cannot afford
to forget in an all-round view of the evidence for survival."

Many books have been published that the authors claimed
were produced through "automatic writing" by communicators working through them. These authors usually discounted
the possibility that such works were the production of their
own subconscious minds. In most instances the quality of the
writing is poor and it provides no real evidence for an outside
source. In the Patience Worth case, on the other hand, the
high quality of the writing, the vocabulary, and the integrity
of the work for the period in which it was set were so far
from Mrs. Curran's life and background that we are hard-
pressed to imagine how the writings could have been produced solely through her own inner resources. The unique-
ness of this case is what gives it strength, but from the
scientific point of view this is also the source of its greatest
weakness. Until we have the opportunity to study other cases
that are closely similar to this one, it may not be possible to
reach any fully satisfactory scientific conclusion about it, an
interpretation that will be acceptable to all. Meanwhile, the
mystery endures—as well as the challenge.

I would like to offer a few words of advice and caution
regarding the use of the ouija board. If it is true, as I have
heard, that the ouija board has been a best-selling game during recent years, there must be tens—perhaps hundreds—of
thousands tucked away in closets or standing on edge out of
sight behind bookcases. Most persons who will dust their
boards and try their luck will approach the matter solely
from a sense of curiosity and with a conviction that if anything puzzling happens, the information received would be
coming solely from the unconscious minds of the successful
operators. This would mean that when the board brings nothing that the persons working it do not already know, the
pointer is in all likelihood powered by unconscious muscular
effort. Even when information comes through that no one
present knows in any normal way, usually nothing more is

involved than ESP. Both of these results can be interesting and quite good fun.

If what looks like ESP results do start to come and then continue for a time, they should not be ignored or wasted, but should, if possible, be brought to the attention of someone experienced in the investigation of psi phenomena.

But what if the purported communicator—the entity that, if taken at face value, seems to be speaking through the board—turns mean or threatening, or insists upon monopolizing the board even if told to go away? This is the time to exercise some caution regarding continued use of the board, because a very small percentage of persons may have a potential danger—one of which they might be quite unaware —that an unpleasant and hidden side of their nature could come out into the open if given the right opportunity to do so. The ouija board is one situation, automatic writing is another, in which such an unhealthy development in personality might occur, a kind of secondary, unconscious personal force that uses the disguise of being a communicator.

My strong advice is that no encouragement should be given to any such evil-appearing force beyond the point at which its unpleasant or evil character is recognized. If its appearance is clearly associated with a particular person whose hands are on the pointer, it will probably be a sufficient safeguard if that person yields his place to another and merely watches while others work the board. Or it may be enough if all agree that the person through whom the "evil spirit" appears can help operate the pointer only as long as friendly communications show up.

Of course, it is not impossible, even if unlikely, for another case like Patience Worth to appear. I do not see that kind of development as, in itself, a bad thing; and if anyone does become a ouija channel for the emergence of such a friendly and gifted "spirit," I hope to be one of the first to hear about it.

POSSESSION

*"The devil took hold of me in that picture show. He
would pull my head down and throw me against the wall.
When that devil come out, hallelujah, thank you, Jesus,
I seen his face and I was speaking in tongues, praise God."*
—*Young man on WDCA, April 14, 1974, testifying to his
experience after seeing* The Exorcist

The idea of demonic possession seems to go back to pre-
history. Skulls have been found with holes chipped out,
trephined, with stone instruments, presumably to free the
victim from the possessing entity. The Bible refers in many
instances to possession by unclean spirits. Martin Luther was
a believer in the phenomena.

The Archbishop of Canterbury, the Most Reverend Arthur
Michael Ramsey, was in the United States soon after the
movie *The Exorcist* was released. He stated, "Genuine cases
of demonic possession are a minority. If there's an immense
craze on the subject, it is a sign of spiritual immaturity."

Billy Graham said, "Don't go to see that movie."

Frederic W. H. Myers, a pioneer parapsychologist, made
the flat statement that there was no evidence for demonic
possession: "A devil is not a creature whose existence is independently known to science; and from the accounts, the
behaviour of the invading devils seems due to mere self-
suggestion."

The Catholic Church guardedly admits that the individual's experience may sometimes be more than mere
self-suggestion. Father John J. Nicola, assistant director in
Washington at the National Shrine of the Immaculate Conception, was engaged by Warner Brothers as a technical
consultant for the filming of William Blatty's book *The
Exorcist*. In seminary, Father Nicola had done a paper on
demonology which led to further research. He advises that

persons thinking themselves possessed first get a medical or psychiatric examination. Self-deception or fraud must be ruled out before considering the possibility of demonic intervention.

In 1949 Gaither Pratt was working with Rhine at the Duke Parapsychology Laboratory when letters were received from a Lutheran minister concerning the case upon which Blatty, twenty years later, was to base his book. The victim was a boy, not a girl as in the fictional version; fortunately, his identity was protected and he is now grown and living a normal family life with his wife and children.

According to the minister's report, the family first became aware of scratching noises that seemed to come from the walls and ceilings of their home in suburban Washington. They called in an exterminator, but he was unable to find any signs of rats or mice. The scratching noises increased, and now they began to hear squeaking footsteps in the hall. Furniture moved all by itself, dishes flew about, and the bed of their thirteen-and-a-half-year-old son trembled so violently that he had difficulty in sleeping. Often the covers would be pulled off, and if he tried to hold on to them, they would be jerked away with such force that he would be dragged from his bed.

All the manifestations revolved about the boy, and even followed him when he spent the night at the homes of neighbors. At school his desk moved in an apparently paranormal way, and unexplained marks appeared on his body. His distraught parents were so sure that the trouble was caused by an evil spirit, possibly that of a recently deceased relative, that they sought help from their minister. Prayer meetings were held; the family took communion; the boy was sent to a mental-health clinic. Nothing had any effect.

The clergyman had come to the house and seen some of the occurrences for himself, but when they had persisted for about six weeks, he took the boy, by then exhausted from lack of sleep, to his own home.

Here, too, the bed began to shake. At midnight the boy went to try to sleep in a "heavy chair with a very low center of gravity. The chair moved several inches; then he placed his knees under his chin, with his feet on the edge of the chair. The chair backed up three inches against the wall. When it could move no further in that direction, it slowly tipped over . . . throwing the boy to the floor." The minister said he was so fascinated by the slow tilting of the chair that he couldn't move forward to stop it, but just stood there watching. All this happened while the light was on.

A bed was then made out of blankets on the floor in the center of the room to get away from the danger of tipping furniture. The light was left on, and twice the man saw the boy and his bedding move slowly to a spot under the bed. His head and hands were in full sight and his body appeared to be rigid.

Early in March the boy and his mother left to visit relatives in St. Louis, hoping to escape the annoying "spirits." There the rites of exorcism were conducted separately by a Lutheran minister, an Episcopal priest, and at least two Jesuit priests. Although the boy underwent thirty-five traumatic days of anti-demonic prayer and ritual, the phenomena persisted periodically and did not disappear altogether until after he returned home in April.

Dr. Henry Ansgar Kelly, an English professor at UCLA, and author of *The Devil, Demonology and Witchcraft*, wrote as follows in the Catholic magazine *Commonweal*: "Diabolical possession is caused by belief in diabolical possession— possession without the devil remains simply an autosuggestive trance or hysterical fit."

Citing instances of purported possession that were full of "diabolical wonders," Dr. Kelly said, "The temptation to exaggerate in such cases is almost irresistible." He seemed to feel there had been exaggeration in this case. In his opinion, the boy was the center only for poltergeist manifestations, and it was not until the rites of exorcism were under way that he began to show the symptoms of the possession syndrome.

Most members of the Catholic clergy deplore the publicity given to such cases. One said, "It would be blasphemous if it were not funny." Another called the idea of devil-possession "Dangerous nonsense which appeals to the prurient interest in the supernatural."

Possession of quite another kind, angelic rather than demonic, was believed to have taken place nearly a hundred years ago in the town of Watseka, Illinois, when the gentle spirit of a girl named Mary Roff, dead twelve years, seemed to enter the body of Lurancy Vennum, not quite fourteen.

Despair had settled over the Vennum household on the afternoon of January 31, 1878. Arrangements were under way for their daughter Lurancy—nicknamed "Rancy"—to be admitted to an insane asylum, which was in those days a place of horror. Mr. Asa Roff, a prominent Watseka citizen whom the Vennums knew slightly, was to bring an out-of-town physician, Dr. E. W. Stevens, to look at the girl. But the parents' hopes cannot have been high: two Watseka doctors had already treated her without effect, and the verdict of relatives and neighbors was that the girl was clearly mad. She was subject to "fits," had undergone a frightening personality change, and her mother was on the verge of collapse caring for her.

All of this had begun the previous summer, when the girl described what seemed to have been a nightmare: "Persons were in my room and they called, 'Rancy! Rancy!' and I could feel their breath upon my face." During the summer she had gone into frequent catatonic states, followed by trances during which she described spirits, including those of her dead sister and brother. She had begun having attacks of severe pain, which caused her to double back so that her head touched her feet. From then on, according to Dr. Stevens' detailed account of "The Watseka Wonder," published in the *Religio-Philosophical Journal*, she would go into as many as twelve trances a day, during which she sometimes seemed to be in ecstasy, describing heaven and the angels. At other times she would appear to be possessed by spirits who were anything but angelic, speaking rudely to her distraught parents, calling her father "Old Black Dick" and her mother "Old Granny."

Mr. Roff had known the family slightly when Lurancy was six and the Vennums had lived nearby for a few months, but he was concerning himself with this situation and enlisting Dr. Stevens' help because his daughter Mary, who had died at the age of eighteen, had exhibited similar though even more bizarre symptoms.

Mary Roff, dead now for twelve years, had been obsessed with the idea of ridding her body of blood. At that time bleeding was common medical practice and three of the doctors who had treated her had applied leeches. Sometimes Mary herself would apply them to her temples, reportedly liking the little things and making pets of them. On one occasion she slashed her arm so severely in an apparently deliberate attempt to free her body of blood that she became unconscious from the loss of it. Soon thereafter, to quote from a newspaper in a nearby town, *The Danville Times*, "She became a screaming maniac. Disease dethroned her reason and maddened her brain until she sought her own and others' lives."

Mary, then in her late teens, had been confined in a Peoria institution, where she underwent, without benefit, the "water cure," a treatment that was in use in the Middle Ages and revived in the nineteenth century. This involved immersing the patient in very cold, as well as hot, water; cold douches administered with a hose; tight wrapping in icy sheets; and vigorous friction of the skin.

It is possible that Mr. Roff's firsthand knowledge of his lost daughter's experiences may have caused him to try to persuade the Vennums not to subject Lurancy to "a condition terrible to behold . . . among maniacs, to be ruled and cared for by ignorant and bigoted strangers." Or the fact that he was a spiritualist may have had something to do with it, for the whole town was aware that the girl claimed to be in touch with spirits in the other world. Whatever the reason for his interest, he had been insistent that he be allowed to come on this January afternoon, and to bring Dr. Stevens, who was also of the spiritualistic persuasion.

Lurancy sat by the stove, silent, elbows on her knees, hands under her chin, feet curled beneath her, looking like an old woman. Savagely, she warned Dr. Stevens not to come nearer when he moved his chair, and she refused to be touched or to shake hands.

He asked, "What is your name?"

"Katrina Hogan."

"How old?"

"Sixty-three years."

"Where from?"

"Germany."

"How long ago?"

"Three days."

"How did you come?"

"Through the air."

"How long will you stay?"

"Three weeks."

Now her manner and appearance changed. She was not an old woman, she confided, but a young man, Willie Canning, who had led a wild life and was not here because he wanted to be. Suicide may have been implied, and "here" may have meant the spirit world.

Lurancy turned then upon the doctor, firing rude questions at him rapidly: "Do you lie? Get drunk? Swear? Go to church? Pray?"

Abruptly she stood, flinging up her hands and falling straight back upon the floor, her body stiff, her upraised hands like iron bars. Dr. Stevens took her hands and lifted her, and by means of calm suggestion he soon had her under control. She spoke to him normally, quite rational, except that now she claimed to be in heaven.

She said she knew the evil spirits calling themselves Katrina Hogan and Willie Canning. When asked if she would not rather be controlled by happier, more intelligent spirits, she said there were a great many who would be willing to come, one in particular. "Her name is Mary Roff."

Mr. Roff: "That is my daughter! Mary Roff is my girl! Why, she has been in heaven for twelve years. Yes, let her come, we'll be glad to have her come!"

And come she did, or so the Vennum and Roff families were convinced. The next day Lurancy was insisting that her name was Mary Roff and that she wanted to go "home."

Dr. Stevens says, "From the wild, angry, ungovernable girl, to be kept only by lock and key, or the more distressing watch-care of almost frantic parents; or the rigid, corpselike cataleptic . . . the girl had now become mild, docile, polite and timid, as if among strangers, knowing none of the [Vennum] family, but constantly pleading to go home."

After about a week of that, Mrs. Roff and her daughter Minerva, who was married to a Dr. Alter, came to the Vennum home to see if the rumors they had heard about the transformation were true. When Lurancy looked out the window and saw them coming, she cried, "There comes my ma and my sister Nervie!" She embraced them, cried for joy. But seeing them made her more "homesick" than before. After a few more days of frantic pleading, both families agreed that the girl should go to live in the Roff home.

Happy and appearing normal, Lurancy Vennum took the place of the daughter the Roffs had lost twelve years before. She said, "The angels will let me stay until sometime in May."

It is interesting to read the criticism of the townspeople occasioned by this odd turn of events, although Dr. Stevens called them the sneers and taunting innuendos of an uneducated bigotry. The minister who had arranged to have Lurancy committed told Mr. Vennum, "I think you will see the time when you will wish you had sent her to the asylum." A "friend" of the Vennums predicted that if Rancy ever came home, she would be more trouble then ever, and a relative said, "I would sooner follow a girl of mine to the grave than have her go to the Roffs and be made a spiritualist."

A local doctor who had called the girl's illness "Catalepsy #2" showed both charity and prescience when he said, "Humor her whims and she will get well."

Lurancy now truly seemed to be Mary. Mr. and Mrs. Roff were now "Pa" and "Ma." Dr. Stevens wrote that she knew every person and every thing that Mary Roff had known, remembering hundreds of incidents that had taken place during her life as a daughter in the home. She asked once for a box of her letters, which Mrs. Roff had kept, and when she discovered a little tatted collar that was also in the box, she exclaimed that it was the collar she had made. She recognized old neighbors and friends, greeting them by the familiar names that Mary had used. But when the Vennums and their children visited, she had to be introduced as if to strangers.

May drew near. Except for brief periods of "slipping off to heaven," and an occasional reappearance of the Lurancy personality, the girl was as affectionate and helpful as Mary had been in her lucid intervals. And then on May 19, Lurancy took possession. Henry Vennum, her brother, happened to be at the Roff home, and she threw her arms about him, kissed him and wept, saying she wanted to see her mother and father. They came within the hour. More kissing and weeping. Lurancy said she would come back home in two days.

As Mary, she told the Roff family and neighbors goodbye. As Lurancy, when the final moment came for leaving, she seemed not to know the family and neighbors. She addressed Nervie as "Mrs. Alter" and said dazedly, "Where are we going?" Then, "Oh, yes, Mary told me." When she reached the home she had left three months before, she said she felt as though she had been in a dream.

The *Watseka Republican*, chronicling the girl's return, said: "The meeting with her parents at the home was very affecting, and now she seems to be a healthy, happy little girl, going about noting things she saw before she was stricken, and recognizing changes that have since taken place. This is a remarkable case, and the fact that we cannot understand such things does not do away with the existence of these unaccountable manifestations."

Letters which Lurancy now wrote to Dr. Stevens were, he said, very different in make-up and penmanship from those he had so recently been receiving signed "Mary Roff." He closed his account with a letter from Mrs. Vennum saying that they believed their child was cured by spirit power, and that Mary Roff had controlled the girl, effecting her recovery.

They were, however, afraid to talk to Lurancy about the experience for fear of bringing on "the spells" again. Contented and entirely well, she lived at home until her marriage four years later to a farmer who lived nearby, George Binning. Until she moved to Rollins County, Kansas, she kept in close and loving touch with the Roff family.

The case had received wide publicity, and many wondered what had happened to Lurancy after the events reported. In response to continuing interest, *The Religio-Philosophical Journal*, eight years later, asked Mr. Roff for further information.

In a letter which the *Journal* published, Mr. Roff said that Lurancy had not developed as a medium—as the spiritualists no doubt had hoped. The young farmer whom she had married "never had made himself acquainted with spiritualism and furnished poor conditions for further development in that direction; this with the fact that her many household cares and busy life, together with the charge of her children, has made the exercise of her mediumship extremely difficult." But he said that when Lurancy was alone with the Roff family she would allow Mary to take control and "we enjoyed many happy sessions together."

Nervie also kept in touch, and many years later reported that Lurancy lived to an advanced old age.

J.G.P. COMMENTS:

The possession hypothesis has not been one of primary concern to parapsychologists. The reality of the phenomenon is far from having been proved from the scientific point of view. But cases of disturbed individuals said to have been taken over by an outside force, recorded as they have been throughout history and from all parts of the world, cannot and should not be ignored. Such occurrences are usually given a religious interpretation, and the existence of a devil who can control a person's body is a matter of faith, as is the remedy of using Divine power to drive out the intruder. The rites of exorcism used in the Catholic Church as well as in other religions are the plans of attack against a vicious display of what seems to be evil solely for evil's sake.

The fact that afflictions which look like possessions occur widely and frequently does not mean that the cases provide their own interpretation. The phenomenon is one that deserves critical investigation regardless of the outcome. A

1921 book on this subject by a German philosopher, T. K. Oesterreich, described scores of cases from all races, cultures, and times. The author finished his work firmly convinced that the afflicted persons were only suffering from a particular kind of mental illness and that possession in the literal sense of the word does not occur.

Perhaps Oesterreich's views about psychic phenomena led him to try to close the books on this issue too soon. He believed that all psi occurrences must be explained in terms of capacities existing within the person exhibiting such powers. Logically, he could not continue to hold this view if he admitted that discarnate beings or entities exist and are able at times to take over and use a human body.

Mrs. Hintze has described two cases of supposed possession. The one upon which the novel and movie were based is an example of supposed demonic possession. In a case of this kind, we have no way of establishing the identity of the possessing agency, since the existence of a devil or of evil spirits is a matter of religious faith. The presence of a diabolical influence can therefore only be inferred from what happens to the afflicted person. The events may be so evil that they seem completely out of character for the troubled individual, and they may involve feats of strength that appear to be completely beyond his power. A religious person might therefore say that such acts could be the work only of the devil. But it is not possible to be sure how a severely troubled person might act or what feats of strength he might be able to perform in a state of extreme agitation. That is why the evidence offered for demonic possession is not conclusive.

The Watseka case, on the other hand, is one in which the apparent possessor claimed to be the surviving spirit of a real person. This kind of claim is one that may be settled to some degree by independent evidence. Thus, in the changes that came over Lurancy Vennum we have not only behavior suggesting that her body had become possessed. In addition, the claim of being Mary Roff was directly supported by a whole array of psychological traits—memories, recognitions, emotions, and general personality—that were characteristic of Mary during her lifetime. If we can be sure that such information was not obtained in a normal way before these characteristics appeared, then we need to consider whether the evidence the case provides makes it implausible that the possessed person could have obtained this information by ESP and have used it to dramatize the personality of the chosen "possessor."

In cases of demonic possession, my own view is that a satisfactory scientific conclusion is not possible with the knowledge we have at this time. Even in cases of personal possession, it is difficult to see how a final conclusion favoring this interpretation could be reached, though the possession hypothesis is a theoretical possibility.

Let us now try to evaluate Mrs. Hintze's two cases in the light of the general principles we have been considering. The Washington–St. Louis case that became the basis for *The Exorcist* does not earn high marks as evidence for possession. During the time the Duke Parapsychology Laboratory kept in touch with the case in its initial stage, the events had all the earmarks of a typical poltergeist disturbance. Everything that happened, then, is easily interpreted as the result of PK forces in the boy, perhaps triggered by psychological stresses he was suffering. If the characteristics of the happenings changed after the boy was started on treatment by exorcism in St. Louis, there is a possibility that the manifestations changed to show the characteristics of possession under the influence of suggestion.

The fact that the disturbances ended less than two months after exorcism was begun provides no scientific evidence that the treatment produced the cure. Poltergeist cases do not, as a rule, last as long as that one did, when we add the time covered by the case in the two cities. We may reasonably suppose, therefore, that the case might have ended sooner and with less suffering if the boy had not been taken to St. Louis and treated by exorcism.

It is difficult if not impossible to reach any sound judgment about what happened during the St. Louis phase of the case, since the records have not been made public. Father Nicola, the priest who was a technical consultant during the filming of *The Exorcist*, was not a direct witness of the exorcism, but he has given us a fairly complete account of the events as he learned them from persons closely connected with the case. He says that he did not, however, talk directly with the exorcist or with the afflicted boy.

From his account, we are led to believe that the significant events in St. Louis mainly involved exaggerated forms of behavior centered upon the boy himself. He suffered at times extremely severe spasms. He displayed agility and strength in attacking and injuring the adults who were attending him. He vomited to a surprising degree in relation to what he had eaten. Similarly, his amount of urine seemed large in proportion to his intake of fluids. He was clever in spitting repeatedly into the exorcist's eye in spite of efforts made to prevent his doing so. How can we say that these and other similar types of behavior were not the unconscious reactions of the boy himself to the powerful suggestions that evil spirits were at work in his body?

Nicola does not attempt to conceal his own strong preference for the demonic-possession interpretation, but he admits that the evidence is not compelling. "The understanding and explanation of the facts will depend on the disposition of each reader and on what criterion of truth he accepts or favors. No analysis of the case can disprove other interpretations . . . Only time will issue a definitive judgment."

The Lurancy Vennum case is generally regarded as one of the best instances of apparent possession on record, so it serves as an excellent example of both the strengths and the weaknesses of such evidence. The main source of strength is the published report of Dr. Stevens, which gives us an account prepared by a physician who had firsthand knowledge of the main events and who felt responsible for preserving the case for science.

The chief weakness of the record lies in the possibility that Lurancy could have gained in a normal way some knowledge of events and circumstances in Mary Roff's life. It is impossible for us to weigh accurately today the likelihood that this might have happened. Dr. Stevens' account reveals the fact that the Vennums and the Roffs were fairly close neighbors for a part of one summer when Lurancy was a small child.

We do not know what contacts she had with the Roffs and how alert she was to pick up and retain information about Mary, for whom the family still grieved.

Were the correct recognitions of relatives and of personal and family objects really Mary's memories retained from her earlier life? If so, they would be evidence that the body of Lurancy had become possessed by Mary's returning spirit. But it is necessary to consider also that those puzzling incidents could be attributed to Lurancy, produced by her through either memories of things she had learned or her ESP abilities. We simply cannot now say. In any event, a conclusion that possession occurs cannot be based on a single case. Even though the Vennum-Roff report is perhaps the best of its kind on record, its true value for us today is that it helps to keep the possession question open.

The frequency of cases of apparent possession and the trouble they cause for the persons directly involved as well as for their families has naturally been of concern to psychiatrists. The orthodox psychiatric position is that the symptoms and the suffering can be very real, but the causes of the changes in personality and behavior can be found entirely within the afflicted individual's own mental system. Outside influences, consisting of cultural, environmental, and psychological factors, may trigger the mental illness of a so-called possession case, but the psychic forces involved are only those of the troubled person. They were there all the time, though previously hidden. Such cases are known in psychiatry and abnormal psychology as multiple personalities or split personality, and it is difficult to define a sharp boundary line separating such cases from what would be properly classified as possession. But in principle there is a clear distinction, which is that in multiple personality nothing new is added to the person but only a shifting of priorities occurs regarding elements that were already present. In a true possession case, on the other hand, some outside force takes over the body and displaces the ordinary personality.

The difficulties of applying parapsychological study are due in part to the fact that cases of apparent possession are so rare. When a disturbance does occur, by the time the persons who are caught up in the events are ready to accept the possession interpretation they want release, not research.

Even though the logistics are difficult, there are two excellent reasons why the possession hypothesis merits attention from parapsychologists. First, cases that lend themselves to this interpretation usually exhibit psi phenomena as the multiple-personality cases usually do not. Things happen that cannot be explained in terms of the normal capacities of the afflicted individual. If careful study should reveal that all of the cases can be explained without the concept of possession, well and good—but the psi aspects still may show that some kind of parapsychological interpretation is required. Second, possession is a conceivable possibility that may eventually help us to gain a better understanding of other psychic phenomena, particularly those connected with mediumship, survival, and reincarnation. We can not afford, therefore, to ignore the cases from everyday life that directly raise the possibility of possession. This psi phenomenon has not yet been established as a scientific reality. But neither has it been disproved by other discoveries in science.

The possession hypothesis implies that personal agencies or entities, whether human or nonhuman, exist independently of living physical bodies. It also implies that such a psychic force can under some circumstances take over a body and use it. Either of these possibilities would, if true, have tremendous importance for a better understanding of the universe and of our place in it.

THE MEDIUMS

*"Glendower. 'I can call spirits from the vasty deep.' Hotspur.
'Why, so can I, or so can any man; but will they come
when you do call for them?' "—William Shakespeare,*
King Henry IV, *Part I, Act III*

The so-called "golden age" of mediumship lasted nearly fifty years, and it ended just about that long ago. Now that interest in psychic phenomena is picking up momentum, it may be about time for the cycle to begin again. Unfortunately, some rather suspicious characters seem to be leaning from the mediumistic merry-go-round these days, hands out for the money of those who wish to be taken for that particular ride.

A young man, age twenty-one, calling himself a medium and ESP expert, appeared in our town recently. For about a week the local paper had been carrying advertisements saying that he and two other "experts" would soon be in our midst: one was a "Celebrated Author and Religious Scholar" and the other a "Noted Psychologist from Stanford." The proceeds were to go, so the ad said, to the National Parapsychology Foundation.

The admission fee was five dollars, and for an additional twenty-five dollars one could have a fifteen-to-twenty-minute private session with the boy wonder. Now, it so happened that this talented trio had performed in Chattanooga the week before. A letter to the editor of the *Chattanooga Times* described the performance as a "snow job," which had ended with demands for money back, calls to lawyers, and even to the police, but unfortunately, a copy of that news story did not reach our town in time to alert all those who turned out for the session. It was, so I have been told, inept, immature, and an insult to intelligence. Some members of the audience left before the performance was over, voicing audible objections.

And yet the line-up of those with twenty-five dollars in their hands was so long that it was one o'clock in the morning before the last person had received his private reading.

Maybe there is such an organization as the National Parapsychology Foundation, but the parapsychologists of my acquaintance never heard of it, and at least one attempt to place a call to the San Francisco address given resulted in the information that there was no such listing. As J. Richard Sells, writer of the letter to the *Chattanooga Times*, said, "I regret that persons such as these three can so easily besmirch the study of parapsychology at a time when real and beneficial advances are being made in the field."

The long lull in mediumship may be due partly to the undeniable fact that fraudulent mediums from the middle of the last century did a great deal to besmirch the field. Even some of those who are believed to have real mediumistic ability did, upon occasion, cheat. Apparently it is easier to cheat than to turn on psychic energies upon demand. But Rex Stanford makes the point that even if some of them are known to cheat ninety-nine times out of a hundred, parapsychologists must concern themselves with that one time out of a hundred when there seems to be evidence of genuine mediumistic ability.

There have been, moreover, a few mediums who have never had the least stigma attached to their reputations. Leonore Piper of Boston was one of those. William James was the discoverer of her extraordinary powers. He and his wife sat with her many times, and he said that he knew of no way in which, normally, she could have acquired the richly detailed and intimate knowledge of the James family life. Many serious investigators were convinced that her information came from the deceased; others felt that her knowledge was telepathically acquired from the living. But Gardner Murphy, one of the world's most distinguished living psychologists, says, "She was never involved in any suspicious circumstances." (See chapter XIV for the Bennie Junot case in which she acted as medium.)

The most documented, most thoroughly investigated medium of all time was Gladys Osborne Leonard, an Englishwoman. She was discovered by Sir Oliver Lodge in 1915 and was studied by many interested persons for over fifty years. As did many other mediums, Leonard had "controls," spirits from the "other side" who facilitated communication between herself and the deceased. Mrs. Leonard's control was Feda, whose English was sometimes a bit peculiar, for supposedly, during her lifetime, Feda had been Gladys Leonard's great-great-grandmother, born in India.

Other mediums, too often, have brought messages, purportedly from the other side, that have been dismaying in their banality: "Do not grieve." . . . "I am happy." . . . "Time does not exist here." It seems to me that I could spend a day in Peoria and have more of interest to relate. William James himself once made the wry comment that about half the messages seemed to have been written by the same person.

But Mrs. Leonard, time after time, ventured into specifics that defy a normal explanation. She made "book tests" that seem to suggest that some sort of communicable consciousness may persist. For instance, on many occasions, not knowing the identity of the person who was sitting, she would deliver a message from a discarnate entity directing the sitter to go home to a certain library shelf and choose, let us say, the second book from the right on the top shelf, turn to a certain page, and on a specified line find a message of special meaning, perhaps reminiscent of shared experience between the sitter and the deceased. The following varies somewhat from the typical book test, but it illustrates the kind of communication her sitters found convincing.

Mrs. Hugh Talbot gave neither her name nor her address when she attempted, through Mrs. Leonard, to contact her dead husband. After receiving what she considered a very good description of his personal appearance, she became aware that he was terribly anxious to convince her of his identity. She said in a letter describing the séance: "Incidents of the past, known only to him and to me, were spoken of; belongings trivial in themselves but possessing for him a particular personal interest . . . were minutely and correctly described . . . Also, I was asked repeatedly if I believed it was himself speaking."

Some of the usual statements about death not being much different from life came through, and then Mrs. Talbot wrote:

"Suddenly Feda [the control] began a tiresome description of a book, she said it was leather and dark, and tried to show me the size. Mrs. Leonard showed a length of eight to ten inches long with her hands and about four to five wide." Mrs. Talbot was not very much interested; she was sure she knew which book was meant, but thought she had either thrown it away or it was in a place not readily accessible. "Feda began a wearisome description all over again, adding that I was to look on page 12 . . . that it would be so interesting after this conversation . . . 'He says he is not sure it is on page 12, it might be on 13 . . .' "

Somewhat indifferently, Mrs. Talbot said she would try to find it. "But this did not satisfy Feda. She started all over again, becoming more and more insistent, and went on to say, 'He is not sure of the colour . . . There are two books, you will know the one he means by a diagram of languages in the front . . . Indo-European, Aryan, Semitic languages . . . There are lines . . . going out sideways from one centre.' Then again the words 'A table of Arabian languages, Semitic languages . . .' It all sounded absolute rubbish to me. I had never heard of a diagram of languages . . . and she kept on and on 'Will you look at page 12 or 13? If it is there, it would interest him so much after this conversation. He does want you to, he wants you to promise.'

"By this time I had come to the conclusion that what I had heard of happening at these sittings had come to pass, viz., that the medium was tired and talking nonsense, so I hastened to pacify her by promising to look for the book, and was glad when the sitting almost at once came to an end."

Mrs. Talbot said that she might never have looked for the book had she not reported to her niece that same evening the fact that the medium had "talked a lot of rubbish about a book." Her niece begged her to look for the book at once. "I wanted to wait till the next day, saying I knew it was all nonsense. However, in the end, I went to the bookshelf, and after some time . . . I found one or two old notebooks . . . One, a shabby black leather, corresponded in size to the description given, and I absent-mindedly opened it, wondering in my mind whether the one I was looking for had been destroyed or only sent away.

"To my utter astonishment, my eyes fell on the words, 'Table of Semitic or Syro-Arabian Languages,' and pulling out the leaf . . . I saw on the other side, 'General Table of the Aryan and Indo-European languages.' It was the diagram of which Feda had spoken."

Feda's description of lines going out from the center was also correct. Mrs. Talbot said that she had never looked inside the book before. She was so taken aback that it was some minutes before she remembered to look at "page 12 or 13." On page 13 she found this extract from "Post Mortem," author anonymous, published in 1881 by Blackwood and Sons:

"I discovered by certain whispers which it was supposed I was unable to hear . . . that I was near death . . . Presently my mind began to dwell not only on happiness which was to come, but upon happiness that I was actually enjoying. I saw long-forgotten forms, playmates, schoolfellows, companions of my youth and of my old age, who one and all, smiled upon me. They did not smile with any compassion, that I no longer felt that I needed, but with that sort of kindness which is exchanged by people who are equally happy. I saw my mother, father, and sisters, all of whom I had survived. They did not speak, yet they communicated to me their unaltered and unalterable affection. At about the time when they appeared, I made an effort to realize my bodily situation . . . that is, I endeavoured to connect my soul with the body which lay on the bed in my house. The endeavour failed. I was dead . . ."

It will occur to the skeptic that there was a possibility that Mrs. Talbot only *thought* she had not seen the book before, that the information was there in her subconscious mind all the time, and that Mrs. Leonard picked it up telepathically. This is the sticking point for most serious investigators: whenever telepathy is even remotely possible, then the message coming through the medium loses much of its value as evidence of survival.

There is one medium who, at times, seems able to by-pass this stickler, Hafsteinn Bjornsson of Reykjavik, Iceland. Ian Stevenson says that of all the mediums of whom he has personal knowledge, Hafsteinn is the greatest now living.

Few laymen outside of his own country have heard of him. Few, including myself, know very much about Iceland beyond some rather vague ideas about volcanoes and sagas and those long, long nights. But this little Kentucky-size republic is a land of surprises: winter temperatures along the coastal regions where most of the people live seldom get down below freezing. Not only is Reykjavik a city of parks, with the buildings and the year-round outdoor swimming pools heated by underground hot springs, but it is a city of bookstores. In proportion to the population, twenty times more books are published there than in the United States. The vivid tale-spinning of Halldor Laxness, a recent Nobel Prize winner, has reminded the world of the great narrative art of the sagas of the eleventh and twelfth centuries. It is little wonder that they originated there, for Icelandic nights are twenty hours long in the depth of winter. Not much work can be done, and so, for these hundreds of years—not an unattractive thought—the people have groped their way to each other's houses for companionship. There they sang and danced, and still do. They told and retold the old stories. And they held séances.

Iceland is one of the two countries in the world, the other being Holland, where psi is accepted matter-of-factly, and considered to be a real and natural part of life. The Icelandic Society for Psychical Research is a very active one.

Hafsteinn Bjornsson is a full-time employee of a Reykjavik radio station, but he has been acting as a medium for nearly forty years. In common with most mediums, his paranormal powers became evident in early childhood. In his ordinary waking state, he claims to be able to see deceased persons near the living. In a trance state, he uses controls who sometimes seem to speak directly through him.

What is unusual, however, and this is a talent few mediums possess, is his ability for getting full names of people and places, very often a generation or two—or more—removed from the sitter. Not only is this knowledge concerned with relatives in the sometimes rather distant past, but of friends or even casual acquaintances of these relatives, persons of whom the sitter has almost certainly never heard, thus all but disposing of the possibility that Hafsteinn is telepathically tapping the mind of the sitter.

Upon at least one occasion, he has exhibited another rare talent, that of xenoglossy, the ability to speak a language he does not know in a non-trance state, as well as responsive xenoglossy, the ability to carry on a dialogue with someone who is speaking in that language. We have an account of one instance when a visiting professor from Denmark was enabled to carry on, through Hafsteinn, a conversation in the Eskimo language with a dead Eskimo friend who had lived in Greenland. Hafsteinn did not know the language at all, but the Danish professor had lived in Greenland for many years and knew the language well.

Hafsteinn was barely twenty-three at the beginning of the long winter in 1937–38 when he started acting as a medium with a group of sitters who met at a private home in Reykjavik. Fairly soon, a rather bizarre personality began to manifest himself while Hafsteinn was in a trance state. He was what parapsychologists refer to as a "drop-in" communicator, which is to say a discarnate personality whom nobody was trying to contact, nobody had ever heard of, a stranger who simply comes barging in like an uninvited guest at a party. When this rude intruder was asked to identify himself, he said, "What the hell does it matter to you what my name is?" When they asked him what he wanted, he said, "I am looking for my leg." His leg, he said, was "in the sea."

This group was meeting once or twice a week, proof that they were pretty serious about the whole thing, and after the first novelty of the strange interruption, it must have become a nuisance to have him keep butting in, demanding his leg and refusing to say who he was.

The next fall when the nights began to lengthen, the group started meeting again. Some new sitters had been added and now they were meeting at a different house, but back came the "drop-in" with the same refusal to tell his name and the same annoying insistence that he wanted to have his leg.

Soon after the first of the year, a newcomer joined the group, Ludvik Gudmundsson, who knew some of the members but had not previously known Hafsteinn. Ludvik lived in Reykjavik, but he also owned a house in Sandgerdi, about forty miles away. To his bafflement, the nameless intruder expressed pleasure in meeting him, because, he said, the missing leg was in his house in Sandgerdi!

This made no sense to Ludvik. And as time went on, it was making less and less sense to the members of the circle to allow this intrusive personality to take up so much of their time. His presence was unmistakable, for his personality was so different from that of the medium. He would demand snuff, which Hafsteinn does not use. Once he said that the hostess had something in a glass in the back of the kitchen cupboard which he would like. It was rum, used for cooking, and he grumbled when it was refused to him. A glass of wine once or twice a year is about Hafsteinn's limit where alcoholic beverages are concerned.

An ultimatum was delivered: either this obnoxious personality should reveal his identity or he would have to stop bothering them.

They were able to have several peaceful, uninterrupted sessions, and then, as if he had decided he'd sulked long enough, he came back abruptly, interrupting another, gentler communicator to say that he had decided to tell who he was. "My name is Runolfur Runolfsson. And I was fifty-two years old when I died . . ."

Now there follows an example of Hafsteinn's rare ability to get names of people and places. I shall not attempt to give very many of them, but later they facilitated the exhaustive checking that was done on this case.

Runolfur (eventually to be called "Runki" by the group, that being the Icelandic nickname for Runolfur) had been drunk on that fateful day when he started for his home at Klappakot. The weather had been bad, and when he stopped at the house of friends they insisted that he must not leave in that condition unless somebody went with him. Ridiculous —especially to someone in an intoxicated condition—for home was only a fifteen-minute walk away. He became angry and said he would not go at all if he could not go alone. They let him go.

Wet and tired, he set out. But he sat down on a rock when partway home, took out his bottle and drank some more.

The tide came in. He was carried out to sea. When the tide washed his body back up on the shore, the dogs and ravens came and tore him to pieces. That was in October, and the year was 1879. The remains of his body were not discovered until January. They were buried in the Utskalar graveyard not far from Sandgerdi.

It was never established that those who found the remains noticed that a thigh bone was missing, but Runki said it was. He said, "It was carried out to sea again, but later washed up at Sandgerdi. There it was passed around and now it is in Ludvik's house." He said proof of all this could be found in the Utskalar church book.

Now the sitters had something concrete to go on. They examined the church book, which by then had been transferred to the National Archives in Reykjavik, and found this note, which concurred with what Runki had said: "On October 16, 1879, Runolfur Runolfsson, living in Klappakot, was missing on account of some accidental or unnatural occurrence on his way home . . . during a storm with rain near his farm in the middle of the night. He is believed to have been carried along by the storm down to the beach south of the farm boundary . . . from where the sea carried him away because his bones were found dismembered much later and his clothes were also separated."

A further note said that he had been decently buried on January 8, 1880. The church record book said nothing about the missing thigh bone.

Ludvik recalled that when he had bought the house at Sandgerdi he had heard some talk about its being haunted. Two skulls had been found there, and he thought it possible that other bones might be there too. He questioned some of the elderly men of the village, and some of them recalled that a thigh bone had been "going around" but they did not know what had happened to it. Someone thought rather vaguely that the bone had been placed downstairs in the northern part of the house between the inner and outer walls.

In Iceland, if we may judge from what followed, considerable importance is attached to human bones. Ludvik, although he had no way of knowing where in his large house

the missing bone might be—if, indeed, it was there at all—
was now determined to find it. Following a suggestion that it
might be in a wall between two windows, that wall was torn
open. Nothing was there. Now a carpenter who had worked
on the house was located. Yes, he remembered the bone that
had been washed up on the shore, and he also remembered
exactly where he had placed the missing relic some twenty
years before. He indicated the spot. The wall was opened,
and there was a bone. Was it *the* bone that Runki had made
all the fuss about? Possibly. At any rate, it was very long,
substantiating his statement that he had been very tall.

Dr. Ian Stevenson and Dr. Erlendur Haraldsson, Department of Psychology, University of Iceland, made an exhaustive study of this case, and Stevenson has a picture of this
bone which was made after it was placed in the little coffin
that Ludvik had constructed for it. The bone, apparently
accepted by all concerned as having belonged to the man
who had died in the sea almost sixty years before, was buried
following traditional procedures for such occasions. The
clergyman gave a sermon eulogizing the long-deceased
Runolfur Runolfsson; the choir sang; then those who had
gathered for this little service went to the clergyman's house
for a pleasant but dignified reception.

Hafsteinn was not among those present, but he held a
séance immediately following the burial service for the bone.
Runki, naturally, made his presence known, expressed grati-
tude, and said that he had been present at the churchyard
ceremony and the reception following. He described it all in
satisfactory detail, even to the different kinds of cakes served
at the clergyman's home.

Now that everything had been taken care of in such a
tidy fashion, Runki began to undergo a personality change.
He appeared often at Hafsteinn's séances, and as time went
on he became gentler, helping other communicators. For
many years he has been one of Hafsteinn's chief controls.

Stevenson and Haraldsson went to great lengths to establish the verifiable facts of the foregoing case. They interviewed a large number of persons in an effort to see whether
or not Hafsteinn could have obtained all his information in a
normal way. They even seriously considered disinterring the

remains of Runki's body, as well as the thigh bone, to see if the bones "matched." This would have gone a long way toward establishing paranormality.

They received permission from the grandson and granddaughter to have the bones disinterred. But where were the bones? The cemetery at Utskalar is rather large; many graves are unmarked; and since they had no clue as to where the single thigh bone rested, to say nothing of the other remains of Runolfur Runolfsson, they had to agree with the clergyman at Utskalar that the search would be an almost impossible one.

J.G.P. COMMENTS:

That mediumship flourished during a half-century-long "golden age" was perhaps due to the combination of practicing mediums and qualified investigators. The fading may not have resulted from the disappearance of the mediums but because the parapsychologists turned their attention to other lines of work. Thus the mediums were left to serve only the members of the public who visited them in the hope of getting in touch with loved ones who had died. Their talents were overlooked by the scientists.

Now there are clear signs that the situation is changing. A new generation of scientists has come upon the scene, and the recent reports of the successful tests of the Icelandic medium Hafsteinn Bjornsson are perhaps only the first signs of a renewal of scientific interest in mediumship.

The explanation that it was not the mediums who disappeared but the research workers who took their leave is not an indictment, but only a description of the historical developments. There was not, however, so much a loss of interest in this line of research as there was a realization that the previous efforts had fallen short of the goal of answering the survival question. What was needed, the investigators generally agreed, was more secure ways of evaluating mediumistic material, in order that future research efforts might yield more objective and convincing results. In contrast with the intense interest of previous years, the attention given to mediums during the past half-century looks like neglect, but parapsychologists never got completely away from an interest in them. In particular, we needed ways of conducting the mediumistic sittings and checking the records that guarded against the possible effects of suggestibility and the will to believe in the checking of the records.

The end product of a séance is a mass of verbal material, general statements of a personal kind, some vague and some specific, that may or may not apply to the sitter. The first problem is to decide whether this record contains accurate information that was not available to the medium in any normal way and thus ESP of some kind was involved. The second question, assuming that ESP really took place, is: What is the source of the information? We have learned how to deal satisfactorily with the first issue, but the question regarding whether the information is from persons who have died and thus is direct evidence of their survival is more difficult.

During the thirties I supervised a study of the mediumship of Eileen Garrett, with the purpose of improving the methods of evaluating the accuracy of her trance statements. Each sitter sat in an adjacent room, out of the medium's sight and beyond the reach of her voice. The medium worked in a self-induced trance, which my publication on that study described:

"Mrs. Garrett seems to be able to go into and come out of trance at will; at least, she never failed while under the observation of those connected with these investigations. To bring on the trance, she sits in a soft chair, slumps down or 'sprawls' with her feet far forward and her head thrown back. She appears to relax completely. Her eyes roll upward in their sockets. After a few moments her breath begins to come in short gasps, and she utters low moans. The eyes are by this time closed, though during the trance the lids seem to flicker continuously. In a short while she crosses her arms across her breast and begins to sway back and forth in her chair. The voice of the control then makes its appearance with a low, masculine quality. His first utterance seldom varies from the stereotyped phrases: 'It is I, Uvani, I bring you greetings, friends.' Uvani claims to be the spirit of a deceased Arab. He is very cooperative in experimentation. Upon being told that a subject is ready . . . in the next room with the intervening door closed, he begins his remarks for that subject and continues until he talks himself out. He never tries, as far as I have observed, to get leads from the subject or those present. Sometimes he apologizes because he does not feel that he is having much success. He announces when he is finished, and asks if there is anything more desired from him for this time. Two or three long experiments may be conducted during one period of trance, consuming from one to two hours. When Uvani is dismissed, Mrs. Garrett arouses herself by stretching and yawning as though coming out of a natural sleep. She appears to be fully normal in about a minute's time."

A total of twelve sitters took part in the study. All of the utterances of the medium were taken down in shorthand, and the records were later typed out in full. Each sitter left without knowing anything about what the medium had said. A brief description of how the material was handled will illustrate the care investigators now use in checking mediumistic utterances.

To check the results, the twelve records were arranged in a random order. Then all statements, such as the day of the week or the hour of the day, that might provide a clue regarding which records were intended for which sitters were removed. Finally, the material was divided into separate items of information to be checked by the person scoring the material. Thus the material was converted into a kind of true or false test.

Each of the twelve participants received a complete set of the mediumistic records, but with each individual's statements embedded in an unknown position among the records given for the other eleven sitters. Thus each participant had to check each item as true or false without knowing whether the medium intended it for him. In this way we attempted to eliminate the possibilty that a particular sitter might have accepted too many of the medium's statements as correct because of the knowledge that the medium intended them to apply. The method also avoided errors of the opposite kind: if a skeptical sitter had known which was his own record, he might have rejected statements even though they were true.

When the results were combined for all twelve sitters, they were so much beyond the level expected on a purely chance basis that the odds against finding such results merely by luck were approximately 1,700,000-to-1. The results thus led to the conclusion that ESP was involved in the sittings, though the findings did not tell us whether the medium was receiving communications from beyond the grave.

The Runki case had its beginning in Iceland not long after this study was made with Mrs. Garrett. Although that work with Hafsteinn did not follow such a formal procedure, one feature of the communications made them difficult to explain in terms of the psi abilities of the medium and thus gave them more weight as evidence of survival. This is the fact that Runki was not known to any of the people who were at the séance, so there was no information about him in any-one's mind that the medium could pick up by telepathy. It is conceivable, of course, that the medium could have obtained some of the information by clairvoyance, but it is not easy to see what purpose Hafsteinn would have had in using his own ESP abilities to dig up information about this obscure stranger. On the other hand, Runki, if he survived death, had a strong reason to communicate. He wanted his lost thigh bone found and given a decent burial.

A communicator who is unknown to the medium and the sitters at a séance may lead to the investigation of what is called a "drop-in" case. Such instances are especially interesting because the wish to communicate seems to belong to the deceased persons who claim to be giving information about themselves. The strength of such a case depends upon how well it stands up in an investigation that covers two areas of inquiry. The first task is to look for documentary evidence that a person fitting the description given by the drop-in communicator really lived and died. If this is successful, the other step is to find out whether the medium could have obtained the information about that person in any normal way. Both of these stages of the investigation of the Runki communicator were carried out with thoroughness and with results that strongly support the genuineness of the case. We are justified, therefore, to choose the obvious interpretation of the facts—that Runki was the initiator of the information about himself and therefore some part of his personality must have survived death—but we would not be justified to say that this case alone establishes survival.

While there is a common denominator of similarity in the way that all mediums work, each one has unique individual characteristics. Mrs. Piper dropped her head onto pillows arranged on the table at which she sat, and during the trance the communications came through automatic writing while the sitter moved the paper to keep the pencil from running off the edge or the words from piling one on another in an illegible scramble. Only during the brief periods of coming out of trance were words spoken in the Piper sittings. Mrs. Leonard usually spoke in the girlish voice of her control, Feda. With Hafsteinn, most of his sessions involve trance, with Runki or some other controlling "personality" acting as messenger or intermediary for the supposed discarnates who wish to communicate. But Hafsteinn also holds sittings in which he does not go into trance but simply gives impressions that come to him in a waking state.

Haraldsson and Stevenson have reported a series of sittings of the latter kind that they carried out with Hafsteinn. When the medium visited New York in 1972 they arranged to have him give waking or "clairvoyance" readings for ten volunteer subjects who had lived in Iceland. The ten subjects were taken one at a time in random order for individual sittings. The subject and the medium did not see each other, and the sitter wore earplugs as well as earphones through which loud music played, while Hafsteinn, back of a heavy curtain, was giving his impressions in Icelandic. After each reading the subject left the building without seeing those who were awaiting their turns. When the sitters later read the records —each one read all ten—four of them were successful in selecting the one that Hafsteinn gave while they were outside the curtain. By mere chance, only one of the sitters would be expected to choose correctly, and the probability is that as many as four would do so only once in a hundred times. Getting such a result the first time means that the experiment was significant. The investigators saw their study as a valuable one chiefly because it shows that Hafsteinn's ability is still working and that it can be studied in controlled experiments.

Over the years investigators have taken a special interest in the controls that appear to take over mediums when they are in trance. Efforts to find out if the controls are the surviving spirits of persons who have died have not supported their claims to such identities. Rather, the weight of the evidence favors the interpretation that the control is a dramatized imaginary creation built up by the medium. Even when, for example, a Hodgson control took over in the Piper sittings after Hodgson, her long-time investigator, died, we have no real reason to think this was anything more than a dramatization.

It is interesting to consider whether the Runki case must be considered an exception to this rule. In this instance Runki appeared first as a communicator, which means that he was, at most, only temporarily in control of the medium on each occasion when he appeared. The evidence became strong, as we have seen, that Runki was a real person who had lived and died in Iceland. Later a control calling himself Runki became a fairly regular feature of Hafsteinn's trance séances. We are told that Runki as a control was a reformed, well-behaved personality as compared with Runki the original communicator. I suggest that only the names are the same, and that the Runki control is, after all, only the medium's dramatization of a "personality" for that role based in a general way upon what had been learned in earlier sittings about a real person of that name.

Suppose, on the contrary, that we had found that the controls are discarnate beings that take over the bodies of the mediums during the trance state. In that eventuality, mediumship would be a form of possession, and instead of a paucity of evidence for that hypothesis, we would have abundant support for it.

The place of the controls in mediumistic trance is a complicated question. The suggestion that they are fictional characters seems to apply to most of the regular controls who take over the mediums during trance to introduce and assist those who wish to communicate from the other side. But occasionally a communicator appears to take control of the entranced medium and to speak directly in a different voice —even one that the sitter may recognize as that of the dead person who is supposed to be speaking. These occasions seem more like possession of the medium by a surviving personality. While the evidence is not conclusive, it is surely so strong that further research is amply justified.

SURVIVAL

"I write in full consciousness of the low value commonly attached to inquiries of the kind which I pursue."— F. W. H. Myers, Human Personality and its Survival of Bodily Death *(1903)*

I took notes on the final day of the 1972 Parapsychological Association Convention in Edinburgh when the topic for a symposium discussion was: "What evidence, if you had it, would convince you of survival?"

DR. HANS BENDER: "I cannot reconcile myself to the terrible waste of death with no survival. I feel that survival is likely, indeed most probable, but I see no possibility for definite proof."

DR. JOHN PALMER: "The only evidence that would convince me would be my own survival."

DR. IAN STEVENSON: "I am in a different position from that of the other members of the panel: I am already convinced of survival beyond physical death." (He added later, "I do not mean to imply that everyone else should be convinced by the evidence that has persuaded me—indeed, I am sure that even the best evidence we have is imperfect and not necessarily compelling.")

ROSALIND HEYWOOD (from the floor): "The analytical half of me finds it very difficult to envisage the possibility of survival. The other half of me has had the experience, eight or nine times, of apparently being instructed by the recently dead to do something unexpected for somebody they had loved on earth. But each must have his own firsthand evidence. If all of you had had the evidence I have had, you would be as convinced as I am."

When psychic research began almost a hundred years ago

it was sparked by interest in survival. Religious concepts were beginning to sway before the battering rams of materialistic science, and survival of bodily death was considered by many to have been a mere superstition. Ignoring ridicule, the founders of what came to be known as parapsychology began their investigations by concentrating on human personality. They viewed historical evidence, the brilliant Swedenborg's impassioned testimony, the remarkable experiences of the Wesley family. They investigated the mediums of their day, good, bad, and terrible. And they collected thousands of spontaneous cases, many of which are still the classics of parapsychological literature.

Are we to believe that this research added up to merely thousands of lies, swallowed whole by credulous men? Consider what giants they were: F. W. H. Myers, Henry Sidgwick, and Edmund Gurney were brilliant scholars connected with Cambridge University; William Crookes, Oliver Lodge, and William Barrett were knighted for their eminence in the physical sciences. Eminent psychologists William James and William McDougall joined their ranks, as did Nobel Prize winners Charles Richet and Henri Bergson.

Some of the investigators were never able to accept the idea of survival; others, notably Sir Oliver Lodge, became deeply interested in spiritualism. As that cult flourished in the second half of the nineteenth century, claiming at one time as many as eleven million members, so did the mediums multiply. Many of them were such flagrant frauds that their cheesecloth ectoplasm all but smothered the voices of the few who were worth listening to.

Most parapsychologists are of the opinion that although the séances held during the years between 1880 and 1930 provide much evidence of ESP, they offer little that can be considered compelling evidence of survival. Still, some of the carefully detailed records of séances make interesting "period piece" reading. Henry Holt, in his *On the Cosmic Relations*, gives several verbatim accounts. His favorite case seemed to be that of Bennie Junot (pseudonym) and he devoted a long chapter to sittings conducted by Dr. Richard Hodgson with Mrs. Piper as the medium through which Bennie's ostensible communications were made known.

Although Mrs. Piper had never known Bennie, and the Junot family was introduced to her anonymously, there may be little that cannot be explained by the assumption that Mrs. Piper had unusual telepathic ability. And yet it is a moving chronicle of one family's desperate attempt to establish evidence that their son still lived after death.

Bennie Junot was seventeen when he died of an unspecified illness. The communication is exactly the sort that would be typical, particularly of that day, when a seventeen-year-old boy has suddenly been taken from a warm and loving family. He was concerned about the health of family members: he mentioned his mother's illness, his sister's sore throat, his brother's head injury suffered during a hockey game, his father's tiredness, and even the trouble an aunt was having with her teeth.

Other relatives and friends were discussed back and forth with detail that would be trivial except for the circumstances. At one time his father asked, when they were talking about a trip they had taken, "Who was with you on the ride out West?" and Bennie answered with the name of a cowboy who had accompanied him on a long ride.

Family pets were often mentioned. When instructed by Bennie to "give my horse to my little sister," Mr. Junot wired home just in time to stop the horse's sale. On one occasion Mr. Junot asked Bennie to enlist the help of a coachman, dead some months, in finding a dog. The coachman had left the family's employ before his death, taking a favorite dog of theirs, Rounder, with him. This is the message that came through when Dr. Hodgson, in the absence of the Junot family, was asking questions through Mrs. Piper, who produced automatic writing while in trance.

BENNIE: "John Welsh has Rounder."

DR. HODGSON (apparently not remembering the name of the dog that Bennie's father previously had asked about): "John Welsh was round her?"

BENNIE: "John Welsh has Rounder. Tell this . . . tell . . . tell . . . John Welsh has Rounder."

DR. HODGSON: "John Welsh *is* round her?"

BENNIE: "Has . . . has . . . It's I, Bennie, don't you see me? I, Bennie!"

Even Mr. Junot had never heard of a man named John Welsh, but when this information was conveyed to him later, he was able to recover the dog.

Again, when Dr. Hodgson was acting as sitter with no family members present, Bennie said, "I can hear the piano going now, is it Helen?" That afternoon Hodgson sent a telegram to Bennie's mother, asking if Helen, the sister, had been playing piano at twenty-five minutes past eleven that morning. She replied that Helen, usually at school at that hour, had stayed at home because of a cold and bad weather, and that she had indeed been playing the piano at that time.

The account tells of a sitting when Mrs. Junot said, "Do you remember that day you were sick and we talked so long?"

BENNIE: "Oh, yes, I do very well. You thought you knew about this, and I remember you were somewhat troubled, but I told you I was going to be all right."

MRS. JUNOT: "Yes, Bennie, you did tell me. You said you were better."

BENNIE: "Yes, and I was right. Believe me, dear, I am all right. Do you remember you said you did not know what you should do if anything should happen to me, and I answered don't worry, I shall come out all right?" (The father remembered this conversation.)

MRS. JUNOT: "Yes, Bennie, but I didn't want you to leave us, to leave me."

BENNIE: "But I did not leave you, dear, don't you see? I—I did not leave. I am really Bennie . . ."

Holt, in his comments on this case, admitted that the séances may have provided consolation for this family, but he said, "I incline to think that for many people, probably for the vast majority, the medium habit would not be a good habit."

Although few today look to mediums to provide evidence of survival, Dr. Gertrude Schmeidler has suggested that an experiment, using a medium, might provide interesting and evidential material. This would involve enlisting the cooperation of those who knew they didn't have long to live. Psychological testing could determine how their minds worked, speech patterns, what kind of jokes appealed, and so on. Then after death any message which mediums might be able to get, purporting to come from those who had been tested, could be evaluated. If they met the testing criteria, this would be consistent with the survival hypothesis. Schmeidler points out, however, that this would not be absolute proof.

The Rhines were seeking evidence of survival when they began their studies of psychic phenomena fifty years ago. Their work has been a magnificent sidetrack, so involving that it has postponed concentration on this single question. The findings have spawned so many questions that it is hard to conceive of the kind of evidence that would provide a conclusive answer. On the other hand, the more that was learned about psi capacities, the more the Rhines and other researchers saw that man has qualities that make the theory of survival more acceptable.

A few years ago a rather curious phenomenon was hailed by some as a real breakthrough on the survival question—in fact, a book with the title *Breakthrough*, by the late Dr. Konstantin Raudive, psychologist and philosopher, was published in the United States in 1971. It was subtitled: "An Amazing Experiment in Electronic Communication with the Dead."

It all began when Friedrich Jurgenson, a Swedish painter and film producer, found that voices seemed to have been recorded on tapes he had made of bird sounds. They had not been audible when he made the tapes, and he could not account for them by normal means. In the months that followed, he heard words and sentences in the splashing of rain, the dripping of water, even the rustling of paper, which seemed to be giving him personal messages. One female voice, heard repeatedly on tape, demanded that he maintain contact with the machine and said, "Listen. Please to listen."

This might have been dismissed as the imagining of a sick mind, but when Jurgenson invited scientists to listen, some of them were able to hear the voices too. In 1964 he published a book in Sweden, *Voices from Space*, which was issued with a recording of the voice sounds.

Other experimenters became interested and reported success. In Germany, Dr. Raudive set up his own laboratory and at the time *Breakthrough* was published he claimed to have recorded seventy-two thousand voices.

They have a peculiar rhythm, and most of them are unintelligible unless one is told what to listen for. The polyglot mixture of languages makes for further difficulty.

Dr. Hans Bender, of the University of Freiburg, said in his discussion of the voices that after making his first investigation of Jurgenson's tapes, he believed that because of Jurgenson's reputation for integrity, fraud was ruled out. He felt a paranormal origin was probable, but inclined toward a psychokinetic explanation: in some way, unconsciously, the mediumistic abilities of the operators were being transformed into word sounds. He said, however, that before paranormal origin can be claimed, there must be an elimination of projection of illusionary semantic contents onto normal speech or accidental interfering noises, uncontrolled utterances of persons present, and fragments of radio transmission, which can often be picked up by tape recorders functioning as radio receivers.

The idea of extending the power of the ordinary senses is not new. Myers mentions shell hearing, which goes back to ancient times and is analagous to crystal gazing. Those with psychic sensitivity often claimed that above the "roar" of the sea in the shell, they could hear voices.

David Ellis, awarded the Perrott-Warrick Studentship by Trinity College, Cambridge, for research on the voices, tells of a legend that seems to be based on a similar idea. Fishermen will not visit a certain Cornwall beach at night because they say they can hear the voices of dead sailors calling to them from the sea. He suggests that the "white sound" of breakers on the beach might have a parallel with the voice phenomenon. A further comment which he made about the way meaning can be projected onto almost any random sounds reminded me of the way two of my children used to argue, sometimes heatedly, over what our creaky old rocking chair was "saying."

Ellis, who started his research in 1970, concentrating mainly on Raudive's recordings, says that the voices, though very faint and difficult to distinguish from background noises, are in many instances clearly recognizable as human voices. A number of the voice phrases he heard were relevant to the experimenter, with Latvian (Raudive's native language) predominating, telling him about deceased friends or answering questions put by persons present.

Most of what comes through is trivia or even foolishness. But survival is the central theme of the most meaningful statements that have been obtained. "The dead live, Konstantin." "Kosti—" (Raudive's nickname) "we are." "Please believe." Margarete Petrautski, for ten years secretary to Dr. Zenta Maurina, Raudive's wife, was always skeptical about survival, but she is reported to have come through clearly, saying, "Just think! I am!" Ellis says that all samples of Margarete's voice, recorded over a period of five years, had the same frequency characteristics.

I talked with David Ellis in 1972 and it was no surprise to me to learn that he ended his study of the phenomenon less enthusiastic than when he started. Few parapsychologists have admitted that the Jurgenson-Raudive voices have accomplished a breakthrough. Interest in the phenomenon has been world-wide, but opinions vary, from Raudive's own obsessive conviction that survival has now been proved, through a let's-wait-and-see attitude, to flat denial that the voices are anything other than a mixture of voice sounds picked up from radio broadcasts in many languages. Even Peter Bander, translator of *Breakthrough*, who had once been convinced that he had heard the voice of his dead mother on a tape, said in his preface to the book, "It would be wrong to expect that tomorrow we can dial M for Mother."

Those with strong religious convictions concerning an afterlife need no proof of survival, but this is not to say they do not welcome the reinforcing mystical experience which—as Nils Jacobson says in his thoughtful book *Life After Death?* —brings its own absolute wisdom and certainty. *The Spiritual Frontiers Fellowship Newsletter*, December 1974, told of an incident which brought comfort to bereaved parents of a four-year-old boy, even though it was experienced by someone who had never seen the child.

Melissa Siebert, a graduate student at Loyola University in Chicago, was working late at a small suburban gift shop. All alone in the deserted shop, she was concentrating on an inventory spread on the floor when she felt the impulse to look up. Standing a few feet in front of her was a small boy.

Melissa said, "He was looking at me with a direct and solemn expression. I judged him to be four or five years old, with red hair and a strong little chin. The fact that he seemed to have a blue light around him and that I could 'see through' the edges of his body seemed to be nothing unusual while he stood there. Neither did his yellow Doctor Denton pajamas appear odd, until he literally melted into nothingness a few seconds later. It was then I realized that my little visitor was not of mortal flesh.

"Why had he come? I felt no fear, only a surprising natural-ness at his visitation . . . Relating the event to the shop owner, she told me some rather startling news. Until his death the previous June, the four-year-old red-haired Tommy had been a frequent, chatty visitor at the gift store with his mother and older sister Susie. Since his death, his bereaved parents had desired communication with their child and the confirmation of an afterlife and the power of love over death.

"When I met his parents and described the apparition in detail, I felt rather silly describing the yellow Doctor Denton pajamas . . . When I had finished, there was silence for a minute. Then Tommy's mother said, 'He died in those pajamas. And he came back to us by way of a stranger who would have had no way of knowing him or the details sur-rounding his death.' "

Canon J. B. Phillips, a well-known writer of many books including *The New Testament in Modern English*, may not have needed reinforcement for his faith, but his account of the appearance, twice, of C. S. Lewis, deserves inclusion in this consideration of the survival hypothesis.

The late C. S. Lewis was Professor of Medieval and Ren-aissance English at Cambridge University until his death in 1963. He was a Christian mystic, the brilliant and humorous author of *The Screwtape Letters* and many other books, including science-fiction books for young people.

J. B. Phillips' own account of his experiences appears in his book *Ring of Truth*:

"Let me say that I am incredulous by nature, and as unsuperstitious as they come . . . I laugh . . . when the predictions of celebrated clairvoyants turn out to be false, as they mostly do . . . I mention this because I am not the sort of person who is readily taken in by the fraud and the plausible liar. Experience as Vicar of a parish soon cures you of this if nothing else will! . . . I have had first-hand incontrovertible experience of extra-sensory perception, and a little of precognition. But the experience I want to mention here is relevant to the nature of the Resurrection.

"Many of us who believe in what is technically known as the Communion of Saints must have experienced the sense of nearness, for a fairly short time, of those whom we love soon after they have died. But the late C. S. Lewis, whom I did not know very well, and had only seen in the flesh once, but with whom I had corresponded a fair amount, gave me an unusual experience . . ."

It was while Phillips was watching television that Lewis "'appeared' sitting in a chair within a few feet of me, and spoke a few words which were particularly relevant to the difficult circumstances through which I was passing. He was ruddier in complexion than ever, grinning all over his face and, as the old-fashioned saying has it, positively glowing with health. The interesting thing to me was that I had not been thinking about him at all. I was neither alarmed nor surprised nor . . . did I look up to see the hole in the ceiling that he might have made on arrival. He was just *there*— 'large as life and twice as natural!'

"A week later when I was in bed reading before going to sleep, he appeared again, even more rosily radiant than before, and repeated to me the same message, which was very important to me at the time. I was a little puzzled by this, and I mentioned it to a certain saintly Bishop who was then living in retirement here in Dorset. His reply was, 'my dear J . . ., this sort of thing is happening all the time.'"

Andrew MacKenzie and K. M. Goldney, writing in the *Journal of the Society for Psychical Research* (London), reported that they had questioned Canon Phillips concerning his health at the time. He replied that although the state of his health was excellent, he had been feeling a mental and spiritual depletion for several years. "A sort of greyness of spirit had descended upon me which robbed life of colour and to some extent meaning."

This lends significance to the words which Lewis spoke. On both occasions he used the identical words: "It's not as difficult as you think, you know."

In answer to further questions put by MacKenzie and Goldney, Phillips said, "From a very early age it has never seemed to me that the physical world, which we for the time being inhabit, is anything more than a temporary one . . . Thus, at the time, being fairly familiar with the thoughts and ideas of the personality of C. S. Lewis, it did not seem at all strange to me that he should become physically visible and audible after his death. Indeed it was only afterwards, when relating the occurrence to my wife or one or two trusted friends, that it struck me as 'odd' at all. It would be honest to say that I felt more happy than anything else. For his message seemed to me to bear considerable reassurance. The trials and tribulations of this life were now behind him and from his point of view the emotional strains and stresses from which I was suffering were seen to be transient and relatively unimportant."

In both appearances, Lewis was about four to five feet away, seated, and Phillips says that his attention had been drawn to him much as if his wife had come in quietly and taken a seat near him. He estimated that each appearance lasted no more than a minute and a half. The figure, each time, was dressed in well-worn brown tweeds. "This did not strike me as remarkable at the time until I realised some weeks later that I had never seen him in ordinary clothes. In fact, despite a sporadic correspondence over the years, I had only seen him once before 'in the flesh.' This was on Ascension Day during the war in Southwark Cathedral and he was wearing a black cassock . . . It was several months after his 'appearance' that, in reading one of the several books about him, I learned that it was his habit to wear tweeds that would be comfortable rather than smart . . . The voice was his natural voice . . . His features were the same as I remembered them in life except that any lines of strain or anxiety were lost in what I can only call his grin of joy."

In their discussion of the case, MacKenzie and Goldney commented upon the several features common to apparitional cases: the sudden appearance and disappearance, and the fact that the figure was lifelike, solid, not transparent. They mentioned that it is rare, however, for an apparition to say anything, and particularly worthy of note that the figure appeared a second time and delivered the same message.

MacKenzie, struck with the frequency with which such manifestations appear while the percipient was reading or otherwise concentrating, wrote to Dr. Robert H. Thouless about this, and received this reply: "Your observation of the frequency with which apparitions are seen while reading is an interesting one. It seems to suggest that detachment of attention from the immediate problems of adapting to the external world may be a favourable condition for psi-experience . . . Every new oddity noted is a contribution to the pattern of the psi-phenomena. When we know the total pattern, the explanation of all its parts will become clear."

Phillips knew, of course, that Lewis was dead, which led MacKenzie and Goldney to revive a last-century debate between F. W. H. Myers and Frank Podmore. The latter doubted the evidential value of an apparition of a person already known to be dead. Myers felt otherwise and defended his stand rather tartly. Citing a case where a daughter had seen a vision of her father and received a message from him after she heard of his death, he granted that although it might be *superfluous* for the deceased to inform his daughter that he had died, "he might deem it worthwhile to inform her that he was still living."

According to a Gallup Poll taken in 1968, seventy-three percent of the population of the United States believes in survival. It may follow, therefore, that a great many dying persons have indicated that they glimpse, in the hour of death, something that seems to mean they are about to make the transition to another world.

Dr. Karlis Osis is the director of research for the American Society of Psychical Research. In 1961 he published a monograph, *Deathbed Observations by Physicians and Nurses*, giving the results of a pilot study in which he had questioned five thousand doctors and five thousand nurses.

This area, in which little exploration had been done, not only confirmed earlier indications that apparitions of the deceased very often appear to the dying, but also gave evidence that although death is almost universally feared, a significant number of patients seemed to experience exaltation at the hour of death.

Recently, a new study has been inaugurated by Dr. Osis and repeated in India with the cooperation of Dr. Erlendur Haraldsson. This incorporates the report of seventeen hundred medical personnel about their dying patients. The final evaluation has not been made, but in an interim report published in the *ASPR Newsletter* (Winter, 1975) Osis made two classifications of the visions seen by the dying: the first he calls "Disneyland"—rambling, based on this-world concerns; and the second he calls "mountain" experiences, which seemed to be consistent with the idea of another world.

As an illustration of the latter, he gives an account of a woman tortured by terminal cancer who "saw" her husband, who had predeceased her. In the words of the attending physician: "All of a sudden she opened her eyes . . . She had the most peaceful, nicest smile, just as if she were going to the arms of someone she thought a great deal of. She said, 'Guy, I am coming.' She didn't seem to realize I was there. It was almost as if she were in another world, as if something beautiful had opened up to her . . ."

Realizing that different nations often have different fantasies (the Irish have their leprechauns; the Norwegians, trolls; the Chinese, flying dragons), the decision was made to go to India, where a very different culture prevailed from that in the United States.

It was discovered that death experiences differed from those in the United States in only a minority of cases. In spite of very different religious beliefs, they had characteristics in common which neither the Bible nor the Indian religious literature (Hindu or Moslem) seems to suggest. One characteristic noted was the apparent arrival of deceased relatives who had come to take the dying person away.

Anticipating a possible question as to whether or not this

sort of hallucination was only wish-fulfillment, Osis said he did not think so, because often very strong wishes were evident on the part of the dying to see living persons who were unable to be there and in only a very small fraction of cases was a desired living person hallucinated. He said that "messengers" came just as often to patients who expected to recover as to those who expected to die. "As a matter of fact, we had cases where the patient was so violently opposed to being taken away by the 'visitor' that he screamed for help, asked the doctor to protect or hide him. One young girl implored the nurse to hold her tight so she could not be taken away, and died in that position."

Osis concluded his interim report by saying, "My personal impression, gained from wading through literally thousands of computer print-out pages, is that we have been seeing the 'mountain' not 'Disneyland.'"

J.G.P. COMMENTS:

Many who in the past worked on this issue became personally convinced of the reality of survival. This does not mean, however, that they considered that the evidence was scientifically conclusive, nor do we now. We first have to consider whether the evidence can be explained in terms of the psi abilities of the living, such as the medium who gave the information. If, for example, the information already existed in somebody's mind, the medium might have obtained it by telepathy. Or if it existed in some personal record that was known only to the apparent communicator, the medium could, conceivably, have got it from that source by clairvoyance.

Nevertheless, much of the evidence that has been collected on survival is so striking that it is difficult to explain it in terms of what we have learned about psi in other contexts. If the survival evidence is all due to the psi capacities of the living, then some mediums who think that they are transmitting communications from surviving spirits are capable of demonstrating extraordinary powers of ESP—so extraordinary that it has been dubbed "super-psi." Some parapsychologists go so far as to say that we should abandon all scientific effort on the survival problem unless we can rule out the super-psi hypothesis.

It seems to me that there is another choice open to us, one that is to be preferred because it offers a better prospect of achieving a significant advance in scientific knowledge. *Research effort should be increased when we are confronted with an "either/or" situation, and we should actually favor the more novel explanation, in this case the possibility of survival, during the evidence-gathering stage of the research.* If as a consequence, the novel explanation should eventually prove to be the correct one, science would have benefited through our venturesomeness.

I remain highly skeptical regarding the claims that messages from surviving personalities have been recorded on tape. Mrs. Hintze has already sufficiently exposed some of the difficulties that complicate the survivalist interpretation of the findings turned up by this method. Other problems are also inherent in this method that the proponents have not clearly recognized.

One is the lack of relevant personal details in the supposed communications. There is nothing on the tapes comparable to the kind of detailed personal information obtained through the best of the mediumistic sittings and which the communicators gave to support their claims of survival beyond death. The statements on the tapes, on the other hand, are so cryptic that they provide little, if any, evidence of personal identity.

Another problem is the failure (particularly in the work of Raudive) to verify that the sounds on the tapes are really the words that he has personally taken them to be. This would require that different persons listen to the same recordings and indicate what they hear—each doing so without knowing what others hear. Instead of working in this way, Raudive begins a "test" by carefully instructing the listeners in advance regarding what they are supposed to hear (which means that he has already decided what the message is). This difficulty exists for those cases when the recording is very faint and difficult to interpret, which is the situation for most of them.

Occasionally, we are told, the words are unmistakable. In those instances we have the questions: Where did they come from? How did they get on the tape? The danger of picking up snatches of ordinary radio broadcasts is one that must be taken into account and clearly excluded before we could conclude that we have recorded the voices of the dead. Also, the possibility that words are somehow put on the tape by PK (mind over matter) from the living—Dr. Bender's preferred explanation—is a real alternative. It has become more attractive for me since I discovered in the recent poltergeist case described previously that faint tappings, low rhythmic knocks, and grunting sounds that were not heard in the room were nevertheless picked up on the tape. We attributed these sounds to the unconscious PK influence of the central person in the case, a ten-year-old girl who had reached puberty before she was nine. The recording of those inaudible sounds makes it easier for me to consider that inaudible *words* can also occasionally be put on tape by PK from the living.

I suggest that the future of this whole approach might be made more clear if tapings are first taken from the living. Let it be some standard test phrase, such as "Mary had a little lamb, Its fleece was white as snow." Then when one of these persons later wishes to prove that he has survived death, the message should be only his name, plus "Mary had a little lamb, Its fleece was white as snow." The evidence of survival would rest upon comparing the voice prints of the "before" and "after" recordings. If they matched, this could well go far toward providing the super-psi-proof evidence that the two samples are from the same person, one made before the death of the body and the other after that event. This result, I feel, would be strong evidence for survival.

In making studies of mediums to explore the possibility of survival, investigators tried to take nothing for granted. The fact that the medium in trance was apparently under the guidance of some controlling personality was not accepted uncritically as literally true. Rather, the controls were considered to be only imaginary personalities which were dramatic creations of the mediums.

Several of the investigators who had taken a leading part in the survival research died around the turn of the century. Following their deaths, they apparently began to play an active role as participants in the research from the other side. They themselves became frequent communicators in the research and sometimes even became the principal controls, displacing those who had seemed to be entrenched in that role before they died.

Dr. Hodgson had moved from London to Boston in 1887, where he devoted most of his time to the investigations of Mrs. Piper until his death in December 1905. In February 1906 William James wrote to his friend Théodore Flournoy in Switzerland about the sudden death of Hodgson and stated his opinion that all aspects of Mrs. Piper's mediumship had been fully explored. Yet in July 1906, just six months later, he wrote that a great deal of automatic writing was now coming through Mrs. Piper that seemed to originate from Hodgson and that he (James) had agreed to organize the material and report it. The task grew as the material continued to accumulate, and the report of more than a hundred pages was finally published in 1909, just a year before James's death.

A new and striking stage of survival evidence was reached in Britain during the first two decades of this century. This was in the form of literary puzzles that were based upon a detailed knowledge of Classical Greece, which had been Frederic Myers' special field of academic study. Following Myers' death in 1901, a few of the members of the Society for Psychical Research had attempted deliberately and successfully to receive "messages" through automatic writing. When they appeared to be receiving worthwhile material, they started to send it to key persons in the SPR for safekeeping and analysis. The examination of these records from several automatists quite unexpectedly revealed that the records received by different automatists, separated as widely as India, Britain, and America, were hinting at common classical themes, but doing so in such a way that it was possible to tell what was being communicated only when the separate pieces of the puzzle were assembled from the different records. Furthermore, the communications made it clear that this was an experiment planned from the other side, one intended to make it more difficult to attribute the communications to the psi capacities of the automatists.

This material was quite complex, and only those few investigators who were sufficiently well informed about the literature and culture of Classical Greece were qualified to appreciate it at first hand. But these difficulties were also the strengths of this special evidence, because the nature of the information made it that much more difficult to suppose that pieces of the puzzle could have been assembled by the ESP powers of persons of ordinary educational talents, such as Mrs. Piper.

It would be a mistake to consider that the strictly mediumistic material stands alone as evidence relevant to the survival question. To it must be added the evidence from everyday life covering such psychic experiences as apparitions of dying persons or of those who had recently died when the persons seeing the lifelike visions had not yet learned of the death. Also, there are cases on record, thoroughly investigated, in which a dreamer received a particular message that seemed to come from the spirit of a deceased person, bringing information that the apparent communicator would have wished to convey. Also relevant here are haunting cases in which an influence appears to be associated with a particular location, such as the events related earlier in the book about Oakland Farm. Such experiences do not prove survival, but they are a part of the complex pattern making up the woven fabric of evidence relevant to the issue.

We can see more clearly now, also, the relevance to survival of the experiences of separation of the center of consciousness from the physical body. While it is true that the lines of research, as discussed earlier, on altered states of consciousness have not yet reached the point of conclusiveness, they have made a start, and we may reasonably hope for further findings that will advance such investigations to the point for a decision.

The research by Osis and Haraldsson on the deathbed

observations of physicians and nurses is a novel approach—
one that is a welcome addition to the methods of studying
the survival question. Their work is a good illustration of
how scattered claims from real-life situations can be turned
to advantage by ingenious research methods.

In another direction, following a method published by Ian
Stevenson, I have set the combination of a lock, and it can be
opened only by twisting the dial to match three two-digit
numbers. I chose the combination by taking an arbitrary
starting point in a table of random numbers and then reading off the first six digits. Afterward I made up a six-word
sentence in which the initial letters of the six words, decoded
according to the procedure published in the Stevenson paper,
correspond to the six digits. Then I set the combination on
my lock using the three two-digit numbers and conforming
with the secret sentence, a device used solely as an indirect
aid in remembering the combination.

All of this procedure was carried out entirely in my head,
so there was not at any time any written record or any
spoken description of any of the steps that might be used as
a target for clairvoyance. Nor shall I ever permit myself to
make a record while I am living that could make my combination available after my death through the ESP abilities of
a medium or anyone else who may successfully get the six-
word sentence (or the combination directly) that opens my
lock.

During the four years that have passed since I prepared
the test, I have annually closed myself in my office and
have taken out the lock and proved, by silently opening the
lock, that I still recall my memory device. Now I am ready to
have anyone try to learn my secret by telepathy while I am
alive. Anyone is welcome to try, but I will not promise to
help. In fact, I intend to see that all such efforts fail while I
am living, if I can do so.

In the event that I find myself surviving death, I intend to
communicate the sentence that will open my lock. If I succeed, that will be evidence that I have survived. By itself it
will not be conclusive proof of survival, but if such evidence
can be obtained from a number of persons who have died, it
could become strong support of the survival hypothesis.

Already a number of people have set locks. As we die, failure to receive the necessary communications to open any of the locks will not disprove survival. We simply do not know whether the nature of an afterlife makes it possible to carry over into that existence a simple secret memory and to act successfully on the strong resolve to make it known to those still living on earth. Even if the intention to communicate is still clear after death, success of this test will depend upon whether a suitable medium or other channel of communication can be found. My thought is to try first making contact through the Icelandic medium Hafsteinn, if he is still living. If that channel is closed for any reason, I will seek another; or even, for safety's sake, two or more.

The idea of leaving behind some kind of sealed or coded message is not new, since some of the early investigators, including Sir Oliver Lodge, did this. But the method favored in those early days was to prepare a secret sealed package in the hope that the contents could be accurately described through a medium after the preparer's death. But when a message that seemed reasonable had been received, the only way of checking on its accuracy was to open the package. The act of checking-up put an end to the test, regardless of whether the message was right or wrong. So far, the sealed-message tests have all failed, and even if such a test should succeed, the results could be easily explained by clairvoyance by the medium.

Dr. Robert Thouless was the first investigator to recognize the importance of finding a method which would not involve destroying the test in order to check up on the accuracy of a single trial. He published in 1948 a literary passage with its meaning concealed in a code that could not be broken without the use of a verbal key that only he knows. He also has challenged persons in contact with good mediums to try to get the key from his mind while he is living. If they do not succeed, it is his intention to try to reveal the key after his death as evidence that he has survived, and the proof of success will lie in the fact that it will then be possible to translate into plain English the coded passage he has already published.

I welcome also the test proposed by Dr. Schmeidler, as

described by Mrs. Hintze, in which persons are tested to register their individual personality characteristics. If one of those persons claimed to be communicating through a medium after death, the same tests would be given again and the two sets of results compared to see if they could only have come from the same person.

MEMORIES OF ANOTHER LIFE

*"Reincarnation, to most Europeans and Americans . . .
is regarded, if it is thought of at all, as a fantasy of the
Oriental mind, to which in our country a motley crew
of frustrated elderly women, dim-witted cultists, gullible
Theosophists, and generally unintelligent crackpots have been
attracted, like so many pathetic moths to an illusory
flame . . . But to the materialistic thinker . . . a 'soul' is a
ridiculous notion and even its survival after death, much
less its evolution through repeated earth-experiences, quite
unthinkable."—Gina Cerminara, Ph.D.,* The World Within
(1957)

In a paper written for the 1968 annual convention of the
Parapsychological Association in West Germany, Ian Stevenson said, "Belief in reincarnation is accepted (in some
cultures) as axiomatic. Some of my informants express
astonishment or amusement that money should be spent in
the investigation of something so obviously true."

Reincarnation is by no means accepted as obviously true in
the Western world, but investigation suggests there may be
as many children in our culture as in any other who when
very young make statements which indicate they may be
remembering a previous life.

Such statements usually are not taken very seriously. A
friend says she has been told that when she was about three
she frequently made such comments as, "When I was old—
when I was eighty, before I was born . . ." She has no recollection of this, and since her mildly puzzled parents never
pressed their little girl for an explanation, whatever memories she may have had were never explored.

According to Ian Stevenson, parents in India are much
more apt to take such statements seriously, but many of them,
although believing in reincarnation, fear that such children

do not live long. Consequently, they feel that such "memories" should be forgotten, and the sooner the better.

One of the cases which Stevenson investigated over a period of several years was that of Bishen Chand Ghulam, born in 1921 into the family of B. Ram Ghulam, a poor government clerk in the city of Bareilly, India. Apparently he was a much-desired child, for the mother had gone to a temple to pray for another son before his conception. By the time he was ten months old, the family noticed something that puzzled them: instead of confining his utterances to simple, babyish syllables, the little boy was trying to say "Pilibhit."

There was a town of that name, but it was about fifty kilometers away and the family knew no one there. He began to ask definite questions about the town when he was about a year and a half old: How far was it? When would his father take him there? It became obvious that he believed he had had a previous life there.

Distressed though the family may have been, they did listen. As time went on, he was talking incessantly of his former life in a city he had never visited.

Bishen Chand was four years old when his father took him by train to a wedding at a town beyond Pilibhit. On the way back home the little boy heard the name of the station Pilibhit announced. Excitedly, he demanded to get off the train, saying this was where he used to live. Quite naturally, his father refused, and the child cried on the way back to Bareilly.

By the summer of 1926, when he was five and a half, his memories of a previous life seemed clear and explicit. He said his name had been Laxmi Narain, and that his father had been a wealthy landowner. He also described a man as "Uncle" Har Narain. Later it was found that Har Narain actually had been Laxmi Narain's father, but since a Bareilly neighbor of that name was known to the little boy as "Uncle" Har Narain, the coupling of "Uncle" to the name was perhaps only natural.

He described the house in which he lived, saying it had a shrine room and separate quarters for the women. Often they had enjoyed the singing and dancing of nautch girls, professional performers who not infrequently double as prostitutes. Similar parties had been held at the home of a neighbor, Sunder Lal, who lived in a "house with a green gate."

His contempt for the conditions under which he now had to live were expressed freely and often. "Even my servant would not eat the food cooked in this house!" When his demands for meat and fish, prohibited by his family's caste, were not met, he sometimes satisfied his cravings at the homes of neighbors.

He tore his cotton clothes off when they were put on him and demanded that he be dressed in silk, saying that the cotton clothes were not fit to be given to his servants. In his lofty way, he told his father to give him money, and cried when his poor father would not give it to him.

Once when his father mentioned that he was thinking of buying a watch, little Bishen Chand said, "Papa, don't buy. When I go to Pilibhit, I shall get you three watches from a Muslim watch dealer whom I established there." He even gave the name of the dealer.

His sister Kamla, older by thirteen years, said he talked about his former life every day during these years of early childhood. Alcohol was forbidden by the caste to which the family belonged, but they kept some in the house for medicinal purposes. When the dwindling supply was noted, Kamla caught Bishen Chand drinking brandy. With his customary arrogance, the child informed her that he was used to drinking.

Dr. Stevenson puts it mildly when he says it must have been a bore for the family to put up with all this.

Before he was five and a half, the boy said to his father, "Why don't you keep a mistress? You will have great pleasure from her." One can imagine the consternation of this poor father, barely able to support one wife and three children, but with his usual patience he asked, "What pleasures, my boy?" The youngster told his father, "You will enjoy the fragrance of her hair and feel much joy from her company."

Since the fantasy life of even a very precocious little boy could hardly be expected to include the idea of a mistress, Dr. Stevenson made a recheck of the notes which had been made about this by Professor Pal, a former magistrate and professor of a college in Bengal, and it seemed certain that the use of the words indicated that he understood very well the difference between a mistress and a wife.

It is not clear whether he spoke now or a little later of having had a mistress himself in his former life. Her name was Padma. She was a prostitute, but he seemed to have considered her his exclusive property, for he told his family proudly of having killed another man he once saw coming from her apartment.

Along about now the story of his obsessions with memories of another life came to the attention of K. K. N. Sahay, a lawyer in Bareilly. He went to Bishen Chand's home, made a record of the astonishing things the lad was saying, and then arranged to take him, together with his father and older brother, to Pilibhit.

It is not hard to believe that a crowd soon collected, for crowds collect in India for any unusual event. Not quite eight years had elapsed since the death of Laxmi Narain, whom this little boy was claiming to have been in his former life. Nearly everyone in the town must have known of the wealthy family and the profligate son who had been involved with the prostitute Padma, still living there, and of how, in a fit of jealous rage, Laxmi Narain had turned to the servant who accompanied him, seized the gun he was carrying, and shot the rival lover dead.

Although the young murderer himself had died from natural causes a few months after the killing, justice had hardly been served, for the family's influence had enabled the charges to be suppressed.

It is known that the crowd following the boy included the superintendent of police, who said, perhaps trying to catch Bishen Chand in an error, "Now tell us about your wife and children—" to which the boy replied, "I had none. I was steeped in wine and women and never thought of marrying."

He did make two errors: He said that as Laxmi Narain he had been twenty years old when he died, instead of giving the correct age, which was thirty-two. He was also wrong about the part of town in which he claimed to have lived.

It seemed also that he might be wrong when he was taken

to the government school which he said he had attended, but now did not recognize. However, this was the newly built school, and later when he was taken to the old school (now with the headmaster in tow) he ran up the stairs to where his classroom had been. Somebody produced an old picture, and he recognized in it the face of one of Laxmi Narain's classmates who happened to be in the crowd. When the classmates asked him about the teacher, he correctly described him as a fat, bearded man.

In the part of town where Laxmi Narain had lived, Bishen Chand recognized the house of Sunder Lal, which he had previously described as having a green gate. The lawyer Sahay, writing the report later for the national newspaper *The Leader* in August 1926, said, "I saw the gate myself. It had a green varnish which had grown faint by lapse of time." The lad also pointed to the courtyard where he said the nautch girls used to entertain with singing and dancing. Shopkeepers in the neighborhood agreed that this was true.

But what of the home that the child had described so glowingly? Once almost palatial, it had fallen into ruins, and when he saw it he burst into tears and said, "Nobody cared even to repair my house after my death." For all his precocity, the child didn't seem to realize that the reckless generosity and self-indulgent spending of Laxmi Narain had been largely responsible for reducing the family to destitution.

He designated the shrine room and the place where the women's apartments had been. Pointing to what was now only a pile of bricks and mud, he said that this had once been a staircase. Although Bishen Chand's family did not know Urdu, they were aware that the boy seemed to have a knowledge of the language. And at this time he used the Urdu word for the women's apartments, and also the one for lock.

The sole male survivor of the family brought an old picture of Har Narain and his son, and the boy put his finger on the picture and said, "Here is Har Narain, and here I."

In the accounts published by *The Leader*, lawyer Sahay wrote: "The name of the prostitute with whom the boy associated in his previous life was repeatedly asked by . . .

people [in the crowd]. He reluctantly mentioned the name 'Padma,' which the people certified as correct."

Sometime during this remarkable day, the boy was presented with a set of tablas, or drums. The father said he had never seen the tablas before, but to the astonishment of his family he played them skillfully. Dr. Stevenson makes the point that playing well on the tablas requires training and practice, and does not consist merely of tapping on a drum.

It is not quite clear just when Bishen Chand first met the mother of Laxmi Narain, but a strong attachment was immediately apparent between them. Bishen Chand answered the questions she asked, including significant details about boyhood incidents such as the time in the previous life when he had thrown out her pickles. He named Laxmi Narain's personal servant correctly, describing him as having been black and short, and also gave the caste to which the servant had belonged.

The mother later spent some time with Bishen Chand's family, and he frequently visited her. At one time the boy urged his father to let her come to live with them. His sister and brother said that he preferred her to his own mother, and later he confirmed this himself.

Laxmi Narain's father was thought to have hidden some treasure before his death, but nobody knew where. When Bishen Chand was asked where the treasure was, he led the way to a room of the ruined mansion. The child's claims for his previous life gained additional credence when the treasure, consisting of gold coins, was found here later.

This child with his strange store of memories was also to meet the other woman who had been important in the life of Laxmi Narain. While he was still very young, Padma came to see him with her younger sister. The sister was about the same age as Padma had been at the time of her former lover's strong attachment for her, and it was to this sister that the little boy went, climbing upon her lap. Although Padma was only in her mid-thirties then, she is reported to have said, "You are a small child, but I have grown old."

Much later, when Bishen Chand was twenty-three, Padma came back into his life briefly. He was then working in another town at the Central Excise Office and Padma happened to be living in a nearby village. When she came into the office one day with some other women, Bishen Chand recognized her.

Apparently she did not make herself known to him, and perhaps had not even known he was there. When he asked, "Are you Padma?" she said, "Yes." He embraced her, but was so overcome by emotion that he fainted.

To Dr. Stevenson, Bishen Chand admitted later the intensity of his newly aroused affection, and told him that that evening he went out to her home with a bottle of wine. But Padma, much older and obviously wiser, discouraged any ideas he may have had of continuing the relationship that she had had so many years before with Laxmi Narain. She told him, "I am an old woman, like your mother. Please go away. You lost everything in your previous life. Now you want to lose everything again."

So she broke the bottle of wine and sent him away. The next year she died, and during the following year Bishen Chand married a girl with whom he has lived with apparent faithfulness and happiness ever since.

Bishen Chand is now middle-aged. When Stevenson talked with him in 1969 and again in 1971, he said that the only thing he still remembers of his life as Laxmi Narain is the killing of Padma's lover. This still persists with vivid clarity.

Memories of that other life had begun to fade by the time he was seven. Personality traits, such as his arrogance and hot temper, also changed as the different circumstances of his life asserted themselves. Gradually he resigned himself to accept the humble life into which he was born. And yet even now he remembers somewhat wistfully that the freedom provided by wealth in that previous life gave him more happiness.

Of the hundreds of cases he has studied, Ian Stevenson considers this to be one of the most interesting. It is of particular value to the scientific literature in the field because an early record was made by a highly regarded lawyer when the child was very young and when many of the principals in the case were still alive. Nearly all of the statements made by the child before going to Pilibhit were verified. Certainly the family had nothing to gain by trying to establish a link with a family whose fortune had been dissipated.

Stevenson sums up the case by saying, "I cannot imagine any motive his parents could have had for promoting the sort of attitudes that Bishen Chand showed as a child. Or can someone seriously suppose that the father wanted to hear his son boasting of a murder he had committed, and deriding his family for their poverty?"

J.G.P. COMMENTS:

In 1960 Ian Stevenson published a forty-three-page essay with the title "The Evidence for Survival from Claimed Memories of Former Incarnations." This was, in its first part, a survey of cases then available in the literature in which claimed memories of an earlier life contained information beyond the limits of knowledge acquired in normal ways. A total of forty-four apparently paranormal cases were found.

A second part of the essay discussed the possible ways in which such evidence might be interpreted, including fraud, memories acquired normally but with the source being subsequently forgotten, racial memory, ESP of facts that are mistaken for memories, retrocognition (ESP of past events), precognition of facts brought to light during subsequent efforts at "verification," possession, and reincarnation. The writer expressed the opinion that the reincarnation hypothesis best covered the facts, and he concluded his essay with the following paragraph.

"The evidence I have assembled and reviewed here does not warrant any firm conclusion about reincarnation. But it does justify, I believe, a much more extensive and more sympathetic study of this hypothesis than it has hitherto received in the West. Further investigation of apparent memories of former incarnations may well establish reincarnation as the most probable explanation of these experiences. Along this line we may in the end obtain more convincing evidence of human survival of physical death than from other kinds of evidence. In mediumistic communications we have the problem of proving that someone clearly dead still lives. In evaluating apparent memories of former incarnations, the problem consists in judging whether someone clearly living once died. This may prove the easier task and, if pursued with sufficient zeal and success, may contribute decisively to the question of survival."

This essay was read by Mrs. Eileen Garrett, president of the Parapsychology Foundation, who provided Dr. Stevenson with a grant to go to India to study some of the cases covered in this survey as well as new cases.

The field research was successful beyond all expectations. The first trip in 1961 was followed up by others, made possible through the generous support of another donor, and by 1966 a book, which was to become a classic, was published presenting the first harvest of thoroughly investigated cases, most of them brought to light for the first time by Stevenson. This book had the title *Twenty Cases Suggestive of Reincarnation*, and it presented cases from India, Ceylon, Lebanon, Brazil, and Alaska. Since the book's publication, Dr. Stevenson has made numerous further field trips to those parts of the world where the cases are most plentiful.

As of July 1974 the files on reincarnation cases in the University of Virginia Division of Parapsychology contained a total of 1339 distinct instances of persons claiming such memories that had been reported directly to the investigator or to his associates in the field or reported through correspondence. Only a small number of these cases has been thoroughly investigated. Dr. Stevenson scrupulously collects all of the memories expressed by the "present personality" and uses the information these contain to check with the family of the "previous personality" and verify the degree to which the memories were correct.

Evidence is increasing that these cases are more numerous in the West than is commonly supposed. Of the 1339 certified cases on file, the United States has the most, with 324 cases (not counting Indian and Eskimo), and the next five countries in descending order are Burma (139 cases), India (135), Turkey (114), and Great Britain (111). These figures should not be taken, however, as giving the relative density of cases in the various countries, since the conditions that influence whether or not existing cases will be reported to the investigator vary widely from one part of the world to another. However, they do seem to indicate that this phenomenon is not purely an Eastern one.

A special feature of Dr. Stevenson's work, which greatly strengthens the rebirth hypothesis, lies in the birthmark cases. These are instances in which the children who have the memories of a former life exhibit striking birthmarks that resemble the scars of healed wounds. Among the memories given by the children in these cases are those covering the circumstances of a violent death that ended their previous life. They describe, for example, being shot in particular parts of their body, and these remembered wounds correspond in location to the scarlike birthmarks on the body of the child. Dr. Stevenson has in several instances been able, after the previous family has been identified and located, to find the medical records covering the death of the previous personality and has confirmed that the location of the wounds did indeed correspond with the child's memories as well as with the locations of the birthmarks.

In 1972, at the Edinburgh convention of the Parapsychological Association, Dr. Stevenson presented an imaginary "perfect" case of reincarnation which would be the most convincing evidence for survival. He said, "The subject was a boy born in a village of France who had several distinct birthmarks. When he began to speak he indicated that in his previous life [in Ceylon] he had been shot and killed with bullets hitting him at the sites of these birthmarks."

The speaker went on to detail how this hypothetical boy would have the memories of a dead person, his skills and personality traits, and knowledge of his language. If these details could be exactly verified, Dr. Stevenson asked, "Would not the interpretation that this deceased man had, in fact, been reborn seem more probable than any other interpretation of the case?"

Undetected fraud is, of course, a conceivable possibility, but it seems to me extremely unlikely as the explanation of all the reported cases, or even a small proportion of them. In a number of instances the parents objected strongly to the child's memories of another life. Often the special demands placed upon the family caused great inconvenience.

The ESP interpretation of the cases also encounters a number of difficulties. The children with memories about an earlier life do not, as a rule, show any signs of being generally gifted with ESP ability. If their "memories" are really only disguised ESP, why should it be exhibited in such a specialized, narrow way? These children would, in any event, have to be credited with super-psi in order to acquire such a large number of correct details about the life, relatives, and circumstances of a particular dead person. ESP, even of this special and peculiar kind, could not account for the existence of special skills without practice, and the birthmark evidence is clearly beyond the scope of ESP.

Dr. Stevenson does not hesitate to say that the reincarnation hypothesis, in his opinion, fits the facts better than any variant of the ESP hypothesis. I find that I must agree. But he goes on to say that the present facts do not conclusively establish reincarnation. Rather, he says, they show that the cases present a challenge and an opportunity for scientific investigation that is eminently worth pursuing. Again, I fully agree.

Dr. Stevenson's research on reincarnation cases deserves, I feel, the place of distinction at the end of the book that we have given it. It is work still very much in progress, which I think is the normal state for research. Like Dr. Stevenson, I do not say that the findings prove reincarnation. But I emphatically say that this could well be the ultimate outcome of the new field of research that he has, almost single-handedly, opened up. And if we can all put aside our Western prejudices for a time, we might all agree that the concept of the "spirit" of a human being, often of someone who died early in life from acts of violence, being able to take up a new abode in an infant human body is one that will, if fully established and generally accepted, profoundly affect our outlook on life.

BIBLIOGRAPHY

I. By Extrasensory Means: Can Mr. A Communicate with Mr. B?

Heywood, R. *Beyond the Reach of Sense.* New York: Dutton, 1961.

McMahan, E. A. "An Experiment in Pure Telepathy." *Journal of Parapsychology*, 1946, Vol. 10, pp. 224–242.

Moss, T., and Gengerelli, J. A. "Telepathy and Emotional Stimuli: A Controlled Experiment." *Journal of Abnormal Psychology*, 1967, Vol. 72, pp. 341–348.

Palmer, J., and Dennis, M. "A Community Mail Survey of Psychic Experiences." In: J. Morris (Ed.), *Research in Parapsychology 1974.* Metuchen, N.J.: Scarecrow Press, 1975. (Abstract)

Soal, S. G., and Bateman, F. *Modern Experiments in Telepathy.* New Haven: Yale University Press, 1954.

Stevenson, I. "The Substantiality of Spontaneous Cases." In: W. G. Roll (Ed.), *Proceedings of the Parapsychological Association*, 1968, No. 5, pp. 91–128.

Stevenson, I. *Telepathic Impressions: A Review and Report of Thirty-five New Cases.* Charlottesville: University Press of Virginia, 1970.

Targ, R., and Puthoff, H. "Information Transmission Under Conditions of Sensory Shielding." *Nature*, 1974, Vol. 251, pp. 602–607.

Ullman, M., Krippner, S., and Vaughan, A. *Dream Telepathy.* New York: Macmillan, 1973.

White, R. A., and Dale, L. A. *Parapsychology: Sources of Information.* Metuchen, N.J.: Scarecrow Press, 1973.

II. $X+Y=Z$

Mitchell, C. W. *X + Y = Z, or The Sleeping Preacher.* New York: W. C. Smith, 1876.

Morris, R. L., Roll, W. G., Klein, J., and Wheeler, G. "EEG Patterns and ESP Results in Forced-Choice Experiments with Lalsingh Harribance." *Journal of the American Society for Psychical Research*, 1972, Vol. 66, pp. 253–268.

Myers, F. W. H. *Human Personality and Its Survival of Bodily Death*. London: Longmans, Green, 1903.

Pratt, J. G. *A Decade of Research with a Selected ESP Subject: An Overview and Reappraisal of the Work with Pavel Stepanek*. Proceedings of the American Society for Psychical Research, 1973, Vol. 30.

Prince, W. F. *Two Old Cases Reviewed*. Bulletin XI, Boston Society for Psychic Research, 1929.

Schmidt, H. "Clairvoyance Tests with a Machine." *Journal of Parapsychology*, 1969, Vol. 33, pp. 300–306.

III. Precognition: A Few New Instances

Ashby, R. H. *Quarterly Journal of Spiritual Frontiers Fellowship*, Spring, 1972.

Kelly, E. F., and Kanthamani, B. K. "A Subject's Efforts Toward Voluntary Control." *Journal of Parapsychology*, 1972, Vol. 36, pp. 185–197.

Krippner, S., Honorton, C., and Ullman, M. "A Second Precognitive Dream Study with Malcolm Bessent." *Journal of the American Society for Psychical Research*, 1972, Vol. 66, pp. 269–279.

Pratt, J. G. *Parapsychology: An Insider's View of ESP*. New York: Dutton, 1966.

Roll, W. G. "The Problem of Precognition." *Journal of the Society for Psychical Research*, 1961, Vol. 41, pp. 115–128.

Saltmarsh, H. F. "Report on Cases of Apparent Precognition." *Proceedings of the Society for Psychical Research*, 1934, Vol. 42, pp. 49–103.

Schmidt, H. "Precognition of a Quantum Process." *Journal of Parapsychology*, 1969, Vol. 33, pp. 99–108.

IV. Testing: Do You Have ESP?

Heywood, R. *ESP: A Personal Memoir*. New York: Dutton, 1964.

McConnell, R. A. *ESP Curriculum Guide*. New York: Simon and Schuster, 1971.

Rhine, J. B., and Pratt, J. G. *Parapsychology: Frontier Science of the Mind.* Springfield, Ill.: Thomas, 1974. (Fifth Printing)

Stanford, R., and Palmer, J. "EEG Alpha Rhythms and Free Response ESP Performance." In: W. G. Roll, R. L. Morris, and J. Morris (Eds.), *Research in Parapsychology 1973.* Metuchen, N.J.: Scarecrow Press, 1974. (Abstract)

Thouless, R. H. *From Anecodote to Experiment in Psychical Research.* London: Routledge & Kegan Paul, 1972.

V. ESP in Animals

Morris, R. L. "Psi and Animal Behavior: A Survey." *Journal of the American Society for Psychical Research,* 1970, Vol. 64, pp. 242–260.

Parkes, A. S. "General Discussion." In: G. E. W. Wolstenholme and E. C. P. Millar (Eds.), *Extrasensory Perception: A Ciba Foundation Symposium.* New York: Citadel, 1956.

Pratt, J. G. "Testing for an ESP Factor in Pigeon Homing." In: G. E. W. Wolstenholme and E. C. P. Millar (Eds.) (Preceding citation)

Pratt, J. G. (As cited for chapter III)

Rhine, J. B., and Feather, S. R. "The Study of Cases of 'Psi-Trailing' in Animals." *Journal of Parapsychology,* 1962, Vol. 26, pp. 1–22.

Rhine, J. B., and Rhine, L. E. "An Investigation of a 'Mind-Reading' Horse." *Journal of Abnormal and Social Psycology,* 1929, Vol. 23, pp. 449–466.

Rhine, J. B., and Rhine, L. E. "Second Report of Lady, the 'Mind-Reading' Horse." *Journal of Abnormal and Social Psychology,* 1929, Vol. 24, pp. 287–292.

Warren, K. "Wonder Mare Is Hopeful of Better Times in 1932." *Richmond News-Leader,* January 2, 1932.

VI. Altered States of Consciousness

Braud, W. G., and Braud, L. W. "Preliminary Explorations of Psi-Conducive States: Progressive Muscular Relaxation." *Journal of the American Society for Psychical Research,* 1973, Vol. 67, pp. 26–46.

Cousteau, J. J. *Life and Death in a Coral Sea.* Garden City, N.Y.: Doubleday, 1971.

Heywood, R. (As cited for chapter IV)

Honorton, C. "ESP and Altered States of Consciousness." In: J. Beloff (Ed.), *New Directions in Parapsychology*. London: Elek Science, 1974.

Honorton, C., Drucker, S. A., and Hermon, H. C. "Shifts in Subjective State and ESP Under Conditions of Partial Sensory Deprivation: A Preliminary Study." *Journal of the American Society for Psychical Research*, 1973, Vol. 67, pp. 191–196.

James, W. *The Varieties of Religious Experience*. New York: Modern Library, 1929. (Originally published in 1902)

Palmer, J., and Vassar, C. "ESP and Out-of-the-Body Experiences: An Exploratory Study." *Journal of the American Society for Psychical Research*, 1974, Vol. 68, pp. 257–280.

Stanford, R. G., and Lovin, C. "EEG Alpha Activity and ESP Performance." *Journal of the American Society for Psychical Research*, 1970, Vol. 64, pp. 374–384.

Tart, C. T. "A Physiological Study of Out-of-the-Body Experiences in a Selected Subject." *Journal of the American Society for Psychical Research*, 1968, Vol. 62, pp. 3–27.

SPECIAL NOTE: For other leads on lines of research discussed in this chapter, consult the index of the annual scientific publication of the Parapsychological Association, *Research in Parapsychology*, published by Scarecrow Press, Metuchen, N.J.

VII. The Aberrant Creatures of Oakland Farm

Eisenbud, J. *The World of Ted Serios*. New York: Morrow, 1967.

MacKenzie, A. *Apparitions and Ghosts*. London: Barker, 1971.

Maher, M., and Schmeidler, G. R. "Confirmation of a Family's Report of an Apparition." In: J. Morris (Ed.), *Research in Parapsychology 1974*. Metuchen, N.J.: Scarecrow Press, 1975. (Abstract)

Moss, T., and Schmeidler, G. R. "Quantitative Investigation of a 'Haunted House' with Sensitives and a Control Group." *Journal of the American Society for Psychical Research*, 1968, Vol. 62, pp. 399–410.

Schmeidler, G. R. "Quantitative Investigation of a 'Haunted House.'" *Journal of the American Society for Psychical Research*, 1966, Vol. 60, pp. 137–149.

Tyrrell, G. N. M. *Apparitions*. New York: Macmillan, 1962 (paperback). (Originally published in 1942)

VIII. Poltergeist: The Racketing Ghost

Bender, H. "Modern Poltergeist Research—A Plea for an Unprejudiced Approach." In: J. Beloff (Ed.) (As cited under Honorton for chapter VI)

Glanville, J. *The Full and Plain Evidence Concerning Witches and Apparitions*. London: Collins, 1681.

Owen, A. R. G. *Can We Explain the Poltergeist?* New York: Garrett Publications, 1964.

Pratt, J. G. *ESP Research Today: A Study of Developments in Parapsychology Since 1960*. Metuchen, N.J.: Scarecrow Press, 1973.

Pratt, J. G., and Roll, W. G. "The Seaford Disturbances." *Journal of Parapsychology*, 1958, Vol. 22, pp. 79–124.

Roll, W. G. *The Poltergeist*. New York: Nelson Doubleday, 1972; New American Library, 1973 (paperback).

Roll, W. G., and Pratt, J. G. "The Miami Disturbances." *Journal of the American Society for Psychical Research*, 1971, Vol. 65, pp. 409–454.

IX. Kulagina

Herbert, B. "Kulagina Cine Films: Summary." *Journal of Paraphysics*, 1970, Vol. 4, pp. 160–165.

Keil, H. H. J., and Fahler, J. "A Strong Case for PK Involving Directly Observable Movements of Objects Recorded on Cine Film." In: J. Morris (Ed.), *Research in Parapsychology 1974*. Metuchen, N.J.: Scarecrow Press, 1975. (Abstract)

Keil, H. H. J., Herbert, B., Pratt, J. G., and Ullman, M. *Directly Observable Voluntary PK Effects: A Survey and Tentative Interpretation of Available Findings from Nina Kulagina and Other Known Related Cases of Recent Date*. Proceedings of the Society for Psychical Research, 1975, in press.

Pratt, J. G., and Keil, H. H. J. "Firsthand Observations of Nina S. Kulagina Suggestive of PK Upon Static Objects." *Journal of the American Society for Psychical Research*, 1973, Vol. 67, pp. 381–390.

Rhine, L. E. *Mind over Matter: Psychokinesis*. New York: Macmillan, 1970.

Van Dine, A. "Minutes From Nope." *Saturday Review*, June 3, 1972.

X. The Miracle Healers

Barry, J. "General and Comparative Study of the Psychokinetic Effect on a Fungus Culture." *Journal of Parapsychology*, 1968, Vol. 32, pp. 237–243.

Grad, B. "Some Biological Effects of the 'Laying on of Hands': A Review of Experiments with Animals and Plants." *Journal of the American Society for Psychical Research*, 1965, Vol. 59, pp. 95–129.

Haraldsson, E., and Thorsteinsson, T. "Psychokinetic Effects on Yeast: An Exploratory Experiment." In: W. G. Roll, R. L. Morris, and J. Morris (Eds.) (As cited under Stanford for chapter IV)

Jacobson, N. O. *Life Without Death?* New York: Delacorte Press, 1973.

Krieger, D. "The Laying-on of Hands as a Therapeutic Tool for Nurses." Paper presented at a symposium held at the French and Polyclinic Medical School and Health Center, New York City, February 20, 1974.

Nolen, W. A. *Healing: A Doctor in Search of a Miracle*. New York: Random House, 1974.

Smith, M. J. "Paranormal Effects on Enzyme Activity." *Human Dimensions*, 1972, Vol. 1, pp. 15–19.

Travel-King, Inc., et al. Initial Decision of Chief Administrative Law Judge Daniel H. Hanscom, February 28, 1975. Docket #8949.

Watkins, G. K., and Watkins, A. M. "Resuscitation of Anesthetized Mice." *Journal of Parapsychology*, 1971, Vol. 35, pp. 257–272.

Weatherhead, L. D. *Psychology, Religion, and Healing*. Nashville: Abingdon Press, 1954.

West, D. J. *Eleven Lourdes Miracles*. New York: Helix Press, 1957.

Worrall, A., and Worrall, O. *The Gift of Healing*. New York: Harper & Row, 1965.

XI. *"Again I Come—Patience Worth My Name"*

Curran, P. "A Nut for Psychologists." *The Unpartisan Review*, March-April 1920.

Litvag, I. *Singer in the Shadows*. New York: Macmillan, 1972.

Prince, W. F. *The Case of Patience Worth*. Boston: Boston Society for Psychic Research, 1924.

Thouless, R. H. Review of Heywood, *The Sixth Sense*. *Journal of the Society for Psychical Research*, 1959, Vol. 40, p. 142.

XII. *Possession*

Kelly, H. A. "Death of the Devil?" *Commonweal*, November 6, 1970.

Nicola, J. J. *Diabolical Possession and Exorcism*. Rockford, Ill.: Tan Books, 1974.

Oesterreich, T. K. *Possession: Demoniacal and Other*. New Hyde Park, N.Y.: University Books, 1966.

Pope, D. (Ed.), "A Report of a Poltergeist." *Parapsychology Bulletin*, No. 15, August 1949.

Stevens, E. W. *The Watseka Wonder*. Chicago: *Religio-Philosophical Journal*, September 1879.

XIII. *The Mediums*

Haraldsson, E., and Stevenson, I. "A Communicator of the 'Drop-in' Type in Iceland: The Case of Runolfur Runolfsson." *Journal of the American Society for Psychical Research*, 1975, Vol. 69, pp. 33–59.

Haraldsson, E., and Stevenson, I. "An Experiment with the Icelandic Medium Hafsteinn Bjornsson." *Journal of the American Society for Psychical Research*, 1974, Vol. 68, pp. 192–202.

Pratt, J. G. *Towards a Method of Evaluating Mediumistic Material. Bulletin XXIII*, Boston Society for Psychic Research, 1936.

Sells, J. R. "Snow Job." *The Chattanooga Times*, September 4, 1974.

Sidgwick, Mrs. H. "An Examination of Book-Tests Obtained in Sittings with Mrs. Leonard." *Proceedings of the Society for Psychical Research*, 1921, Vol. 31, pp. 241–400.

XIV. Survival

Ducasse, C. J. *The Belief in a Life After Death*. Springfield, Ill.: Thomas, 1961.

Holt, H. *On the Cosmic Relations*. New York: Houghton Mifflin, 1914.

James, W. "Report on Mrs. Piper's Hodgson-Control." *Proceedings of the Society for Psychical Research*, 1909, Vol. 23, pp. 2–126.

Le Clair, R. C. (Ed.). *The Letters of William James and Théodore Flournoy*. Madison: University of Wisconsin Press, 1966.

Myers, F. W. H. (As cited for chapter II)

Osis, K. *Deathbed Observations by Physicians and Nurses. Parapsychological Monographs*, No. 3. New York: Parapsychology Foundation, 1961.

Osis, K. "What Do the Dying See?" *Newsletter of the American Society for Psychical Research*, Number 24, Winter, 1975.

Pratt, J. G. (As cited for chapter III)

Raudive, K. *Breakthrough*. New York: Taplinger, 1971.

Saltmarsh, H. F. *Evidence of Personal Survival from Cross Correspondences*. London: Bell, 1938.

Stevenson, I. "The Combination Lock Test for Survival." *Journal of the American Society for Psychical Research*, 1968, Vol. 62, pp. 246–254.

Symposium: "What Evidence, If You Had It, Would Convince You of Survival?" In: W. G. Roll, R. L. Morris, and J. Morris (Eds.), *Research in Parapsychology 1972*. Metuchen, N.J.: Scarecrow Press, 1973.

Thouless, R. H. "The Cipher Test of Survival." *Theta*, July 1963.

Vaughan, A. "Interview: Gertrude Schmeidler, Ph.D." *Psychic*, February, 1972.

XV. *Memories of Another Life*

Cerminara, G. *The World Within.* New York: Sloane, 1957.

Stevenson, I. *Twenty Cases Suggestive of Reincarnation.* (Second Edition, Revised and Enlarged) Charlottesville: University Press of Virginia, 1974.

Stevenson, I. "The 'Perfect' Reincarnation Case." In: W. G. Roll, R. L. Morris, and J. Morris (Eds.) (As cited under Symposium for chapter XIV) (Abstract)

Stevenson, I. "Some New Cases Suggestive of Reincarnation: II. The Case of Bishen Chand." *Journal of the American Society for Psychical Research,* 1972, Vol. 66, pp. 375–400.

Stevenson, I. "The Evidence for Survival from Claimed Memories of Former Incarnations." *Journal of the American Society for Psychical Research,* 1960, Vol. 54, pp. 51–71; 95–117.

INDEX

About the Authors

NAOMI A. HINTZE's first mystery novel, *You'll Like My Mother*, received an Edgar Allan Poe Special Award from the Mystery Writers of America. Her other books include *The Stone Carnation, Aloha Means Goodbye, Listen, Please Listen* and *Cry Witch*. They have been sold to the films, selected as Book-of-the-Month Club Alternates, and published in magazines in this country as well as in Europe, South Africa, and Australia. Mrs. Hintze has three grown children. She and her husband have traveled to many parts of the world and have lived in most sections of the United States, but they make their home now in Charlottesville, Virginia.

J. GAITHER PRATT began ESP research while he was a graduate student at Duke University. After completing his study of psychology, Dr. Pratt joined the research staff of the Duke Parapsychology Laboratory in 1937, where he remained for twenty-five years. Since 1964 he has worked in the Division of Parapsychology at the University of Virginia. He has traveled abroad numerous times to visit scientists in his field, is a past president of the Parapsychological Association, and in addition to his books—*Parapsychology: An Insider's View of ESP* and *ESP Research Today*—he has published more than a hundred scientific papers. He and his wife live at High Fields, a farm home in Albemarle County. They have three grown sons and a daughter.